Backroad Mapbook

Welcome to the premier edition of the Backroad Mapbook for the Chilcotin and Central Coast.

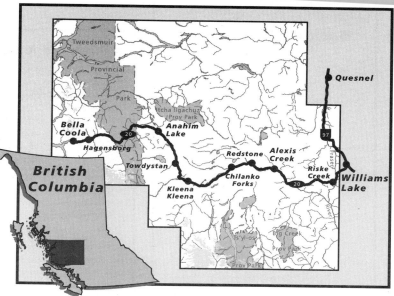

Taking you from the rolling plateau of the Chilcotin, deep into the spectacular Coast Mountains, the Chilcotin Backroad Mapbook helps open up one of BC's final frontiers. This is a place like no other in the province. There are places far removed from the nearest road and relatively untouched by human development and industry. It is an area to preserve and to treasure.

Highway 20 bisects the Chilcotin and provides a lifeline for the small communities out west. Names like Bella Coola and Alexis Creek might not mean much in the bigger cities of the south, but out here they are the big cities. South of the highway lies an area of high elevation plateau, and open forest that slowly runs into the Coast Mountains (in the west) and the higher mountains of the South Chilcotin (in the east). North of the highway, the Chilcotin roles on, slowly transitioning into the Interior Plateau south of Prince George.

Anglers and hunters love the plateau, with its plentiful game and lakes full of wild Chilcotin rainbow. For the avid hiker, mountain biker or horseback rider, there is a lot of country out there to discover. It is also a chance to take in a bit of history and to follow one of the historical trade routes that have been used for thousands of years.

Tweedsmuir Park helps transform the dry, high elevation plateau into the lush Central Coast region. Although access beyond Bella Coola Valley and trails within the park is limited, this beautiful region should not be missed. It is an area dominated by rugged terrain with towering, glacier-clad mountains forming an impressive background.

The Backroad Mapbook will help you explore this vast and wonderful section of our province. In addition to the maps, the writing will let you dream of places not so far away. So sit back and enjoy what we have to offer.

Backroad Mapbooks

DIRECTORS
Russell Mussio
Wesley Mussio
Penny Stainton-Mussio

COVER DESIGN & LAYOUT
Farnaz Faghihi

PRODUCTION
Adrian Brugge
Alfred Berger
Shawn Caswell
Farnaz Faghihi
Brett Firth
Grace Teo
Dale Tober
David Widgington
Heather Yetman

SALES /MARKETING
Shawn Caswell
Jason Marleau

WRITERS
Russell Mussio
Wesley Mussio
Trent Ernst

*National Library of Canada Cataloguing in
Publication Data*

Mussio, Russell, 1969-
Mussio Ventures presents Backroad mapbook. --
3rd ed.

Includes indexes.
Cover title.
Prepared by Russell and Wesley Mussio; vols. 3, 7
by Russell Mussio, Wesley Mussio and Trent Ernst.
Incomplete contents: Vol. 1. Southwestern B.C.
-- v. 2. Vancouver Island and the Gulf Islands. -- v.
3. Kamloops/Okanagan. -- v. 7.
Chilcotin. ISBN 0-9697877-0-7 (v. 1). -- ISBN
1-894556-10-0 (v. 2). -- ISBN 1-894556-21-6 (v.
3). -- ISBN 1-894556-19-4 (v. 7).

1. Recreation areas--British Columbia--Maps. 2.
British Columbia--Maps. I. Mussio, Wesley, 1964-
II. Ernst, Trent, 1970- III. Title. IV. Title: Back-
road mapbook.
G1170.B23 1998   912.711   C00-002450-8

Published by:

232 Anthony Court
New Westminster, B.C. V3L 5T5
P. (604) 438-3474   F. (604) 438-3470
E-mail: info@backroadmapbooks.com
www.backroadmapbooks.com
Copyright © 2003 Mussio Ventures Ltd.

Acknowledgements

This book could not have been compiled without the relentless effort of Trent Ernst. He headed the research and writing effort and did a fabulous job of digging up countless recreational opportunities and describing them in a creative, yet appealing way. We are also indebted to Stuart Kenn for helping us add the relief shading to all of the maps. Combined with the talented people at Mussio Ventures Ltd., Adrian Brugge, Alfred Berger, Shawn Caswell, Farnaz Faghihi, Brett Firth, Dale Tober, Grace Teo and Heather Yetman, we were able to produce the most comprehensive guidebook for a wonderful region of British Columbia.

This book is dedicated to all the former Forest Service Recreation Officers. Thank you for everything you've done. We're going to miss you. We'd like to give a special tip of the hat to Dalton McArthur, who knew the most about the Spruce Lakes Trail area and was one of the driving forces behind the discontinued Spruce Lake Map. He's now up in Fort Nelson.

Our maps and writing got a whole lot better when we stumbled across people like Petrus at Eagle's Nest Resort or Chris at Nuk Tessli Alpine Experience. They were a wealth of information on the many historical routes around Anahim Lake. If you get a chance stop in and check out the Eagle's Nest Resort Library. Further east, Andy Motherwell helped shape and refine many of the historical trails and maps in the Nazko area. In Bella Coola, we had lots of help from trail experts Duane Pederson and Reinhard Maag. We couldn't have made it to the hot springs if not for the boat ride from Mike, at Just for the Halibut Adventures. Information on mountain biking around Bella Coola was provided by the folks at Rick's Re-Cycling. Thanks to Les and Pierre from the New Caledonia Canoe Club, who told me which rivers were paddleable, and which weren't. Tammy Helfrich in Nazko was our source of local knowledge for trails and paddling in that area and Terry at the DFO helped us sort out where to fish in the salt chuck. We cannot forget the Bryant's, Gail and George for their pictures and tips on the Bella Coola River, and David for the map and his 'conservation' measures.

The trails section would have been even smaller if it weren't for the help of Fritz Mueller and Sandy Hart in Tatlayoko Lake. Information was also provided by Betty Motherwell and Dwight Dodge from the Telegraph Trail Society, and Dan at Chaunigan Lake Lodge. Least we forget John Woodsworth, the true pioneer of the Alexander MacKenzie Heritage Trail.

Herb Carter, Joanne McLeod and most everyone at the Water Land and Protection Office in William's Lake answered incessant questions about where the trails are in Itcha Ilgachuz and what's happening in the Spruce Lakes area (short answer, who knows?) and

Thanks also to various folks out hiking, canoeing, fishing or otherwise enjoying themselves before some strange guy with a camera asked them if he could take their picture for this project. A special thanks goes out to Allen Cazes, who played both model and driver for most of the research trip.

Finally we would like to thank Allison, Devon, Nancy, Madison and Penny Mussio for their continued support of the Backroad Mapbook Series. As our family grows, it is becoming more and more challenging to break away from it all to explore our beautiful country.

Table of Contents

Outdoor Recreation Reference Section

Map Section

Foreword

The Backroad Mapbook is truly a unique product. No other source covers the Chilcotin and Central Coast of BC with as much detail or information on all types of outdoor recreation activities.

The Backroad Mapbook is simple to use. There are two sections in the book, the reference section and the maps. If you know the activity you are planning, simply turn to that reference section and find the area that you are interested in. If you are planning a trip to a specific area, you should consult the index to find the appropriate map(s) and look for the various recreational opportunities highlighted in green and red.

The reference section found in the guide includes information on both saltwater and freshwater fishing, hot springs, paddling routes, parks and wilderness camping (recreational sites), multi-use trails (hiking/biking, and off road trails), wildlife viewing and winter recreation. Countless hours have been spent in researching this book, making it the most complete compilation of outdoor recreation information you will find on the region anywhere. This information can be enjoyed by anyone who spends time in the great outdoors.

Our maps have been developed and updated using a wide variety of sources including the current forestry and logging road maps. Therefore, our maps are very detailed as they show a myriad of logging roads in addition to the various trail systems available. We provide a map legend at the start of the maps to illustrate the region we cover as well as how to decipher the various grades of roads and symbols used on the maps. You may also notice the overlapping of maps on the map key. This was done to help readjust the maps to true north.

New to the maps is relief shading. It should be pointed out that this relief is included to give readers a general idea of topography. The accuracy is 25 metres/82 feet with a sun angle of NW & SW. We have also included UTM Grids (datum NAD 1983; projection Albers Equal Area) and Longitude and Latitude reference points for GPS users. We must emphasis that these are for reference only. We cannot guarantee the accuracy of all sources we use to update the maps.

Although the Backroad Mapbook is the most detailed and up-to-date resource available to recreationists, it must be noted that it is only a planning and access guide. We have gone to great lengths to ensure the accuracy of the book. However, over time, road and trail conditions change. Always be prepared and please respect private property!

Backroads of the Chilcotin

More than almost anywhere in the province, the Chilcotin is a land of backroad travel. Even the 450 kilometre long Highway 20 hasn't been completely conquered by civilization. Between Anahim Lake and the bottom of The Hill, the Freedom highway has yet to be paved. There are a few other incursions of pavement into the area (the Nazko Road and part of the Blackwater Road), but these are the exceptions that prove the rule.

The highway system and majority of the paved roads are obviously well maintained and even ploughed in the winter. So too are the main (logging) roads. But with the Ministry of Forest pulling out of both recreation and out of road maintenance, the times they are a' changing for backroad explorers.

There are 45,000 km (27,450 miles) of backroads in the province. Most of those roads (35,000 km/21,350 miles) will be maintained by the industry, with the Ministry maintaining a nominal percentage (1,300 km/793 miles) as Community Roads (usually for First Nations Communities).

This leaves just about 9,000 km (5,490 miles) of road to the elements. They will be classified as Wilderness Use Roads, and will not be graded or brushed. These roads will remain open, as long as they are safe, or if they are important for forest fire access. Roads added to help control the beatle kill problem are being deactivated as quickly as they are added.

For folks with 4wd vehicles or ATVs, this is a good thing. However, for people without 4wd vehicles, access into these areas will become increasingly difficult.

In the Chilcotin and Coastal regions, as with other areas of the province, most of these roads that will be turned into Wilderness Use Roads are the ones that lead to really interesting destinations (like the Jay Lakes area above Bella Coola). Add in the overzealous cross-ditching practices of the 90's along with the muddy road conditions in early spring and backroaders will need a lot of patience when they get off of the main roads. So slow down and allow a bit of extra time to get to that trailhead or mountain lake.

This mapbook is an accurate picture of the road and trail system as it stands at the time of publication (Summer, 2003). However, things change rapidly out there. If you come across a road that has been deactivated, please let us know, at updates@backroadmapbooks.com.

Backroad Attractions

People venturing about on the Backroads of BC are blessed with an amazing variety of sights and sounds. From old-growth trees, to cascading waterfalls and impressive mountain vistas, there is always something to see and do. Some of these are marked on the maps (usually with a star) but many are simply yours to discover.

Below, we have picked a few points of interests that have always intrigued the people exploring the Chilcotin and Central Coast regions of BC.

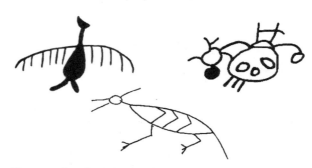

Hot Springs

While the Central Coast is one of the more active geothermal areas of BC, hot spring-wise, almost all the springs fall outside the scope of this mapbook. Most of these hot springs are boat access only, and see little use in the course of the year. Within the scope of our maps are arguably the nicest springs in the area (Tallheo Hot Springs), but other springs that bear investigation are Eucott Bay and Nascall Bay (the latter is on private land, and a user fee is charged).

Tallheo Hot Springs (Map 12/C3)

This beautiful set of hot springs is located in the south Bentink Arm, far, far away from the nearest road access. Even if a road ran close (and none do, the old Clayton Creek Road to Larso Bay, which kayakers used to use to access the hot springs, has been deactivated), most people would still be out of luck, as the springs are on the far side of the fjord. For those with a boat (there are charters out of Bella Coola) or float plane, these are some of the nicest springs you'll find in the province. The short access trail from the beach is a bit rough, but the springs themselves, carved into the rock and covered with a canopy of thick rainforest, are a delight. The fjords from Bella Coola offer little in the way of landing spots, so kayaking to the springs is not recommended. The main soaking pool is about 69°C (156°F), but the entire area is full of hot seeps.

Thorsen Creek Springs (Map 12/F1)

There are reports of a hot spring up Thorsen Creek, but very little is known about them, other than that, yes, they are there. Where exactly, we do not know. The amount of flow or how warm they are has also not been reported. People interested in exploring these springs should be prepared to bushwhack up the river.

Petroglyphs & Pictographs

These two distinct forms of First Nations rock writings were created by two unique cultures. Petroglyphs are rock carvings that are commonly found in the Coastal Culture, while pictographs are rock paintings that are more common to the interior. Both types of writing were created as a way to record events and to stand the passage of time.

If you do venture into one of the sites, stay awhile. Not only will the change in lighting reveal new images but it is also a chance to introspect. The sites are often found in special places and can only really be appreciated by those who take the time to try to get a feel for the area.

Bull Canyon Pictographs (Map 18/G5)

Now preserved as a provincial park, the Bull Canyon has been a significant area with First Nations people for thousands of years. A set of pictographs can be seen from the highway at the base of the cliffs atop a rock slope. The site is at the second cave from the westernmost slope.

Dog Creek Pictographs (Map 11/G5)

This site is found in a cavern that is visible from the community of Dog Creek. Please seek permission from the Dog Creek Indian Band before proceeding to the sacred cave.

Farwell Canyon Pictographs (Map 11/C1)

Visitors to Farwell Canyon will understand why this site was chosen as a pictograph location. The canyon itself is spectacular. The area is also a traditional fishing area. The site is found very close to the junction of the road and the river.

Thorsen Creek Petroglyphs (Map 21/F7)

Found on a terrace above Thorsen Creek, is an art display created hundreds of years ago. The trail up to the site is rather steep and narrow and it can be slippery near the ledge. So be careful. To get a true sense of the images, we recommend contacting the Bella Coola Tourism office. They will set you up with a Nuxalk First Nations guide.

Towdystan Pictographs (Map 15/F3)

These pictographs are well known and in very good condition. Look for them 5.5 kilometres south of the settlement of Towdystan right beside Highway 20. They can be seen on a boulder about 30 metres (100 feet) from the road.

Accessing the Chilcotin/Central Coast

The Chilcotin/Central Coast area of British Columbia is a unique somewhat isolated place to visit. For visitors coming from far, there are several interesting ways to gain access into this vast, yet beautiful area:

From the West

Bella Coola is a port city that is serviced by BC Ferries. The Queen of Chilliwack runs from Port Hardy on Vancouver Island to Bella Coola several times a week during the summer. It is an exhilarating voyage that brings vehicles and passengers through the famed Inside Passage of BC.

From the East

The two major centres that border the Chilcotin in the east are Williams Lake and Quesnel. Williams Lake marks the start of Highway 20, which is the main corridor through the region. Further north, Quesnel also provides good access into the northeast portion of this book. Both the Nazko and Blackwater Roads are easily travelled as they are the only paved backroads in this book.

From the South

Visitors will need to make their way west from Lillooet towards Goldbridge. Both the Yalakom Forest Service Road and the Tyaughton Lake Road branch north from the Carpenter Lake Road and access the South Chilcotin Mountains. Access into the spectacular wilderness surrounding Spruce Lake is restricted to non-motorized vehicles. The Southwestern BC Backroad Mapbook helps visitors gain access into the South Chilcotins.

From the North

Prince George is the largest city in the central interior and is found just north of this mapbook. The paved Blackwater Road is a popular road for recreationists to travel. Branching from this artery are roads of all shapes and sizes. Other main haul logging roads lead south from Highway 16 towards the big lakes of the Nechako Reservoir. These road systems are highlighted in the Central BC Backroad Mapbook.

Freshwater Fishing
(Lake, River and Stream Fishing)

Saltwater Fishing

Anglers come from around the world to test their luck in the myriad of small islands, inlets and coves that make the mid-coast such a great fishing destination. Unfortunately most of these areas, such as the famed Hakai Pass and Rivers Inlet lie just outside the scope of this mapbook. Due to the complex nature of the islands and the fact the Hakai Pass is such a remote area, we recommend going with an experienced guide. There are 9 lodges operating in the area, with most of the inland sportfishing occurring around the Koeye River during the latter part of August when coho congregate there. Feeder spring (smaller wintering chinook salmon) can be found in Burke Channel, but most of the tidal effort occurs in the outside waters of Area 8. A big boat and someone who knows the waters is highly recommended when fishing the outside.

Our mapbook only shows portions of the Dean Channel, and the North and South Bentink Arms. These water bodies are fed by fast flowing glacial streams that create murky water and poor fishing in the summer. Although there isn't much fishing in these arms, anglers can do okay trolling for chinook from Tallheo to Green Bay.

Lake Fishing

The Chilcotin is notorious for big mountains, sprawling plateaus and big fish. This is also an area that promises of excellent fishing in an often secluded lake. The fact that Nimpo Lake is the floatplane capital of BC and many of the lakes in the area are only accessible by plane (or a long, long walk) helps make this a great place to fish for the Chilcotin's famous wild rainbow trout.

Although a few of the lakes here are free of ice in April, there aren't many. Fishing usually gets under way mid-May, but at some of the higher elevation lakes, you will have to wait until June before you can access them. Summers can be long and hot, and fishing in smaller lakes will slow down as the water warms up. The lakes to the south are generally deeper and colder, as they are fed by glacier streams running off the Coast Mountains. Lakes to the north are warmer and often shallower, but this is by no means a rule, just a general guideline.

The clear water lakes in the area hold a lot of leeches and freshwater shrimp. This not only helps the trout grow rapidly, but allows fly anglers a chance to test their luck throughout the ice-free season. Chironomids, mayflies, stoneflies, caddis flies and dragonflies are other common insects in the area. The hot dry climate also allows for some exciting dry fly action. Anglers interested in trolling will find the gang troll continues to be the gear of choice. Outside of a few popular fishing holes, the remote nature of the area does allow the fisherman to use pretty well anything he or she chooses.

Below we have listed most of the lakes that hold resident sportfish. There are many other lakes, but most of these only hold coarse fish (chub, sculpin, squawfish & suckers), are too shallow to maintain a fishery or too remote to access. Stocking is not as prevalent as in other parts of the province, partly due to the secluded nature of the area. The lakes that do hold wild stocks generally hold larger fish.

If you do find a new lake or see our information is lacking or incorrect, please e-mail the report to updates@backroadmapbooks.com. If you send along a picture or two, chances are we will publish it in the next edition of the book or on-line.

Abuntlet Lake (Map 24/A4)

Abuntlet Lake is found at 1,067m (3,468 feet) in elevation and covers 230 hectares. Fishing is best near where the Dean River flows out of the lake. The lake contains cuttbows (a cross between rainbow and cutthroats), most of which will weigh less than 1.5 kg (3+ pounds).

Aktaklin Lake (Map 16/A2)

Found at 1,200 metres (3,940 feet), this 207 hectare lake offers fishing for rainbow. Road access is best from the south. Alternatively, the Lt. Palmer Trail skirts the north shore of the lake.

Alexis Lake (Map 18/E1)

A constant producer of rainbow in the 30 cm (12 inch) range, Alexis Lake has an electric motor only restriction. Fishing remains good from May to October. The lake is accessed off Alexis Lakes Road, a good 2wd road, which is in turn accessed off Highway 20, west of Alexis Creek.

Anahim Lake (Map 24/B5)

The town of Anahim Lake is the heart of fly-in fishing country, but the lake itself is a popular destination without the need to fly-in. There are cuttbow (a cross between rainbow and cutthroats) trout reaching up to 1.5 kg (3+ lbs) in the lake. Fly fishing is the most popular method of angling here, although spincasting and trolling are also effective. Fishing is good throughout the season, but is best in early summer when the waters are cooler and the hatches more prolific. The inflow from Little Anahim Lake is the best place to find trout and it is possible to float from Anahim Lake to Abuntlet Lake along the Dean River. The lake is on the Chilcotin Plateau, at 1,083 (3,520 feet), and covers 562 hectares.

Banana Lake (Map 15/A5)

Shaped like a banana, it isn't hard to figure out how this remote lake got its name. It is a long walk along the May Doe Creek Trail into this 221 hectare lake. Those willing to lug in a float tube will find very good fishing for wild rainbow trout. The lake is found at 1,356 metres (4,450 feet) and fishing holds through the summer.

Barton Lake (Map 44/G4)

Barton Lake is a 64 hectare lake located off the Pelican/Barton Road. The popular lake is heavily stocked with rainbow trout, and the recreation site on the lake's shore sees heavy use. In addition to rainbow and brook, there are a number of other species of fish, including whitefish and suckers. The lake is 777 m (2,525 feet) above sea level and best fished in the spring and fall. Shore fishing is possible, but casting towards shore from a float tube or small boat is more effective.

Basalt Lake (Map 33/A5)

Basalt Lake is accessed via a long trail. The remote location and the catch and release (single barbless hooks) fishery helps the fish grow to good sizes. The lake contains bull and rainbow trout, dolly varden, and a handful of other non-sportfish species.

Batnuni Lake (Map 43/F6)

Batnuni Lake is the third lake in a chain that includes Hanham, Snag, and Comstock Lakes. These lakes are linked by the Euchiniko River and all provide similar fisheries. The biggest lake of the chain is located about 161 km (100 miles) from Quesnel along mainline logging roads. The lake sports good fishing for rainbow and kokanee averaging 0.5 kg (1 lbs) as well as dollies. The rainbow are best caught near the shore with fly gear, while the kokanee and dollies are best caught on the troll. There are two forest service sites on this lake. The eastern site, which is much easier to access and sports a boat launch, is definitely the busier of the two.

Beaver Lake (Map 19/E2)

Beaver Lake is a very shallow lake, so during the hot summer months fishing usually drops off. However, early and late season fishing for the lake's large rainbow can be excellent. The last 10 km (6.1 miles) drive into the lake is very rough, and it gets worse in wet weather. 4wd vehicles are sometimes needed.

Becher Pond (Map 20/C7)
Also known as the Riske Creek Reservoir, this small lake is very popular, and is located alongside Highway 20. Even with all the pressure, the small rainbow that inhabit the lake still take well to flies.

Bidwell Lakes (Map 17/F7)
This chain of small lakes is located along Bidwell Creek, which in turn is south of Highway 20. The lake contains a few different species of fish, including rainbow trout. They are not a popular fishing destination.

Big Lake (Map 9/B7)
Big Lake is a fairly popular fishing lake, and while the rainbow are stocked periodically, there are also some native kokanee and lake trout, too. The lake is situated in the low, rolling, forested hills of the Chilcotin plateau and offers great views of the nearby Coast Mountains.

Big Onion Lake (Map 3/C1)
Sandwiched between the Whitewater Road and the Taseko River, this 59 hectare lake contains wild dollies and stocked rainbow trout (about 8,000 annually). Like most of the lakes in the southern Chilcotin, the surrounding scenery is very impressive.

Big Stick Lake (Map 15/E6)
Big Stick Lake was last stocked with rainbow trout a decade ago, and, while some of these still inhabit the 141 hectare lake, the lake is not a popular fishing destination. It does make a nice camping destination (there is a forest service site on the lake), and if you're in the area anyway...

Bishop (Brown) Lake (Map 27/E4)
Is it Brown or Bishop? Regardless, a 235 hectare lake is located just north of Nazko Lake Provincial Park, with access coming from the north along the Honolulu Road. The lake was stocked with rainbow back in 1994, and they have been able to survive with the aid of special regulations. (There is a two trout limit, as well as a single, barbless, baitless hook restriction). Rustic camping is possible at the former forest service site on the northern shore.

Blanchet Lake (Map 39/E5)
Blanchet Lake is found at the end of a 30 km (18.3 mile) trail, which in turn is accessed on the far side of Ootsa Lake, a 5 km (3.1 mile) stretch of open water. Needless to say, the lake doesn't see much fishing pressure for its resident rainbow.

Blue Lake (Map 20/G1)
Blue Lake is a small lake, covering 34 hectares, found 34 km (21 miles) north of Williams Lake. The lake contains rainbow to 2.5 kg (5 lbs), but 0.5 kg (1 lb) is much more common. The lake also contains kokanee in good numbers as well as a number of non-sportfish. Despite the stocking, the rainbow are notoriously hard to catch in the clear waters. Fly anglers are well advised to use long leaders. There is a popular resort and two forest service sites on the lake.

Blue Lake (Map 29/E2)
There are 18 Blue Lakes in the province, three of which are stretched out along the east side of the Fraser River between the Fraser Canyon and Prince George, and two of which are covered by this mapbook. This Blue Lake covers 14 hectares, and is located just off Highway 97 on the Moffat Lake Road, south of Alexandria. The lake is annually stocked with a 1,000-2,000 rainbow fry.

Blue Jay & Gray Lakes (Map 12/C1)
These small lakes have been stocked with cutthroat in the past. Between them they are only 10 hectares in size. Despite the road that seems to wind to the top of the world, the low elevation (~900 metres/2,950 feet) makes these lakes a better spring or fall fishing destination.

Bluff Lake (Map 7/C2)
Located just south of Sapeye Lake and Horn Lake, Bluff Lake is a beautiful lake with views of the Niut Range looking south down the lake.

There is a boat launch at the north end of the lake. It contains bull trout to 5 kg (11 lbs), rainbow trout to 1.5 kg (3+ lbs) and dolly varden.

Boat Lake (Map 44/A7)
Boat Lake is located 2.5 km west of Titetown Lake on the road to Batnuni. Wild rainbow and dolly varden commonly reach 1 kg (2 lbs) in this small lake. Boat Lake offers a forest service campsite and boat launch.

Bobtail (Naltesby) Lake (Map 44/F2)
A centre of recreation activity in this area, you will find rainbow to 1.5 kg (3+ lbs) and kokanee to 0.5 kg (1 lb) in these waters. The lake is stocked annually with 10,000 rainbow, which should give you an idea of the fishing pressure this lake sees. There is a forest service site with a boat launch on the eastern shores of the lake. Fishing drops off in the summer, but is great in the early and later parts of the season.

Brewster Lakes (Map 42/F5)
A good 2wd road leads past the access road into the small forest service site on the 1st Brewster Lake. The 2nd lake is a bit smaller but not very deep (max. 4.3 m/14 ft) and requires bushwhacking from the main road or the 1st lake. Most of the fishing for average size rainbow occurs on the 2nd lake.

Brittany Lake (Map 8/G4)
Found above Murray Taylor Lake, Brittany Lake sits at 1,335 metres (4,380 feet) in elevation. The 149 hectare lake also has coarse fish competing with the rainbow for available food.

Buckskin Lake (Map 20/F2)
Buckskin Lake is accessed via a rough road east from the Rosita Meldrum Road. The lake offers fair to good fishing for rainbow that can reach 3 kg (6.5 lbs). Trolling, fly fishing and spincasting all produce results.

Bushy (Valerie) Lake (Map 29/F5)
Found to the east of the Fraser River, in the hills above Marguerite, the better access comes from the south of the Gibraltar Mine Road. The lake offers an early season fishery that slows considerably in the summer. Fishing picks up again in the fall. There is a forest service site with a cartop boat launch on the lake.

Charlotte Lake (Map 15/B3)
Charlotte Lake is best known for its large rainbow, which average an impressive 2 kg (4+ lbs), and go up from there. The big (6,596 hectare) lake is found southwest of Nimpo Lake and signs directing the way from the highway to the popular lakeside forest service site.

Chaunigan Lake (Maps 8/G6, 9/A5)
A beautiful lake that has yielded some equally beautiful fish, Chaunigan Lake is found in the southern Chilcotin, where the towering Coast Mountains rise above the plateau. Wild Chilcotin rainbow up to 3.5 kg (8 lbs) are caught fairly regularly, though the average is 1.3 kg (2.5 lbs). The lake produces well from late spring to early fall. There is a single barbless hook restriction on the lake.

Cheshi Lake (Map 8/A7)

Sporting a lodge on its northern shore, this lake offers small rainbow trout. A well-developed trail system also leads to a series of lakes to the north.

Chief Gray (Bitch) Lake (Map 42/C2)

This tiny lake, east of the Kinney Dam, is an excellent walk-in lake. The lake is about 4 km from the Forest Service Site at Hobson Lake (the trailhead is about 250 metres/600 feet from the site). There are a few steep grades, but the overall hike is fairly easy. This lake is smaller, but deeper than Hobson, and fishing for good size rainbow (averaging 50 cm/20 inches, but getting up to 65 cm/26 inches) remains strong throughout the summer. The best time to go is during the damsel hatch in late July. The lake is catch and release, with a single barbless, baitless hook.

Chilcotin Lake (Map 17/F1)

Drained by the Chilcotin River, this lake is found in a marshy area that is popular with bird watchers. Anglers will find rainbow trout to 2 kg (4 lbs) if they bring in a small boat or canoe to get beyond the weeds. The lake is 993 metres (3,258 feet) above sea level.

Chilko Lake (Maps 2/D3, 8/C6)

Chilko Lake is a big lake. In fact, it is the longest coastal lake in BC, stretching 84 km (52 miles) into the heart of the Coast Mountains. It is also the largest high-elevation lake in North America. The lake contains large populations of large fish, with bull trout to 4.5 kg (10 lbs) and rainbow to 3 kg (6.5 lbs). The lake is also home to one of the largest runs of sockeye in BC. Which all sounds great, but with so much area to cover (20,032 hectares), it can be difficult to actually find fish. A good place to start is around creek mouths. Trolling or fly fishing near the drop-off and the feed lines can produce some large fish. Check the regulations for gear, boating, and quota restrictions.

Choelquoit Lake (Map 8/B3-D3)

Choelquoit Lake is rumoured to have some very large wild rainbow, but if they are there, they are hard to catch, and as a result, the lake sees very little pressure. Which could be a great argument for going there. Then again, the lake is subject to sudden violent storms which could be an argument against it.

Chutanli Lake (Maps 42/G6; 43/A7)

A lake revered by the First Nations, Chutanli has long been a good fishing lake. The lake is 175 hectares in size and most of this is shoal areas full of insect life. At 9 metres (30 feet) deep, the lake is better for casting than trolling. Rainbow are the main sportfish, but kokanee and whitefish are also available. A forest service site offers camping and a boat launch onto the lake.

Cicuta (Rum Cache) Lake (Map 41/G2)

A naturally barren lake, Cicuta was stocked with Kamloops-born rainbow, which took to the lake like fish to water. The fish quickly became local legend, with 4.5 kg (10 lb) catches fairly normal. With heavy pressure threatening the stock to extinction, the lake is now catch and release only, with single barbless, baitless hooks. It is still an excellent

lake to learn to fly fish on. The unnamed lake that drains into Cicuta (and that trout spawn up) is also catch and release.

Clear Lake (Map 45/D1)

A tiny lake a few kilometres west of the paved Blackwater Road, clear lake has decent fishing for rainbow that can get up to 1 kg (2 lbs). Fly fishing with dry flies in the summer or chironomids in the spring can be rewarding. The access road in is a bit rough and there is a small forest service site at the lake.

Clearwater Lake (Map 15/G6)

Located just off Highway 20, this 214 hectare lake contains wild rainbow, which average 1 kg (2 lbs). Larger fish are taken fairly regularly both on the fly and with small spinning lures. There is a small lakeside forest service site with a cartop launch.

Cleswuncut Lake (Map 45/C7)

Found off the Blackwater-Mud Road, this small lake offers anglers fair fishing for small rainbow. The lake is subject to winterkill, which accounts for the slow fishing. There is a forest service site with a boat launch on the shores of the lake.

Cochin Lake (Maps 7/G2, 8/A2)

Cochin Lake contains wild Chilcotin rainbow trout that can get up to 4.5 kg (10 lbs), although they average only 1 kg (2 lbs). Hot weather can slow the fishing down, but during spring and fall, or during cool summers, the fish are pretty voracious, taking to flies and lures regularly. There is a cartop boat launch at the lakeside forest service site.

Cohen Lake (Map 14/F6)

If you're going to go through the effort to get into Whitton Lake, you may as well make a weekend of it and try your luck at Cohen. This lake is much smaller (at 45 hectares) and is easier to fish than its bigger neighbour. The trouble is the bushwhack in.

Comstock Lake (Map 43/E6)

There is only a short patch of river separating Comstock Lake from its bigger neighbour, Batnuni. As a result, the two share similar fishing patterns. The main event here is rainbow to 2 kg (4 lbs).

Cogistiko Lake (Map 36/B6)

A rough 2wd branch road leads to the southern shores of this 32 hectare lake. It is only 1.5 metres (5 feet) deep, so winterkill is a definite problem. Anglers will find brook trout, rainbow trout and salmon all migrate up the river on occassion.

Crazy Bear and Area Lakes (Map 14/G3)

Located well off any sort of path, beaten or otherwise, Crazy Bear Lake is a fly-in lake southwest of Charlotte Lake. The average wild rainbow is about 36 cm (14 inches) long. The 177 hectare lake has a resort on it and is found in the heart of the Crazy Bear Valley at 1,286 metres (4,220 feet). There are five other lakes in the area (No Name, Secret, Hidden, Shelter and The Pond) to choose from, all of which offer a similar experience. Check the regulations for quota and gear restrictions.

Cuisson Lake (Map 29/F6)

Similar to most lakes in the area, fishing in Cuisson is better in the spring and fall. The stocked rainbow provide for a good fishery, especially if you work the drop-off south of the island. The lake is found off the Gibraltar Mine Road and offers a forest service site with a boat launch at the south end.

Dante's Inferno (Map 10/G1)

A tiny lake in a canyon famous for how hot it gets in summer (thus the name), Dante's Inferno is a good place to catch rainbow to 1 kg (2 lb). That is as long as you try in the spring and fall when the temperature is cooler. Access is along the Dante's Inferno Trail, which is located south of Highway 20 along Beaumont Road.

Eagle Lake (Maps 7/G1, 8/A1, 17/B7)

Eagle Lake runs vaguely parallel to Highway 20, a few kilometres to the south. The clear lake is a popular destination with anglers, with rainbow averaging 1 kg (2 lbs) and smaller kokanee. Some of the trout can reach a chunky 3.5 kg (8 lbs) in size. Angling is good during the summers, providing it isn't too hot and the lake hasn't dropped too much. The lake is heavily stocked and sports a forest service site.

Eleven Sisters Chain (Map 9/E2)
There are a whole series of lakes northeast of Scum Lake (Norma, Nancy, Roxanne, Ruby, etc.) that are connected to Scum Lake, and offer fishing for wild rainbow to 0.75 kg (1.5 lbs). There is limited access to the lakes but it is possible to bushwhack along Haines Creek to get to the more remote lakes in the chain.

Eliguk Lake (Map 33/A5)
Eliguk Lake is a great fly fishing lake, and produces well throughout the year. The dry fly season peaks in late summer and can create stirring action for the abundant rainbow that reach a chunky 1.5 kg (3+ lbs). Access is by floatplane, or via a long hike (eight days from the Tweedsmuir Trailhead) along the Alexander Mackenzie Trail. There is a private resort, or some undeveloped wilderness tenting spots next to the lake.

Elkin Lake (Map 9/A5)
Elkin Lake is found just past Vedan Lake, on the same road, and the two are often referred to in the same breath. Elkin is a smaller lake, but the fishing is pretty much the same, with wild Chilcotin rainbow to 1 kg (2 lbs) and dolly varden to 7 kg (15 lbs). Trolling is the most common method of catching these fish, followed by spincasting.

Euchiniko Lakes (Maps 34/E2-35/C2)
The lakes along the Blackwater River are wonderful trout lakes, taking the already magnificent fishing of the river and making it even better. The problem, as always, is the access. The lakes are accessed by plane, canoe or on foot. (The Alexander Mackenzie Trail is also a very rough 4wd/ATV route, and should be attempted only by multiple self-sufficient vehicles.) In addition to the requisite rainbow (which grow to 2 kg/4 lbs), the lakes also hold lake trout.

Eulatazella (Graveyard) Lake (Map 44/D1)
Accessed from either the Bobtail Road or the Telegraph Trail (there is a forest service site off Bobtail Road) this well-stocked lake (about 10,000 rainbow annually) covers 445 hectares. In addition to the rainbow (which don't get much bigger than pan size), there is a fair kokanee fishery.

Eutsuk Lake (Map 31/C1)
Eutsuk Lake is a large lake (the largest natural lake in BC, at nearly 80 km/50 miles long) that only just touches the northern borders of our maps. Rainbow in this lake have been known to top 9 kg (20 lbs), with the largest being a whopping 15.5 kg (34 lbs). Access is by boat from Ootsa of Whitesail Lake, or by floatplane. If you choose the former option, know that Ootsa is a dangerous lake, full of snags. It is recommended to use a guide to help locate the cruising trout.

Finger Lake (Map 43/C2)
Access to this lake is limited through a private resort, although the whole area is part of the relatively new Tatuk-Finger Provincial Park. The 875 hectare lake offers consistent fishing for rainbow, kokanee and dollies to 1 kg (2 lbs). The two islands and outflow of Finger Creek are a few areas to work.

Fir Lake (Map 19/G2)
This small, shallow lake has a surprising winter survival rate, which creates lots of wary trout that may or may not take you up on your offer. Fly anglers do well by anchoring and casting towards shore, although trolling small leeches or even casting from shore can work too. Mayflies, damsel flies and sedges are other common fly patterns. Regardless of the method, be patient. When the bite is on, the fishing is great. There is a forest service site here and launching a boat is possible.

Fish Lake (Maps 3/C1, 9/D1)
Situated about 16 km (9.9 miles) southeast of the Taseko River Bridge (Davidson Bridge), this small lake is a good place to chase wild rain-

bow. Fish Lake is a good lake to bring younger kids as the trout are fairly indiscriminate in what they eat. The lake offers a small forest service site with a cartop boat launch and a great view of Anvil Mountain. Check the regulations for restrictions.

Fish Lake (Map 42/A2)
A small lake found just east of the Kenney Dam, Fish Lake contains rainbow to 1 kg (2 lbs), which are taken by trolling (usually when turning) or spincasting and fly casting if you can work beyond the weeds. There is a rough boat launch at the popular forest service site.

Fishem Lake (Map 3/B4)
Fishem Lake is one of a series of lakes situated in the broad valley between Ts'ylos and the Taseko Mountain. Fishem contains small rainbow and bull trout.

Fishpot Lake (Map 36/B6)
Accessed off the Michelle-Coglistiko Road, which is in turn accessed off the Nazko Road, this smaller lake has been known to produce rainbow up to 3 kg (6+ lbs). The lake has historically been stocked with about 5000 yearlings annually, but hasn't been stocked for a couple years now. A forest service site provides camping and a gravel boat launch.

Fletcher Lake (Map 10/D2)
Found 26 km (16.1 miles) south of Hanceville, there are accommodations, boat rentals and some services available at Fletcher Lake. There is also a grassy Forest Service Site near the north end of the lake. Wild rainbow up to 4.5 kg (10 lbs) are caught fairly regularly, although the average is only about 1 kg (2 lbs). The lake is best fished from May through October, and trolling seems to be the preferred method.

Graveyard Lake (Map 44/D1)
See Eulatazella Lake.

Grizzly Lake (Map 5/A6)
Grizzly Lake is a small lake, accessed by foot, along the Noaxe Lake to Quartz Mountain Trail. Anglers can find small rainbow later in the year at this mountain lake.

Grizzly Lake (Map 44/D2)

Found east of Bobtail Lake, this Grizzly Lake is a smaller (137 hectare) lake that is stocked annually with rainbow. Fishing can be good at times for quick growing trout. A forest service site provides camping and a boat launch.

Haines Lake (Map 9/D3)

Haines Lake is noted for the biggest trout of any of the Eleven Sisters Lakes. Access is to the lake is along the Taseko Lake Road, and then north on the Newton-Whitewash Road, which can be difficult to drive in wet weather. Fishing is best in spring and fall.

Hanham Lake (Map43/G7)

Hanham Lake is 3 km (1.86 mi) west of Boat Lake. Steep access to the lakeshore of Hanham makes it inconvenient for anything but light boats and canoes. There is a little used Forest Service campsite on the east end of the lake.

Hidden and Secret Lakes (Map 14/G3)

Found in the Crazy Bear Valley, these lakes are only accessible by floatplane. Needless to say, few anglers ever make it into these high elevation lakes and fishing can be very good for wild rainbow. Some trout are over 36 cm (14 inches) long. Check the regulations for quota and gear restrictions.

Hobson Lake (Map 42/C2)

A small lake east of the Kinney Dam, Hobson Lake is a trophy lake, and one of the best fly fishing lakes in the Nechako Reservoir area. The lake is accessed off the Klukus-Kenny Dam Road (500 Rd). A rough 2wd road leads to a forestry campsite with a cartop launch on the shores of the lake. The lake can produce large trout up to and over 5 kg (10+ lbs). The extensive shoals can create exciting sight fishing if the wind isn't blowing.

Horn Lake (Map 7/C2)

One of the nicest forest service sites in the Chilcotin accentuates this lovely lake, which has big views of the Niut Range to the south. The lake contains rainbow to 1.5 kg (3+ lbs) as well as bull trout. The lake produces consistently throughout the open water season.

Hotnarko Lake (Map 23/G6)

In the late 1980's, Hotnarko Lake was the place to fish in the Chilcotin. Unfortunately, as word spread of the 3 kg (6.5 lb) trout that grew to 68 cm (27 inches), boat loads of people came. The trophy trout have all but disappeared and the rainbow usually average about 30-40 cm (12-16 in) in size. The clear lake has many islands and shoals for the fly angler. Similar to most lakes in the area, leeches, shrimp or dragonflies are the most effective fly patterns, especially in the fall. Access is limited to plane, foot or bike as the road that runs past the lake has recently been blocked off to preserve the wilderness setting. Walking in along the road is certainly an option, but fishing from the shore is difficult, and the lake can be very windy, which doesn't bode well for carrying in float tubes. There is a forest service site offering a tenting area next to the lake.

Janice Lake (Map 9/E2)

See Eleven Sisters Chain.

Junker Lake (Map 14/C3)

There are two ways to get to Junker Lake. The first is to hike 16 km (9 miles) from the end of the Tote Rd (a 4wd road that follows the Atnarko River), to Turner Lake, much of that slogging uphill. From Turner Lake, rent a canoe and paddle your way in. The second, and usually preferred way is to fly-in. The seven lakes in the Turner Lake Chain (including Kidney, Turner and Widgeon Lakes) form the headwaters of the Atnarko River, and contain cutthroat trout, which usually range between 0.5 and 1 kg (1 to 2 lbs). Check the regulations for special restrictions.

Kappan Lake (Map 24/A7)

Located south of Anahim Lake on good backroads (usually in better condition than the gravel section of Highway 20), Kappan Lake contains wild rainbow. The lake sees fairly heavy angling pressure and hosts two forest service sites and boat launch. There is a bait ban/single barbless hook restriction on the lake.

Kidney Lake (Map 14/B3)

Part of the Turner Lake Canoe Route, anglers can also fly-in to this beautiful backcountry lake. The seven lakes in the Turner Lake Chain (including Junker, Kidney, Turner and Widgeon Lakes) form the headwaters of the Atnarko River, and contain cutthroat trout, which usually range between 0.5 and 1 kg (1 to 2 lbs). Check the regulations for special restrictions.

Kloakut Lake (Map 9/G5)

Kloakut is an excellent fishing lake, with wild rainbow up to (and over) 4 kg (8+ lbs). The most popular fishing methods are spincasting and trolling, but fly fishing does work, too. June and September are the best months, since fishing slows down in the heat of summer. The lake is subject to winterkill.

Klunchatistli Lake (Map 43/C6)

Located about 20 km (12 miles) past Batnuni Lake on the Batnuni Lake Road, little is known about the fishing at this lake. People have reportedly caught fish here. Anyone on a reconniscence trip can email their reports to us at updates@backroadmapbooks.com.

Kluskoil Lake (Maps 35/G1, 36/A1)

Kluskoil Lake is another lake along the Blackwater River, miles away from anything resembling a road. The Alexander Mackenzie Trail passes this way, but it's an 18 km (11 mile) hike (or bike, or horseback ride, or, for those with a good clearance ATV or 4wd) in from the closest trailhead. Even then, there is a deep crossing of the Euchinko River that will deter most drivers and hikers. Like most of the lakes on the Blackwater, Kluskoil Lake features great fishing for rainbow, plus a good population of bull trout. Kokanee and whitefish are also found in the 471 hectare lake.

Kluskus Lakes (Maps 34/E3-35/A3)

Yet another remote Blackwater River lake that offers excellent rainbow fishing. The problem, as always, is the access. The lakes are accessed by plane, canoe or on foot. (The Alexander Mackenzie Trail is also a very rough 4wd/ATV route, and should be attempted only by multiple self-sufficient vehicles.)

Knewstubb Lake (Maps 41/G4–42/B3)

Part of the Nechako Reservoir, Knewstubb Lake is basically a flooded forest. While this apparently makes for good fish habitat (as the rainbow that are pulled out of here look more like good sized coho, not trout), it can play merry havok with your gear. The lake also contains lake char, which also grow to a considerable size. There is a resort and forest service site on the north shore of the lake.

Konni Lake (Maps 8/G7, 9/A7)

Konni Lake contains wild rainbow, which average 0.75 kg (1.5 lbs), although some get up to 2.5 kg (5 lbs) or better. Trolling is the best method, or at least the most popular, but certainly not the exclusive way to catch fish here. The lake also contains a small contingent of small dollies (to 1 kg/2 lbs). Fishing starts in May and stays strong into October. Boaters should be aware that strong winds are common in this area. While there are no campsites at the lake, the pretty Chilko Lake Recreation Site (arguably the nicest in the Chilcotin) is just down the road.

Lavoie Lake (Map 43/B4)
Lavoie Lake is just south of Tatuk Lake, and contains rainbow to 2 kg (4 lbs). There is undeveloped camping and a cartop boat launch on the lake. Rustic footpaths lead to smaller lakes nearby.

Lessard Lake (Map 24/A3)
Lessard Lake, like many of the lakes in the Upper Dean drainage, contains hybrid cuttbow, which are a cross between a rainbow and a cut-throat. These fish are rare elsewhere in BC, but thrive here. The average catch is about 35 cm (16 inches). The lake also contains wild rainbow, averaging 1.5 kg (3+ lbs).

Lintz Lake (Map 44/D5)
Located along the Pelican Road, this popular lake is stocked annually with rainbow. The 212 hectare lake is best fished for rainbow to 1 kg (2 lbs) by trolling or fly casting. The forest service site provides a good boat launch onto the lake.

Little Anahim Lake (Map 24/B5)
Little Anahim Lake is connected to Anahim Lake by a shallow creek that gets even shallower in summer. Fishing for cuttbows (a cross between rainbow and cutthroats) is similar to the main lake.

Little Bobtail (Ed Fisher) Lake (Map 44/F1)
Found just north of Bobtail Lake, the smaller Bobtail (at 266 hectares) has rainbow to 3 kg (6.5 lbs) that can be caught by trolling or fly fishing. The lake is stocked annually with 5,000 yearlings. At 815 metres (2,649 feet), the lake does warm up during the summer, so fishing is best during the early and late parts of the season.

Little Charlotte Lake (Map 15/A2)
Little Charlotte Lake is located well away from the nearest road. Fortunately, it is accessible by boat across Charlotte Lake itself, and then a short hike in. The 159 hectare lake is known for producing small, but feisty wild rainbow, which take well to fly fishing and spincasting. The lake is over 30 feet deep, on average, and stays cool during summer, so fishing is good throughout the ice-free season.

Long Lake (Map 20/E6)
Located inside the Chilcotin Military Training Area, Long Lake contains rainbow to 1 kg (2 lbs). Please respect all signage and closures in the area.

MacKill Lake (Map 19/A1)
MacKill Lake is accessed by a short, easy hike-in from the road. The stocked lake is designated as a children's fishery, and there are a lot of small fish (average 25 cm/10 inches).

Marmot Lake (Map 36/D6)
Found two kilometres west of the Nazko Store, the 55 hectare Marmot Lake is stocked annually with 15,000 rainbow fry. Mature rainbow up to 3 kg (6+ lbs) have been pulled out of this lake, usually on flies or small spincast lures. The forest service site is now privately run and offers more facilities than most sites in the area. Anglers will appreciate the boat launch and the trail that circles the lake.

Martin Lake (Map 16/E7)
Martin Lake is located just 10 minutes north of the community of Tatla Lake. Martin is stocked with rainbow and is a popular swimming, horseback riding and winter recreation area.

McKenzie Lakes (Map 45/E3)
Found south of Prince George off the Blackwater-Mud Road are three small lakes. They have been stocked with rainbow, which grow to about 1 kg (2 lbs). Fly fishing can be surprisingly good on occasion. There are

recreation sites complete with areas to launch small boats on the first two lakes. The third lake would require bushwhacking to get to.

McLeese Lake (Map 29/F1)
McLeese Lake is situated 43 km (27mi) north of Williams Lake on Hwy 97. It is a popular fishing, swimming and water skiing lake. The lake opens up very early in the year and offers rainbow and kokanee mostly by trolling as well as whitefish. There is good access at the north end of the lake as well as a resort at the south end.

McIntyre Lake (Map 20/F7)
Found so close to Highway 20 and having a forest service site does not bold well for a good fishery. Luckily, this 18 hectare lake is stocked with both rainbow and brook trout. The 5.5 metre (18 foot) deep lake warms quickly in the summer making early spring and fall the best times to fish.

McTaggart Lake (Map 20/B3)
Accessed via a rough 2wd road (high clearance may be necessary), McTaggart Lake offers fair fishing for rainbow that can reach 1 kg (2 lbs). Fly fishing during the hatches can produce well. There is a rough cartop boat launch at the lake but access may be restricted as it lies in the Chilcotin Military Training Area.

Meadow Lake (Map 44/E5)
Meadow Lake contains a number of species of fish, but their numbers aren't great. Fishing is best in the spring and fall for rainbow that do grow to nice sizes (1.5 kg/3+ lbs). A forest service site provides camping and a cartop boat launch.

Meldrum Lake (Map 20/C3)
Stocked in the 1940's this lake still holds a few rainbow trout. Like most lakes in the area, the 167 hectare lake is best fished in the spring and fall due to its elevation (957 m/3,140 ft).

Middle Lake (Maps 6/G4, 7/A4)
Most anglers do not venture beyond Horn and Sapeye Lakes to the north. If they do, they will find a deep lake that is best trolled for bull trout, dolly varden and rainbow in the spring and fall. The 470 hectare lake is found 795 metres (2,608 feet) above sea level.

Miner Lake (Map 6/G1)
Although only 12 metres deep, this lake holds a variety of sportfish including bull trout and dollies, kokanee and rainbow. There is a forest service site with a boat launch on the 147 hectare lake. The lake is at 1,265 metres (4,150 feet) in elevation and is best fished on the fly or by casting from a small boat.

Mons Lake (Map 10/D4)
Accessed by a rough 2wd road system, Mons Lake offers fair fishing for rainbow trout. The 135 hectare lake is found at 1,150 metres (3,773 feet) in elevation and is best fished in the spring and fall.

Moose Lake (Map 33/C3)

Moose Lake is a fly-in lake about 100 km (60 miles) north of Nimpo Lake, which is the best place to find a floatplane. The lake contains rainbow to 1.5 kg (3+ lbs), which take well with spinning lures or fly fishing. Fishing remains strong from late May to September.

Mud Lakes (Map 5/A5)

Access is difficult into these small lakes found south of Swartz Lake. The lakes are known to hold rainbow trout and a float tube is recommended to get away from the mosquitoes and the swampy shoreline.

Murray Taylor Lake (Map 8/F3)

This shallow (7.6 m/25 ft) lake is all but overrun with coarse fish. There are a few rainbow trout in the 95 hectare lake.

Musclow Lake (Map 38/A7)

Another fly-in or boat-in lake found in the northwestern corner of Tweedsmuir (just off the southwest end of Eustsuk), Musclow Lake is a great fly-fishing lake. Rainbow up to 3 kg (6 lbs) make the long journey well worth the effort.

Naltesby Lake (Map 44/F2)

See Bobtail Lake.

Nazko Lake (Map 27/E7)

The second lake (or first, depending if you can get your vehicle down the rough 4wd track to the boat launch at the south end of the lake) in the Nazko Lake chain, this 117 hectare lake was regularly stocked with 20,000 rainbow, up until 2000. No word yet if they are planning on re-instating the stocking program but it is hoped that fewer fish will result in bigger fish. Currently, the fish grow to pan size. Fishing is best in spring, as the fish become muddy as the weather warms up. Powerboats are allowed.

Nimpo Lake (Maps 15/D1, 24/D7)

Like nearby Anahim Lake, Nimpo Lake is often used as the launching off point for fly-in fishing trips in the area. After all, it is the floatplane capital of BC. The lake itself is an excellent rainbow lake, with the average catch in the 1.5 kg (3+ lb) range. Fly fishing is the most popular way of catching these fish but spincasting and trolling is certainly possible.

Noaxe Lake (Map 5/B7)

This trail access, mountain lake offers good fishing for small trout. Due to the elevation, fishing is better in the summer (later June) and holds through the fall.

Norma Lake (Map 9/D2)

See Eleven Sisters Chain.

Olaf Lake (Map 31/A2)

Olaf Lake is a hike-in lake. The thing is, you have to hike-in from a fly-in lake, first. Lake District Air maintains a cabin on Tesla Lake, and it's a 40 minute hike from there to this lake. Expect fast fishing for pan size rainbow.

One Eye Lake (Map 16/A6)

Located right next to Highway 20, One Eye Lake has wild rainbow that get up to 1.5 kg (3+ lbs) and dolly varden to 4.5 kg (10 lbs). The easy access means the lake sees its fair share of anglers. As a result, fishing is fair from June to October. There is a forest service site on the lake with a cartop boat launch.

One Lake (Map 18/E1)

One Lake is the first of a pair of small lakes at the north end of Alexis Lake, and accessed off the Alexis Lake Road. It is possible to line a canoe or small boat between the lakes, which offer fairly similar fishing for rainbow to 2.5 kg (5 lbs) and brook trout to 1 kg (2 lbs). Fly fishing and spincasting yield the best results. There is a forest service site on Two Lake.

Ootsa Lake (Map 40/B1–D2)

Ootsa Lake is a huge lake forming part of the Nechako Reservoir that was flooded by the creation of the Kenney Dam. This is a flooded forest, and there is lots of debris and snags, making boating dangerous. It also makes fishing difficult, as you'll tend to catch a lot of trees. Still, the trout in here are big enough to be salmon, and many folks out trolling for these monsters use salmon trolling techniques (a flasher with hootchie or bait). The lake is subject to strong winds and big, big waves.

Owen Lake (Map 19/F2)

The good news? People have been known to pull trout up to 7.7 kg (17 lbs) from the waters of Owen Lake. The bad news? It doesn't happen all that often. In fact, pulling anything from these waters can be hit and miss at best, but the promise of monsters entices many. There are good mayfly, damsel fly and sedge hatches on this lake. It is also possible to launch small boats from lakeside.

Palmer Lake (Maps 19/A1, 28/A7)

Located a fair ways off the Highway (71 km/43 miles) along the Alex Graham Road, Palmer Lake is a popular fishing destination. The lake produces 1.5 kg (3+ lbs) rainbow regularly, and larger fish every once in a while. The last few kilometres into the forest service site are very rough, steep, and nearly impassible when wet. The lake is subject to sudden storms.

Pamela Lake (Map 9/E1)

See Eleven Sisters Chain.

Pelican Lake (Map 44/D7)

Despite the distance from any major centre, this lake has good road access and the forest service site can be busy. Despite its heavy summer time use, Pelican continues to provide good fishing for wild rainbow.

Poison & Medicine Lakes (Map 24/A3)

A pair of Poison Lakes found just east of the Upper Dean River Road. (You'll have to carry a canoe about 100 metres/325 feet to get onto one of the lakes). They're not really poisonous, in fact the second lake is locally known as Medicine Lake (the antidote of Poison). The lakes are stocked bi-annually with rainbow, which helps maintain a good fishery. Trout that average 1 kg (2 lb) that take fairly regularly to flies and small spinning lures. The odd rainbow can get up to 2.5 kg (5 lbs).

Punchaw Lake (Map 45/D5)

Known for its small rainbow (0.75 kg/1.5 lbs) that take readily to flies, this lake is extremely popular throughout the season. It is easily accessed from both Prince George and Quesnel along the Blackwater

Road. The busy forest service site is RV accessible and sports a boat launch. Trolling and fly fishing are the popular angling methods on the lake.

Punkutlaenkut Lake (Map 25/B5)
Also known as Punky Lake (much to the relief of outsiders trying to ask for directions), Punkutlaenkut Lake contains small, secretive rainbow that are well known for their ability to evade anglers. The lake was stocked during the 40s and 50s, yet the fish remain small, mostly under 0.5 kg (1 lb).

Puntchesakut Lake (Map 37/E5)
Located just off the paved Nazko Road, this lake offers fair fishing for small rainbow to 0.5 kg (1 lb). The lakeshore park offers a nice day-use area including a boat launch.

Punti Lake (Maps 17/G3-18/A3)
This 384 hectare lake is nowhere near as popular as its larger neighbour, Puntzi Lake. The smaller lake does offer a sports fishery for whitefish.

Puntzi Lake (Map 17/F3-G3)
Puntzi Lake is a popular destination that is home to a couple fishing resorts and a forest service site. Most anglers come in search of the rainbow trout that were once heavily stocked (they dumped about 100,000 fish into the lake in the late 1980s), but are now left to reproduce themselves. The result is bigger fish. There is also good fishing for kokanee, which average 0.75 kg (1.5 lbs). Spincasting and trolling are the main angling methods, although fly fishing is quite effective in the early and late parts of the season.

Pyper Lake (Map 17/D5)
Pyper Lake is found less than a kilometre off Highway 20. Needless to say, the forest service site is often quite busy. The lake is occasionally stocked with rainbow (the last time was in 2001).

Rainbow Lake (Map 33/A7)
Rainbow Lake is north of Anahim Lake on a deactivated road system. Even the Upper Dean River Road is very rough beyond Lessard Lake. The lake contains wild rainbow that average about 1.5 kg (3+ lbs), although there are bigger fish in the lake. Despite the name, the lake also contains kokanee and char.

Raven Lake (Map 19/G5)
Raven Lake is a smaller lake northeast of Hanceville and next to a main haul logging road. The lake is found off the Palmer Lake Road, and contains Eastern Brook Trout averaging 1 kg (2 lbs) and rainbow up to 2.5 kg (5 lbs). There is a large forest service site complete with a boat launch on the lake.

Redfish Lake (Maps 38/G7, 39/A7)
After a long boat ride, a short 1.6 km (1 mile) trail leads from the northern shores of Eutsuk Lake to this popular fly-fishing lake. Bringing in a canoe or tube (or waders) will help you work the lake a lot better.

Roxanne Lake (Map 9/E1)
See Eleven Sisters Chain.

Ruby Lake (Map 9/E1)
See Eleven Sisters Chain.

Rum Cache Lake (Map 41/G2)
See Cicuta Lake.

Rushes Lake (Map 10/D3)
Similar to Abrams to the north, Rushes Lake is almost too shallow (4 m/13 ft) to hold fish. Rainbow do migrate up the creek system and can be found by fly anglers working the expansive shoals.

Sapeye Lake (Map 7/C2)
Sapeye Lake is just across the road from Horn Lake, but is situated 50 metres (160 feet) lower, down a steep, narrow access road. The road leads to a forest service site at the north end of the lake. The lake is an excellent fly only lake, with wild rainbow averaging 1.5 kg (3+ lbs). The lake also contains big bull trout, with lots of fish caught in the 2.5 kg (6 lb) size range.

Scum Lake (Map 9/D2)
Despite the name, Scum Lake isn't that bad a spot, and the fishing for wild rainbow to 0.75 kg (1.5 lbs) is pretty good. There are a whole series of lakes northeast of Scum Lake (mostly part of the Eleven Sisters chain: Norma, Nancy, Roxanne, Ruby, etc.) that are connected to Scum Lake, and share similar fishing, to a greater or lesser degree. West of Scum Lake is Haines Lake, which is also part of the group. Scum Lake is found at 1,195 metres (3,920 feet) in elevation and offers a forest service site with a cartop boat launch.

Shesta Lake (Map 45/D2)
A good access road and two forest service sites mean that this lake sees its share of visitors. Fishing can be good for rainbow, which grow to 1 kg (2 lbs). As with most lakes in the area, spring and fall are the best times to fish. Shesta Lake is 60 hectares in size and found at 838 m (2,749 ft) in elevation.

Snag Lake (Map 43/G7)
Snag Lake, located 4 km (2.48 mi) west of Hanham, is a small lake with steep banks. Try fly fishing for wild rainbow.

Spruce Lake (Map 4/E7)
This remote backcountry lake can only be accessed by trail (hike/bike/horse) or floatplane. It forms the hub of the Spruce Lake Recreation Area and offers camping. The lake is known for its excellent fly fishing for rainbow that can grow to 1.5 kg (3+ lbs). Working from a float tube is your best bet since the 40 hectare lake is quite shallow and shore fishing can be quite difficult. There are private cabins found on the lake, which also holds dolly varden and whitefish. The lake is at 1,577 metres (5,174 feet) in elevation and fishing holds throughout the season.

Stillwater Lake (Map 14/D1)
Most people walk right on by Stillwater Lake on their way to Turner Lake. This is partly due to the shallow nature of the lake (it is only 5 metres/16 feet deep). But the Atnarko River feeds the 106 hectare lake and all sorts of sportfish make their way into it. Rainbow, dollies, cutthroat, whitefish and even salmon can be found. The 436 metre (1,430 foot) high lake is best fished in the early spring or fall.

Stobie Lake (Map 11/B7)
Found off the Gaspard-Churn Creek Road, this 59 hectare lake is not well known as a good fishery. There are some rainbow in the lake, which is at 1,305 metres (4,280 feet) in elevation.

Swartz (Fish) Lake (Map 5/A5)
A popular destination with 4wd enthusiasts, this 14 hectare lake holds rainbow trout. The lake is at 1,522 metres (4,993 feet) in elevation and offers fair fishing throughout the ice-free season.

Tagai Lake (Map 44/C5)

Covering 252 hectares, Tagai Lake is not high enough (830 metres/2,698 feet), big enough or deep enough (average 6.5 metres/21 feet) to stay cool in the summer. Anglers will definitely find the fishing much better in the spring or fall. The lake had about 40,000 rainbow trout dumped in it back in the early 80s, and is now a self-sustaining population. The trout come readily to fly gear or by trolling and grow to about 1 kg (2 lbs). The forest service site offers camping and a cartop boat launch.

Taseko Lakes (Map 3/C2–5)

These two high mountain lakes stretch south, deeper and deeper into the heart of the Coast Mountains. While they are not popular fishing lakes (too remote, too windy, too big, too much glacial till and too few fish are some of the more common reasons not to go), the lake does have wild rainbow and dollies. The best-known place to catch these fish is near the outflow of the Taseko River at the north end of Lower Taseko Lake. Spincaster and fly anglers should also have luck near any inflowing creek.

Tatla Lake (Maps 16/F7, 17/B6)

A long, narrow lake that parallels Highway 20, Tatla Lake has a good kokanee fishery. In fact, the average catch is rumoured to be a chunky 37 cm (15 inches). In addition to a forest service site with a steep boat launch, there is a resort with much better access to the lake.

Tatlayoko Lake (Maps 7/G6, 8/A6)

Records show that back in 1927, 146 dolly varden were deposited into Tatlayoko Lake. Although there still are some dollies, and native bull trout, the lake is better known for its rainbow trout fishing. Rainbow average from 1–2.5 kg (2–5 lbs) and can be caught by trolling, spincasting or fly fishing. Boaters should be wary of the heavy winds common on the lake.

Tatuk Lake (Map 43/D3)

Now incorporated into the relatively new Tatuk-Finger Provincial Park, Tatuk Lake is a popular angling destination. In addition to rainbow, which grow to 2 kg (4 lbs), there are abundant kokanee that also grow to about 2 kg. Most people fishing here do so on the troll. There are a few former Forest Service Campsites (which haven't been—and probably never will be—upgraded to BC Parks standard), and a boat launch. This is a beautiful, long and narrow lake, which gets its name from the Carrier word for "three hills." Kluskus, Nazko and Stoney Creek natives used to meet together here to fish in the fall.

Teepee Lake (Map 36/B2)

An old road leads into this lake, which is one of those local hideaways. In fact, an old ranger cabin has been kept clean and stocked by a few individuals. Since few people venture in, the fishing is quite good for rainbow. Please help keep the cabin clean and stocked for the next person to enjoy.

Tesla Lake (Maps 30/G2, 31/A2)

A big Tweedsmuir Park Lake that offers trophy rainbow trout up to 7 kg (15 lbs). The average is much smaller (2.5 kg/5 lbs), but that's still a lot bigger than the biggest fish in a lot of lakes. The fishing is amazing, and the setting gorgeous. Too bad the access is limited to floatplane. Then again, maybe not. There is a fishing lodge (Lake District Air maintains a cabin on the lake) on the shores of the lake.

Thumb Lake (Map 41/D2)

A small lake in the shadow of the Devil's Thumb, this fly-in lake has plenty of rainbow, which get to about 1 kg (2 lbs).

Till Lake (Map 20/F6)

Stocked with rainbow, which can grow up to 2.5 kg (6 lbs), Till Lake is found off the 1100 Road, which in turn is off highway 20. There is a forest service site at the north end of the lake.

Tiltzarone Lake (Map 37/E5)

A small lake just south of the Nazko Road, Tiltzarone Lake is known for producing some fairly big wild rainbow, up to 2.5 kg (5 lbs). The lake is accessed via a short trail.

Titetown Lake (Map 44/B7)

Titetown Lake is located about 24 km (14.88 mi) west of the Nazko-Euchiniko Road junction, and offers anglers an opportunity to fish for wild stock rainbow and dolly varden. There is a recreation site on the east end of this long lake.

Tory Lake (Map 44/G4)

Tory Lake is located alongside the Pelican Road and sports a small forest service site. This small 19 hectare lake is occasionally stocked with rainbow, which don't grow too big. Fly fishing towards the marshy shoreline is the most effective method.

Tsacha Lake (Map 34/B4)

A challenge for you, try placing a fly on the water and retrieve it before it gets inhaled by one of the rainbow that inhabit the lake. Yes, fishing Tsacha can be that good, but you've got to get there first. Tsacha is a remote lake. You can fly-in, paddle along the Blackwater River or access it by foot along the Alexander Mackenzie Trail.

Tsuniah Lake (Map 8/E6)

Tsuniah Lake doesn't produce big fish, but they usually come at your hook fast and furious. Rainbow average up to 1 kg (2 lbs), and are fairly indiscriminate, taking to flies, spinners and trolling gear with equal voracity. Fishing stays strong June through October. The lake is subject to strong winds that filter down the high mountain valley.

Turner Lake (Map 14/D2)

The Tote Road, a rough 4wd road, heads south from Highway 20 to the trailhead for the hike up to Turner Lake. It's 16 km (9 miles) from the end of the road to the lake, much of that slogging uphill. Many people prefer to fly-in. The seven lakes in the chain (including Junker, Widgeon and Kidney Lakes) form the headwaters of the Atnarko River, and contain cutthroat trout, which usually range between 0.5 and 1 kg (1 to 2 lbs). Check the regulations for special restrictions.

Twin Lakes (Map 37/F2)

Getting a boat down onto the Twin Lakes is a difficult proposition, as the banks are very steep, and there is no launch. Most of the fishing for the generally small trout is done from shore or on a float tube.

Two Lake (Map 18/E2)

Two Lake is located just past Alexis Lake. As the name implies, Two Lake is the second of a pair of small lakes, joined together by a short channel (the other lake being, surprise, surprise, One Lake). The lake is well stocked with rainbow that grow to 2.5 kg (5 lbs) and native brook trout to 1 kg (2 lbs). Fly fishing works well, as does spincasting. There is a small forest service site on the shore, and a cartop boat launch for electric motors only.

Tzenzaicut (Fish) Lake (Map 28/G3)

Locals unwilling to wrap their mouths around the name call this Fish Lake, a tribute to both the number and the quality of the fish here. Early summer is the best time to catch wild rainbow. You'll find them in the 20 to 38 cm (10 to 15 inch) range, and they take well to flies, spinning lures or trolling. The road to the lake is in good condition and there is a popular forest service site with a boat launch on the lake.

Vedan Lake (Map 9/A6)

Vedan Lake contains wild rainbow averaging 1 kg (2 lbs), although some can get up to 2.5 kg (5 lbs). But the real draw here is the bull trout, which can get up to 7 kg (15 lbs). Angling remains strong throughout the late spring to early fall, mostly by trolling. Although flies work well for the rainbow, you will have to get deeper to lure the bull trout. There is a forestry recreation site at the lake that provides a good boat launch onto the often windy lake.

Wahla Lake (Maps 30/G1, 31/A1)

Wahla Lake is a hike-in lake, with rainbow to 7 kg (15 lbs). The walk-in is only 20 minutes, along a trail from Tesla Lake. The bad news is that Tesla Lake is a fly-in lake, many, many, many miles from the nearest road. Still, if you've got the time and, more importantly, the money, there are worse places to spend a vacation.

West (Nadsilinch) Lake (Map 45/G1)

West Lake is bigger than many of the lakes in the immediate area, so it sees its share of recreational use. The bigger lake doesn't mean bigger trout. Like most lakes in the area, the rainbow tend to top out at 1 kg (2 lbs). Trolling is the preferred method of fishing. West Lake Provincial Park is a popular place for a picnic and offers a boat launch.

Whitton Lake (Map 14/G5)

Natives call this lake Nuk Tessli Lake, which translates to West Wind Lake. No matter what you call it, few visitors are willing to hoof it into this remote area. At 1,494 metres (4,900 feet) the 235 hectare lake offers good fishing for rainbow trout from June through fall.

Widgeon Lake (Map 14/C3)

Part of the Turner Lake Canoe Route, anglers can also fly-in to this beautiful backcountry lake. The seven lakes in the Turner Lake Chain (including Kidney, Junker and Turner Lakes) form the headwaters of the Atnarko River, and contain cutthroat trout, which usually range between 0.5 and 1 kg (1 to 2 lbs). Check the regulations for special restrictions.

Yimpakluk Lake (Map 36/B1)

Very few people fish this lake, mostly do to the fact that the lake requires bushwhacking to get into it. (Some brave drivers have crossed the Euchinko River in a 4wd vehicle and followed the Alexander MacKenzie Trail to within easy walking distance). The lake has been stocked with rainbow trout, and contains lots of fish in the 1 kg (2 lb) range.

Stream Fishing

This region spans a vast chunk of real estate, and there are two distinct styles of stream fishing to be found here. The world famous Dean River is a classic example. The Lower Dean River is a salmon stream, well known for its impressive steelhead runs. But most salmon bearing streams in this Chilcotin region are tributaries of the Fraser River, and not of the major Central Coast Rivers. The Dean, like the Bella Coola, are notable exceptions to the rule. This is because many of the streams in the western portion of this book plunge too steeply from the Coast Mountains to support a salmon run beyond a certain point.

Rivers in the high country of the Chilcotin Plateau are best known as trout streams. The Upper Dean is like this, separated from its lower reaches by rapids and falls, the Upper Dean is full of feisty rainbow trout. So to, are many of the creeks and rivers that are found east of Tweedsmuir.

Below we have described most of the fishable streams in the area. Access into many of the other streams hinders both the fish and anglers from enjoying these wild waters. There are also many smaller streams that we have not mentioned. Some of these dry out in the summer while others are simply tributaries of the bigger creeks and rivers that have similar characteristics and fish species as the bigger streams.

Atnarko River (Maps 14/G2-22/E7)

One of the most popular angling destinations in the area, the Atnarko is a lovely place to be, even if you don't manage to catch anything. The most popular place to fish in this fast, clean river is the Fisheries Pool (Map 22/G7) in Tweedsmuir Park. There is a strong chinook run in June and July. Consult your regulations before heading out.

Baezaeko River (Maps 35/A7-36/C3)

The Baezaeko River is a fairly long river, but access is limited to a few road crossings, mostly in the Coglistiko Lake area. The river contains native rainbow trout to 2 kg (4+ lbs), and bull trout to 5 kg (10+ lbs). This is an excellent fly fishing river.

Bella Coola River (Maps 21/E7-22/E7)

A combination of the Atnarko and the Talchako Rivers, the Bella Coola has excellent fishing for cutthroat trout during the March fry migration. The river is also a hot bed of activity during the salmon runs. Chinook begin to appear in the river in late May and run through July. Bar fishing with a heavy weight and spin n glow is the preferred method for large fish that reach tyee status (14+ kg/30+ lbs). The other runs include coho (September to November), pink (August and September), sockeye (August and September) and chum salmon (late July through October). These runs do not receive the same attention that chinook do. Most of the property surrounding this river is private and access is limited. Consult the regulations before heading out.

Big Creek (Maps 4/B6-11/A1)

This is indeed a big creek as it flows from Elbow Mountain all the way north to the Chilcotin River. The creek is easily accessed from a number of different roads south of the Chilcotin River and it contains wild rainbow that are best caught by fly-fishing or small spincasting gear. The best time to go fishing for rainbow is July through October. The creek also contains dolly varden in its upper reaches, which can be accessed by trail.

Blackwater (West Road) River (Maps 33-37, 44, 45)

The Blackwater River runs about the colour of tea and finds its source high in the Ilgachuz Mountains. It flows hundreds of kilometres through several lakes to finally join with the Fraser. The river is gentle, and mostly canoeable (with a few notable exceptions; the name West Road comes from its use as a liquid highway in the early days of the province). The river contains rainbow, whitefish and pike minnow. It is a great fly fishing river, with trout averaging 14 inches (35 cm). Access is limited to trail and bushwhacking in the upper regions (above Kluskoil Lake Provincial Park), and there are only a few places where bridges span the river.

Chilako (Mud) River (Maps 43/E4-45/C1)

The Chilako drains Tatuk Lake and crosses a number of forest service roads and continues north of our maps to the Nechako River (see Central BC Mapbook). Despite the good fishing, the river is rarely fished. As a result, there are some nice size rainbow and dollies that are readily taken by fly fishing or spincasting. Due to the dark muddy waters, anglers should use flies with attractants or spinners. Consult the regulations before heading out.

Chilcotin River (Maps 10, 11, 17, 18, 19, 25, 26)

A major tributary of the Fraser, the Chilcotin has resident stocks of wild rainbow and dollies. The fish can be found throughout the river and average about 1 kg (2 lbs) in size. The river is also home to strong runs of steelhead and chinook salmon that run as far upstream as the Chilko River. Check the regulations before heading out.

Chilko River (Maps 8/E4-18/F5)

Flowing out of Chilko Lake and into the Chilcotin River, the Chilko is best known for its wild rapids and great kayaking/rafting. It is only slightly less famous for its great fishing for wild rainbow, dollies, steelhead and chinook. The best fishing for rainbow and dollies is the first 20 km (12 miles) below Chilko Lake. The river is heavily regulated to protect the fishery. Check the regulations before heading out.

Cluculz Creek (Map 44/D1)

Cluculz Creek contains rainbow to 1 kg (2 lbs). The short section shown in this book can be fished after high water has resided (June to July).

Churn Creek (Maps 5/A2-G7)

A waterfall 19 km (11.6 miles) upstream of Churn Creek's confluence with the Fraser creates an effective barrier, dividing the creek in two. Above the falls, the creek contains rainbow and bull trout. Below the falls, the creek also plays host to migrating chinook and pink salmon. Access into this remote stream is very limited.

Dash Creek (Maps 4/E3-5/A4)

Dash Creek contains rainbow and bull trout. These are important populations, as they are isolated from the rest of the Fraser River drainage by a falls on Churn Creek.

Dean River (Maps 21, 22, 23, 24, 30, 31, 32)

The Dean River flows out of Nimpo Lake, through Anahim Lake, and then on into Tweedsmuir Park and eventually down into the Pacific Ocean. The Lower Dean is one of the finest fishing destinations in the province during its steelhead run (which peaks in August), although access is limited to boat or plane. It still sees a lot of pressure, and is surprisingly crowded, for such a remote river. It also sees a strong chinook run in June, and a fair run of coho in August and September.

The Upper Dean River is a completely different river, offering fine fly fishing for resident trout. Access to the Upper Dean is easy, as the river even crosses Highway 20 between Nimpo and Anahim Lake. The Dean is a heavily regulated river, so check the guide before heading out.

Fraser River (Maps 5, 11, 20, 29)

The Chilcotin is defined by the mighty Fraser River. Locals refer to the high elevation plateau west of the Fraser as the Chilcotin. The Fraser is a huge river, the largest in BC, and still moves a lot of water this far north. In this book, fishing is open for rainbow, dollies and whitefish. The best places to fish are usually where streams enter the river. Consult the regulations for site specific and river specific information and restrictions.

Homathko River (Maps 1/A4-G1; 7/E4-G5)

While the Homathko is most certainly fishable south of Tatlayoko Lake, access is fairly difficult. The upper reaches offer fair fishing for small rainbow and dollies, which may weigh up to 0.5 kg (1 lb).

Lone Cabin Creek (Map 5/D4-G2)

There is a set of impassable falls a mere 200 metres up from Lone Cabin Creek's confluence with the Fraser. Below the falls, the river contains rainbow and chinook salmon. Above the falls, the creek contains bull trout. Roaster Lake (Map 5/C4) has been stocked with rainbow, which may also inhabit the system. To date, there have been no solid reports of rainbow in the lonely creek.

McClinchy Creek (Maps 15/A7-16/C7)

Highway 20 parallels this stream for a few kilometers and provides the best access to this fast moving creek. The stream contains small, wild rainbow that have a lot of energy.

Mosley Creek (Maps 1/A3, 6/G6, 7/B4)

A tributary of the Homathko River, Mosley Creek contains wild bull trout. Outside of the upper reaches between Twist Lake (Map 6/G6) and Bluff Lake (Map 7/C3), access is very limited.

Nazko River (Map 27/F5-36/E2)

The Nazko River contains rainbow trout to 2.5 kg (5 lbs), and bull trout to 5 kg (10+ lbs). There are plenty of good access points to the river, as the Nazko and Honolulu Roads parallel the lower and mid sections of this fine river.

Porcupine Creek (Map 5/E2)

A short tributary of Lone Cabin Creek (see above), this creek contains bull trout, and may also contain rainbow.

West Churn Creek (Map 4/F2-5/B2)

West Churn Creek contains rainbow trout and bull trout. The bull trout are only found in the lower reaches as they are unable to get beyond a series of waterfalls.

Paddling Routes

(Lake, River and Stream Fishing)

River Trips

While the Chilcotin is home to one of the province's most famous whitewater trips, the Chilko, it is also home to a number of very small, low flow rivers. Although many of these are not the best paddling routes, there is enough variety and some very, very remote streams to explore.

For each river, we have included the put-in and take-out locations for the most popular runs on that river. Also included are short descriptions highlighting the route as well as the grading system.

We use a modified version of the international scale to grade rivers. The grade of a run tells you how difficult overall a stretch of river is. Class rates individual rapids, chutes and other features. A run might be rated Grade II overall, but one section might feature a Class IV drop. In most cases, portages have been established to allow less experienced paddlers a chance to avoid the difficult features of any run.

Please note that these descriptions given in this book are limited, and may not contain enough detail to navigate certain rivers safely, especially rivers with higher ratings. We recommend that you check the current conditions with local canoeists/kayakers or local outdoor stores before heading onto a river. It is also essential to scout ahead. River conditions can change daily.

Baezeko River (Map 36/A5-C2)
From the put-in near Coglistiko Lake to where it joins the Blackwater, the Baezaeko is a fast-moving, low flow river with lots of rocks and corners. Don't take a boat you love, as you'll probably hit lots of rocks on your way down. The river is probably a grade II+, but is more exciting in higher water levels. This river should be attempted just after spring run-off.

Baker Creek (Map 37/D6-G5)
Extreme kayakers in the central interior stick to a short section of Baker Creek that features a two metre high waterfall and a pair of rapids, rated class IV and class V. But there is 55 km (33.6 miles) of much milder, grade II water featuring some class III sections on the creek. The big rapids come at the 15 km (9.1 mile) mark below the put-in at the bridge over Baker on Tibbles Road (Map 37/D6). To access this section, drive 30.3 km (18.5 miles) along the Nazko Road from Highway 97, and watch for the gravel pit on your left. Portage trails developed by folks running this section can also be used to portage around the rapids. Below these rapids, the river continues on to its confluence with the Fraser. The take-out is in Quesnel, behind the West Park Mall (east of this map; see Cariboo Mapbook).

Blackwater (West Road) River (Maps 33-37, 44, 45)
Also known as the West Road, this river was the main route west for fur traders in the 1800's. The Blackwater River is mostly easy paddling (which means it can be done in an open canoe), it does have a few tricky sections, including a couple enforced portages (like the 4 metre (13 foot) high waterfall between Tsacha and Euchinko). In late summer and fall, the river runs low, and you may need to get out and line through shallow sections, but one of the nicest times to go is after the leaves change in the fall. There are very few alternate take-outs on the river, so travellers need to be self-sufficient.

Put In: Eliguk Lake (Map 33/B5)

Take Out: Nazko Bridge (Map 36/E3)

Access to the trailhead is via a long (very, very long) carry in along the Alexander Mackenzie Trail, or by floatplane. Do yourself a favour; choose the latter. From Eliguk Lake, follow Ulgako Creek to its junction with the Blackwater. You will probably have to carry this first 2 km (1.2 miles) section. Below the junction, the Blackwater is little more than a creek, with narrow rapids, logjams and sweepers, as well as waterfalls interspersed with some sections that can actually be paddled. The river flows into Tsasha Lake, then out again, through a portagable canyon and over the Kusyuko Falls (2.5 km upstream of Euchinko Lakes). Below Euchinko, the river moves quickly (grade II), but keep your eyes out for Chinee Falls below Kluskoil Lake. Past the falls, the river continues to Nazko Bridge and the West Road River Recreation Site.

Put In: Nakzo Bridge (Map 36/E3)

Take Out: Batnuni Bridge (Map 36/F1)

This is one of the easiest sections of the river, defined by easy riffles followed by shallow pools. A great paddle for beginners. For the true beginner, take out at Gilles Crossing, accessed by paddling a short way up the Euchinko (which enters river left). For the last 1.5 km (.9 miles) to the Batnuni Bridge, the river begins to pass through rapids, including a class III+ canyon that is very difficult to portage.

Put In: Batnuni Bridge (Map 36/F1)

Take Out: Blackwater Bridge (Map 45/C7)

Between these two bridges, the Blackwater is a fairly easy (grade I) river with a fair number of class II and class III features to keep you on your toes. Closed boat paddlers will find the long sections of flatwater boring, while inexperienced open boat paddlers will find the rapids too much. But for the experienced open canoeist, this is a great section. Remember, to scout all rapids! One of the most interesting sections is the second canyon, where the river narrows to a mere four feet of calm water. At high water levels, this section becomes a lot harder, and should only be attempted by experienced paddlers.

Put In: Blackwater Bridge (Map 45/C7)

Take Out: Fraser River (Map 45/G7)

This section of the Blackwater is one of the best open craft paddles in the area. Experienced kayakers will find the class II and III features fairly tame, but the same river, run in an open canoe, is much more dangerous and exciting. There are a lot of things to keep your eyes open for; fast rapids, plenty of boulders, standing waves, holes and ledges. Fortunately, there are a lot of eddies, too. The take-out is reached by paddling up the Fraser River for 2 km (1.2 miles) to an old logging landing. The current is a lot easier to paddle against on river left (across the river), but strong tandem paddlers can bash their way upstream on river right.

Chilcotin River (Maps 17/F1-11/E3)
The Chilcotin is one of the major tributaries of the Fraser River. The most popular section of the river is from Hanceville (Map 19/C7) to Farwell Canyon Bridge (Map 11/C1), although this is a difficult take-out up the steep walled canyon. An easier alternative is to take-out at the Durell Ranch, if you can get permission from the owners. The Chilcotin is mostly grade I, with a pair of canyons and rapids up to Class III (Big Creek Rapid). A much less tested route is to continue on past the Chilcotin/Fraser Confluence and take out at the Gang Ranch Bridge, which is a multi-day trip through very remote country. If you get into trouble, there is little chance of outside help, so know what you're doing. Big John Canyon, just above the Fraser Confluence, is one of the most difficult sections of the trip, and is rated class III+ or higher. The Fraser section is mostly flatwater, but it is a big river, and shouldn't be underestimated.

Chilko River (Maps 8, 9, 18)

The Chilko River drains the famed Chilko Lake and makes a great rafting and kayaking river. There are three distinct sections ranging from grades I-III as well as some classic Class IV features to play in.

Put in: Chilko Lake (Map 8/D5)

Take Out: Henry's Crossing (Map 18/E3)

> This section is an easy grade I/II paddle that can be done by canoes. The river is wide and slow moving, with great views of the surrounding mountains.

Put in: Henry's Crossing (Map 18/E3)

Take Out: Taseko Junction (Map 18/C6)

> The Chilko picks up steam below Henry's Crossing, as it passes into a canyon with small rapids (up to Class III), and some big standing waves. Kayakers often put in just above Bidwell Rapid, and the famous White Mile, a mile-long stretch of continual Class IV rapids. Kayakers often take out just after the Eagle Claw Rapid, the last major feature on the river.

Put in: Taseko Junction (Map 18/C6)

Take Out: Bull Canyon (Map 18/G5)

> The last section of the river is rated grade II/III+, with one hazardous spot at Siwash Bridge. The river funnels into a narrow opening between the bridge piers, which is essential to scout ahead (as wood can block the opening). Not a challenging section, but lots of little play features.

Dean River (Maps 24/E7-30/C7)

The Dean River starts at Nimpo Lake, but most people start at Anahim Lake. One option is to arrange for a fly-out at Boy Lake (Map 32/A6). This section is fairly easy, but there are a few rapids that may need to be portaged around, and a couple shallow sections that may need to be lined. Give yourself about five days to get to Boy Lake, as the river wanders across the high country into Tweedsmuir Park. Below Boy, the Dean begins its descent from the Chilcotin Plateau down to the ocean.

This section is most famous for its world-class steelhead fishing, but it is also a classic Class V whitewater adventure through a remote wilderness. Don't underestimate how difficult this section is, as you will face many rapids, cataracts, constricted canyons, and maybe some logjams. Oh yeah, there's also a bunch of waterfalls along the way, too. You will have to arrange for floatplane drop off at Boy Lake, and pick-up once you hit the ocean.

Entiako River/Fawnie Creek (Map 32/G2-42/A2)

This is a wilderness route that passes through a number of lakes, many of them sporting lodges. The best time to go is just after spring runoff, as the water levels get too low in summer. Upstream of Fawnie Creek (Map 32/G2) the river is little more than a trickle. By some odd coincidence, Fawnie Creek is also the farthest road accessible point in the area. Fawnie can be a rough ride; it's not difficult, just shallow. If you treasure the bottom of your boat, you might want to line. More adventurous paddlers can put-in at the bridge over Matthews Creek (Map 33/F3), and ride this constantly moving, rocky stream. (Locals advise that you run most of this section in an empty, soft bottom boat.) The take-out is at Kenney Dam (Map 42/A2), and requires a 30 km (18 mile) paddle along the often windy, snag riddled Nechako Reservoir. (The wind is usually a tail wind; set up a sail and coast home.) The route is rated at grade I/II and watch for sweepers around some of the corners.

Fraser River (Maps 5, 11, 20, 29)

The Fraser is a big river, with more sections and more features than can be accurately described in the space we have here. It ranges from a slow, meandering behemoth to a thundering man-killer. The section that runs through our maps is a mixture of both. From Quesnel (see Cariboo Mapbook) south to Highway 20 (Map 20/G7) the river offers a fast mostly flatwater route. However, there are few access points and the sheer volume of water should not be underestimated. Below Highway 20 to the Dog Creek Road (Map 11/G7), the river enters some dynamic canyons and rapids that need to be scouted and should only be run by the experienced kayaker. The Dog Creek Road put-in marks the beginning of a popular commercial rafting area. If you want to sample this river, we recommend going with a rafting company.

Klinaklini River (Map 6/G2-A2; 15/F7, 16/C7)

This is not a trip for the average Joe. One of the wildest rivers in Canada, the Klinaklini passes through an unrunnable canyon. Portaging around this section would be almost impossible. Currently, the only people running the river are commercial rafters who heli-portage over this section. Elsewhere, the river is known for a pair of class V drops and long sections of class IV rapids that are also very difficult to get around. The Klinaklini is one of the few rivers that starts in the Chilcotin Plateau and flows west, not east to the Fraser. It has to struggle through some of the wildest territory, and some of the most dramatic scenery this province has to offer. We recommend that if you want to make this trip, do it as a rafting trip with Butterfield and Robinson, the only commercial operator running the river.

Nazko River (Map 27/G2-36/E1)

From the 35 km bridge on Honolulu Road (Map 27/G2), it is a five hour, grade II/III trip down the Nazko to the 13 km bridge (Map 27/E1). This section of the river is faster moving than the lower Nazko, and should only be attempted by folks with some experience on moving water. Below the 13 km bridge, the Nazko is an easy (grade I) float down to the Blackwater. Most people continue up to the Euchinko River and the Gilles Crossing take-out. It may be possible to canoe the river from the end of the Nazko Lake Chain, but the river moves very little water, and goes over a number of waterfalls that will be difficult to get around.

Nechako River (Map 42/A1)

While most of this river is found in the Central BC Mapbook, the Nechako flows out of the Nechako Reservoir at Kenny Dam and very quickly over Cheslatta Falls. To avoid the canyon, put-in below the falls. The first section of the river is an easy grade I paddle, with a short class II rapid. The first takeout is found at Cutoff Creek Rec Site (Map 42/B1), but the river continues on to Prince George, and a confluence with the Fraser, rarely getting above grade II in difficulty.

Snaking River (Map 36/G7–D4)

A few people have successfully navigated the Snaking, but the river sports a couple major waterfalls that are nearly impossible to portage around. One group who did it said their only way past the falls was to throw their boats over, then climb down and swim to recover them. If you do attempt this river, collect as much local knowledge as you can.

Taseko River (Map 3/C1–18/C6)

From Taseko Lake, the Taseko River follows a road for about a third of its length, before heading through a mostly untracked wilderness. The river is mostly grade II/III, but there are some class IV features, including Taseko Falls. Expect to take three days from Taseko Lake to the confluence of the Taseko and the Chilko.

Lake Paddling

The Chilcotin is thick with lakes. They are everywhere. And most of them can be paddled. As a general rule, smaller lakes are easier to paddle, because they aren't subject to the same winds that bigger lakes are. Bigger lakes, like Chilko, Taseko, and Tatlayoko Lakes should be left to experienced paddlers, preferably in closed crafts.

Rather than list every lake you can get a canoe into (which is basically any lake you can get to), we have listed the three main canoe routes in the area as well as those lakes with better access. Please note that the canoe routes (Nazko Lakes, Nechako Reservoir and to a less degree Turner Lakes) should be approached with all caution. All three travel through unpopulated areas, and if you run into problems, you need to be self-sufficient.

Alexis Lake (Map 18/E2)

There is a sandy beach at the forest service site on the shores of the lake, and a cartop boat launch, which is where you can launch your canoe to paddle around this small, usually calm lake.

Batnuni Lake (Map 43/F6)

Batnuni is a long, narrow lake, that is actually just a widening of the Euchinko River. There are a pair of forest service sites on the shores of the lake, and a few islands to explore in the middle of the lake.

Big Lake (Map 9/B7)

It isn't really a Big Lake, nor is it that small of a lake. Rather, this is a medium-sized lake that can occasionally kick up a heavy chop. Access is from the Nemiah Valley Road.

Blue Jay Lake (Map 12/C1)

Blue Jay Lake is found high in the Coast Mountains, 26 km (15.9 miles) southwest of Bella Coola. Access is via a steep, often rough forestry service road and the last few kilometres are 4wd accessible only. The lake isn't very big, but it is a beautiful place to paddle about. There is rarely much of a chop, even on windy days.

Bluff Lake (Map 7/C3)

While the road past Horn Lake seems to terminate at a private residence, it actually skirts right around the property and on to this pretty lake. It isn't a large lake, but the valley tends to channel the wind, which can make for a choppy paddle.

Boat Lake (Map 44/A7)

Another in a series of lakes strung out along the Euchinko River. This is a small, round looking lake, with a forest service site on its north shore. The lake is fairly well protected from wind.

Bobtail Lake (Map 44/F2)

There is a cartop boat launch at the forest service site on the east side of Bobtail Lake and a few interesting features to explore. The lake is fairly large, and canoeists shouldn't get too far away from shore in case of wind.

Boot Lake (Map 37/A1)

Located just off the paved Blackwater Road, this small lake is fairly sheltered from the wind, and offers a good place to paddle for both recreationists and anglers.

Chilko Lake (Maps 2, 8)

Chilko Lake is not recommended for open canoes, but for folks in closed boats, especially touring kayaks, this is a marvelous destination. The often windy lake is much like a fjord, although it is actually well above sea level. As you paddle farther south, the mountains get bigger and more impressive. There are rustic camping spots at various creek mouths along the lake.

Eagle Lake (Maps 8/A1-17/B7)

Occasionally subject to heavy chop, this medium sized, shallow lake is a popular fishing lake.

Eleven Sisters Chain (Map 9/E2)

Remote and wild is the best way to describe these lakes. Other than Scum Lake, which has a forest service site, these lakes see few visitors. But the close proximity of the core lakes (Norma, Nancy, Lac LeLievre, Ruby and Roxanne) makes stringing these lakes together into a wilderness paddling route certainly possible. There are no established portages but the nice scenery and good fishing for small, but wild rainbow should make up for the lack of development.

Hanham Lake (Maps 43/G7-44/A7)

Another Euchinko River lake, Hanham is a very small lake with an island in the centre. It is not subject to high winds.

Horn Lake (Map 7/C2)

A popular fishing lake, this mid-sized body of water is long and somewhat narrow. This means that wind can get funneled down the lake, making it a choppy place to canoe on occasion. But the scenic valley offers impressive views down the lake towards the Niut Range of mountains.

Nazko Lakes Canoe Route (Map 27/D7-F5)

If you approach this series of shallow lakes as a challenge, as a place where you can race to the end and back to see some great scenery, you will miss the magic of the lakes. Oh, sure, the lakes are pretty enough, and can be easily done in one very long day, or two shorter days, but they aren't as spectacular as, say, the Turner Lake Chain. The magic comes when you slow down, and watch the eagles, circling in the air or watch the fish jump to catch insects in the evening. Lucky visitors may even be graced with a flight of giant pelicans passing overhead. Go early in the year when the water is high. During the summer a couple of the lakes are very shallow and weed choked, making passage difficult.

Nechako Reservoir Circuit (Maps 31, 38-41)

BC Parks say don't do it, but people do anyway. There are a lot of reasons not to do this trip. For the most part, they are a series of big, windy lakes that pass though a flooded forest with lots of snags that can cause unwanted trouble in a very remote part of BC. But the area offers some remarkable scenery, and, quite frankly, poses a challenge that many avid adventurers can't pass up. If you do go, expect to take a week to make your way around the circuit. There are a few places to launch, as Knewstubb Lake, Intata Reach, Ootsa Lake and Whitesail Lake are all accessed by logging road from the north (see our Central BC edition). There are portages joining Whitesail Lake and St Thomas Bay of Eutsuk Lake as well as linking Eutsuk Lake with Tetachuck Lake. The remote area offers endless areas to pull up on shore and camp but please stick to the designated campsites (marked on the maps) when travelling through Tweedsmuir Park. Many people rig their canoes with

sails to help pass the many, many miles, but that only helps if the wind is going the right way.

We aren't recommending this trip, as it is for experienced wilderness travellers only. The challenges probably outweigh the gratification but in an era of adventure racing, perhaps that is the appeal of this route.

One Eye Lake (Map 16/A7)

There is a forest service site on the shores of this medium-sized lake, just off Highway 20. Most of the paddlers on this lake also bring a fishing rod to test their luck for wild rainbow trout and large dolly varden.

Puntchesakut Lake (Map 37/F5)

A medium sized lake just off the paved Nazko Road, there is a provincial park on the east shores of this lake. It is a popular place to visit for the day and the lake is a good place for a family canoe trip.

Pyper Lake (Map 17/D6)

Although Pyper Lake is still firmly entrenched in the rolling plateau of the Chilcotin, there are great views of the Coast Mountains when looking west down the lake. This is a popular angling lake, but you don't have to bring a rod to enjoy a spin around the lake.

Sapeye Lake (Map 7/C2)

An attractive lake set in a valley below the Westbranch road, this lake is long and narrow. Wind can play havoc with paddlers at times.

Tatlayoko Lake (Maps 1/G1-7/G5; 8/A6)

A big, long, narrow lake, this lake should not be paddled in an open boat, as the winds howl down the valley and can kick up a heck of a chop. For folks in touring kayaks, this can be a fun trip since the lake is set in an impressive valley. The Tatlayoko Lake Road is never far from the east shore, but there are few signs of settlement and ever-improving scenery as you head south.

Turner Lake Canoe Route (Map 14/B3-D1)

One of the most celebrated lake circuits in the province, this superlative-laden trip is nearly impossible to oversell. The trip is second in popularity only to the Bowron Lakes (see Cariboo Mapbook), and only because access to this circuit is limited by a 16.4 km (10 miles) portage from the parking lot. For those not interested in this long uphill 'portage', there are canoes for rent at Turner Lake. The scenery is such that people have even gone through the trouble and expense to fly into Turner to avoid the long haul in. The lakes are located in the high mountains of Tweedsmuir Park and cut through virgin forest set beneath towering, snowcapped peaks. There are beautiful white sand beaches, backcountry campsites and very good fishing along the way.

Parks

(Provincial Parks and Protected Areas)

In terms of numbers, the Chilcotin/Central Coast district has very few parks, compared to the rest of the province. While there are groups working to see new parks developed in the area, it would be difficult to argue that the Chilcotin/Central Coast is lacking in park area. The largest of the BC parks, Tweedsmuir, bisects the Central Coast from the Chilcotin Plateau, protecting a unique and varied wilderness. In addition, the area has Ts'yl-os, Big Creek, Itcha Ilgachuz, and Entiako Provincial Parks and Protected Areas, all of which preserve thousands and thousands of acres of wildland for conservation and recreation purposes. Because of the size and remoteness of the area, many of the parks only offer rustic camping, more akin to a Forest Service site than a park. Indeed, many of the campgrounds are former Forest Service campgrounds. Some notable exceptions are the campgrounds in Tweedsmuir, and Bull Canyon Provincial Park.

Big Creek Provincial Park (Maps 3, 4, 10)

Big Creek Provincial Park protects a section of the much-contended South Chilcotin. While many environmentalists would like to see a greater section of this marvelous wilderness protected, the 65,982 hectare Big Creek is nothing to be ashamed of. It protects a huge swath of land, from the dramatic mountainous terrain in the south to gentler volcanic hills and the flat, forested Chilcotin Plateau in the north. There is limited road access to the north and east park boundary, but for the most part, this is a trail access park with few if any developed facilities. The southern part of Big Creek Park is the more popular destination with hikers and horseback riders, as it encompasses portions of the former Spruce Lake Trail System. The park is home to many species of wildlife, from bighorn sheep and moose to wolves and grizzly bear.

Bobtail Mountain Provincial Park (Maps 44/G1, 45/A1)

A park designated in June 2000, Bobtail Mountain Park protects 1,360 hectares around Bobtail Mountain, a popular hiking destination northeast of Bobtail Lake. The main feature is the unusual outcropping of rock. Access into this area is via the Bobtail Mountain Trail, a 5 km (3 mile) trail that leads to a trio of viewpoints.

Bull Canyon Provincial Park (Map 18/G5)

Bull Canyon is a small park located in a beautiful canyon along Highway 20. The cool, colourful Chilcotin River flows past one of the few developed public campgrounds in the area. In addition to a short walking trail next to the river, the surrounding area supports excellent fishing lakes, bird watching and wildlife viewing opportunities. Bull Canyon is also a site of Indian Pictographs. There are 20 campsites, ranging from small to RV-sized.

Churn Creek Protected Area (Maps 5, 11)

The unique and fragile landscape protected within the boundaries of Churn Creek provides habitat for some of BC's rarest ecosystems, low, middle and high elevation bunchgrass grasslands. The 36,100 hectare park offers opportunities for hiking, mountain biking, horseback riding and wildlife viewing. Road access into the area is through a series of forestry roads that culminate at the Empire Valley Ranch, a working ranch within the protected area. A 4wd vehicle is recommended, as the roads can be extremely slippery and rutted when wet. There is a small camping area with pit toilets at the ranch near the calving barn. Alternatively, camping is possible off the side of various roads. Please camp at existing sites to limit vegetation impact.

Entiako Provincial Park and Protected Area (Maps 32, 33, 40, 41)

Entiako Park and Protected Area is a remote wilderness area east of the northern section of Tweedsmuir. 48,261 hectares of the 121,529 hectares is classified as Class A Park. The area helps protect the gentle rolling woodlands and old pine trees of the region as well as a diverse selection of larger mammals including woodland caribou, moose, bear and wolves. People who do make it into the area can enjoy the opportunity to boat, fish, hunt or hike an area far removed from civilization.

Finger-Tatuk Provincial Park (Map 43/C3)

Surrounding Finger and Tatuk Lakes, this park extends south to include the smaller Turff, Vance, Cory, Bodley, and Harp Lakes, which lie south of the Tatuk Hills. These are popular backcountry fishing lakes containing rainbow and kokanee. Camping at the park is available at former forest service sites at the east and west ends of Tatuk Lake, and on Expansion Lake. These sites have not been upgraded to BC Park's standards, but are open to campers nonetheless. There is a boat launch at the east end of Tatuk Lake as well as at the private resorts on Tatuk and Finger Lakes. Paddling and exploring old roads in the area are other popular pastimes in the park.

Fraser River Provincial Park (Map 45/G4)

Located on the west bank of the Fraser River, this 4,899 hectare park was created to protect a piece of one of BC's greatest rivers. There are no developed facilities at the park.

Homathko River-Tatlayoko Protected Area (Maps 1, 6, 7, 8)

Protecting the Homathko River and Mosley Creek Valleys, this area covers 17,575 hectares of low elevation coastal rainforests and wetlands. This is a spectacular, but remote area, and access is limited.

Symbols Used in Reference Section

⚠	Campsite /Trailer Park
⛺	Road Access Recreation Site
⛰	Trail or Boat Access Recreation Site
⛽	Day-use, Picnic Site
⛱	Beach
🚤	Boat Launch
🚶	Hiking Trail
🚴	Mountain Biking Trail
🐎	Horseback Riding
⛷	Cross Country Skiing
🏂	Snowmobiling
⛷	Downhill Skiing
🏂	Snowshoeing
🧗	Mountaineering /Rock Climbing
🚣	Paddling (Canoe /Kayak)
🏍	Motorbiking /ATV
🏊	Swimming
⛺	Cabin /Hut /Resort
📖	Interpretive Brochure
🐟	Fishing
🔭	Viewpoint
🔫	Hunt
♿	Wheel Chair Accessible
☽	Reservations
$	Enhanced Wilderness Campsite
🍇	Winery

There are no official trails or roads in the protected area but Tatlayoko Lake is accessible by a road and a forestry recreation site along the eastern shore of the lake. Boating Tatlayoko Lake is a popular activity, and consistent afternoon thermal winds also create good windsurfing conditions. For the experienced backcountry traveller there are opportunities for hiking, kayaking, and mountaineering. However, the Homathko River is considered too dangerous for kayakers or rafters.

Itcha Ilgachuz Provincial Park (Maps 24, 25, 33, 34)

Including volcanic landforms, alpine environments, and forest areas scattered with wetlands, this 11,977 hectare area is a unique landscape in the West Chilcotin Uplands. The Itcha and Ilgachuz Ranges, which are examples of isolated shield volcanoes, provide a dramatic backdrop to the area. These high elevation mountains, rising up to 2,400 metres (7,800 feet) above sea level, are home to the largest herd of woodland caribou in Southern BC. Access is difficult, but the area has a number of informal trails that can be hiked or ridden on horseback.

Junction Sheep Range Provincial Park (Map 11/E2)

An area of rolling grasslands overlooking the confluence of the Chilcotin and Fraser Rivers, the Junction Sheep Range Provincial Park is accessible only by a 4wd cart track. The road doubles as a great mountain bike ride and there are other trails/old roads to explore on foot or by bike. The scenery is spectacular, with deep gullies, cliffs and hoodoos breaking the arid grassland. The park is also home to one of the largest herds of California Bighorn Sheep in the province. The 4,573 hectare park does not have any camping facilities, or any facilities beyond a couple of picnic tables and some rather hard-done-by pit toilets near the old ranger's station. A wildfire recently did much damage to the few trees that do survive in the park.

Kluskoil Lake Provincial Park (Maps 35, 36)

The Alexander Mackenzie Heritage Trail passes through this park, as does the Blackwater River. These are the best ways to explore what this 15,548 hectare park has to offer, but there is also a rough 4wd road leading to the eastern boundary. If travelling by canoe, it is 18 km (11 miles) from the upper Euchinko River crossing, to Kluskoil Lake. This route may be inaccessible early in the year because of high water levels at the crossing of the Euchinko. The lake, which can also be accessed by floatplane, has a campsite with space for about three tenting groups.

Nazko Lake Provincial Park (Maps 18/D1, 27)

This 12,319 hectare park is best known for the Nazko Lakes Canoe Route, a relatively easy out and back paddle along a series of lakes strung together by the Nazko River. Nazko Lake is the biggest of the lakes and can be accessed by a rough 4wd road. There are 2wd accessible campsites at Loomis and Deerpelt Lakes (two rustic sites at each lake), and informal camping along the canoe route. Nazko Lake is a popular fishing lake (it is stocked with rainbow) but the real draw to the area is the wildlife, most notably the white pelicans that feed here.

Nechako Canyon Protected Area (Map 42/A2)

Established in July of 2000, this 1,246 hectare protected area was developed around the 7 km (4.3 mile) long Grand Canyon of the Nechako. The Nechako River cut an impressive canyon through a layer of volcanic rock. Since the construction of the Kenny Dam diverted the water west, this impressive gorge with sheer rock walls, towering pinnacles, and overhanging cliffs has been dry. This provides a unique opportunity to view the results of the river's actions on the rock. There are no facilities or trails at Nechako Canyon, although it is possible to hike the dry riverbed. Just outside the protected area is the Cheslatta River Recreation Site. From the recreation site, a forest service trail follows the Cheslatta River to meet the Nechako River at the 18 metre (58 ft) high Cheslatta Falls.

Nunsti Provincial Park (Maps 8, 9)

Located northeast of Chilko Lake in the Chilcotin Plateau, this 20,898 hectare park was established to protect valuable moose habitat. It encompasses abundant wetlands and small lakes. The area is still open to hunting, trapping and cattle grazing. The cows have established a series of game trails that can be followed by folks on foot or horseback.

Punchesakut Lake Provincial Park (Map 37/E5)

Located on the east side of Punchesakut Lake, this park covers 38 hectares of gently rolling aspen forest. The big draw here is the 1,200 metres (3,900 feet) of waterfront, including a beautiful stretch of sandy beach and picnic area. As a result, most recreation activities are lake oriented. Fishing for trout in the spring and fall is perhaps the most popular pursuit, while other popular activities include swimming, sunbathing, canoeing, boating, and water skiing. The day-use park is accessible off the paved Nazko Road.

Ts'yl-os Provincial Park (Maps 2, 3, 8)

Covering 233,240 hectares of what is arguably some of the most spectacular scenery in the province, Ts'yl-os (pronounced "sigh-loss") Provincial Park encompasses rugged mountains, clear blue lakes, glaciers, alpine meadows, and waterfalls. It is bordered by the rugged peaks of the Coast Mountains to the west, and the dry Interior Plateau to the east. The heart of the park is the turquoise-coloured Chilko Lake, the largest, natural high-elevation freshwater lake in Canada. The lake is popular with boaters, kayakers, and anglers. In addition to water sports, the park is home to great backcountry hiking and camping.

There are two main vehicle access routes into the park, and two campgrounds, one at the end of each route. Nu Chugh Beniz Campground (Map 2/D1) is the main site with 15 sites on the eastern shores of the lake, while Gwa Da Ts'ih Campground (Map 8/D5) is a small, rustic campground (formerly a forest service site) with space for eight groups at the north end of the lake.

Tweedsmuir Provincial Park (Maps 13, 14, 22, 23, 30–32, 38, 39)

Tweedsmuir Park is the largest park in the province. Covering 981,000 hectares, Tweedsmuir is so big it runs off both the northern and southern boundaries of this book. Much of that territory is simply protected area, with no recreational value to anyone but the hardcore mountain climber or backpacker. Still, even with most of the park undeveloped, there is still much to do. The park is home to the Turner Lakes Canoe Circuit, one of the premier, canoe routes in the province. It is also home to dozens of trails, ranging from hikes of a few hours to a few weeks (the Alexander Mackenzie Trail). There is good fishing (from fly-in lake fishing, to salmon fishing along the Atnarko River) and the incredible Hunlen Falls to view. Outdoor recreation opportunities are almost unlimited, but those who are not prepared to be completely self-sufficient or who do not wish to employ a professional guide should not contemplate a visit.

Tweedsmuir Park has a very narrow front country, with only two developed camping areas along Highway 20. Atnarko River Campsite has 28 sites nestled amongst an old-growth forest on the Atnarko River, at the bottom of The Hill. The Fisheries Pool Campsite is situated at the junction of the Talchako and Atnarko Rivers, on the site of an old fish hatchery run by the Department of Fisheries and Oceans. This site attracts lots of anglers (in June and July) to its 14 tightly packed campsites. For those that prefer a bed, the Tweedsmuir Lodge is a popular getaway.

In the north, the big lakes of the Nechako Reservoir bisect the park, and boating is not just one of the most popular activities in the area, it is also the only way to travel through the park. The huge Whitesail and Ootsa Lakes frame the northern border of the park. Boaters must use caution when travelling on these lakes, as the shoreline is a forest of drowned trees and floating debris that creates hazardous boating conditions. As a result, canoeing and kayaking are not recommended. Boaters can make a circuit of the lakes, as there is a 350 metre (1,137 foot) rail portage for boats up to 8 metres (28 feet) in size. Hikers wanting to access smaller interior lakes like Glatheli, Ghitezli and Sabina must first find a way across Ootsa Lake to the trailhead (see Central BC Backroad Mapbook).

West Lake Provincial Park (Map 45/F1)

West Lake is a popular 256 hectare day-use park that is easily accessed off the paved Blackwater Road. There are a series of hiking trails that double as cross-country ski trails in the winter but the real attraction is the lake. Fishing, boating and swimming are just some of the water sports enjoyed here.

White Pelican Provincial Park (Map 19/D2)

This 2,763 hectare park was created to protect important nesting habitat for White Pelicans on Stum Lake. This is the only nesting habitat in the province for this rare bird, which are very sensitive to disturbance. The lake is closed to the public from March 1 to August 31. People looking to spot the birds in summer will find they feed in nearby lakes, including those of Nazko Lake Provincial Park.

Trails

The Chilcotin is a big land, with a big history. This is the land that Alexander MacKenzie walked through way back in 1793, and he followed footpaths that had already been in existence for thousands of years.

To some extent, creating this section has been an exercise in frustration. There are many more trails on Crown Land than appear on the maps. Guide trails and old pack trails criss-cross the landscape, leading up into prime hunting territory. But while these trails are on public land, many are not really public trails. The Chilcotin is currently engaged in a Land Use Management Plan that should resolve many of these issues, and trails currently not listed may open up to the public. Keep an eye on our website for any changes, www.backroadmapbooks.com.

In addition, many of the historical trails have fallen into disuse, and out of memory. Trails like the Lt. Palmer Route and the Collins Overland Telegraph Trail and the old Woddington Route (and the Blackwater Wagon Road, and the Beef Trail, and...) are only recently being rediscovered. For folks who like a bit of history with their outdoor experience, trying to find segments of these routes would be a real coup.

To help you select the trail that best suites your abilities, we have included information on elevation gain, return distance and special features wherever possible. Unless otherwise noted, distances and times are for round trip hikes. Also included in each description is a symbol to indicate what the trail is used for—mountain biking, hiking, horseback riding, ATV, etc. Where applicable, multi-use trail descriptions are written from a hiker's point of view.

Due to the hot dry climate of the area, it is highly recommended to bring along plenty of water. We should also note that higher elevation trails and routes (over 1,000 metres/3,000 feet) might have a limited season due to late season snow. Most of these trails are found in the Coast Mountains and in the Tweedsmuir Park. Trail users should leave these trails for late summer and early fall (July until October).

Finding the trailhead is sometimes half the fun (and half the work). For this reason, you should refer to the appropriate map in this book to determine where the trail begins. But remember, our maps are designed only as a general access guide not intended to navigate you through a hidden mountain pass or across an expansive ridge network. If you are travelling on unmarked trails, we recommend that you have mountaineering knowledge and are equipped with a topographic map and a compass. A GPS could also be invaluable to help mark the trail you have taken.

Despite the wealth of trails listed below, it still only represents a fraction of the outdoor opportunities for adventurers, who can follow old game trails, or logging roads to places that few people know about. If you are planning on getting off the beaten path, be careful and always let someone know where you plan to go.

The trails have been divided into the following groups:

Bella Coola Area

North Chilcotin Trails

Spruce Lake Area

South Chilcotin Trails

Tweedsmuir Provincial Park

Bella Coola Area

Hiking in this region stands in stark contrast to hiking in the Chilcotin. Bella Coola is on the sea side of the Coast Mountains, which means that it gets more rain that point's further inland. Even Tweedsmuir receives markedly less rain, on average, than Bella Coola.

Another difference? The valley bottom Bella Coola is in, is just above sea level. Hikes that start down here have almost a kilometre (half a mile) farther to go, vertically, to reach the alpine.

And the look of the place is different, too. Towering mountains and lots of precipitation means glaciers. You don't see many from town (as it is situated in the bottom of a fairly narrow, steep-walled valley), but as soon as you start to gain some elevation, glaciers become one of the predominant visual features. While in the valley, the defining feature is the lush, verdant rainforest with its towering cedars and thick understory. This forest in a matter of years can eat trails, so it is advised that you check locally to make sure that routes and trails mentioned here haven't been consumed by the flora.

Ape Lake Trail (Map 13/C3-E5) 🏕 🚶 📷 🐾

Officially, this trail is only 6 km (3.6 miles) one-way to a viewpoint near Hammer Lake overlooking the rugged, ice-capped Coast Mountains that Ape Lake is located in. The trailhead is found about halfway between the km 28 and km 29 signboards.

Beyond the viewpoint, a rough route extends another 14 km (8.5 miles) to Ape Lake. We cannot overstate how difficult this hike is. One of the worst sections is a 750 metre (2,438 feet) climb up a 2 km wide avalanche slope. There are also a couple of very cold, sometimes dangerous creek crossings along the way. Those with the Chutzpah and skill to hike the 22 km (13.4 mile) route maybe disappointed with the destination. Once one of the most spectacular alpine lakes in the area, the glacier that blocked the outflow of the lake is prone to rise up and allow the lake to drain, leaving the lake about half its size, surrounded by gravel and silt.

Capoose Summer Trail (Map 22/E6) 🚶 🐎 🐾

This historic pack trail rises sharply from the Bella Coola Valley to connect with the Alexander Mackenzie Trail south of Fish Lake. The difficult route is 14 km (8.5 miles) one-way to the intersection with the heritage trail, climbing 1,403 metres (4,600 feet) along the way. The trail continues into Tweedsmuir as the Capoose Trail (see Tweedsmuir Section).

Cook's Trail (Map 22/B7) 🚶 📷 🐾

Named after local explorer Frank Cook, this trail climbs steeply, and was not in very good condition, at last report. It will take great route finding skills, and a lot of determination to whack your way along this route, which follows part of Olaf Odegaard's trapline into Mosquito Pass. While it is a struggle up to the pass, (it is pretty once you break out of the trees), there is access to a number of peaks in the area.

Gray Jay Lake Trail (Map 12/C1)

Like many of the Bella Coola Trails, the most difficult part of this short hike will be getting to the trailhead, high in the mountains along a rough forestry road. The easy 2 km (1.2 mile) hike starts behind the campsite at Blue Jay Lake Trail, and traverses some sensitive wetlands to a spectacular viewpoint over the South Bentinck Arm.

Lost Lake (Map 22/B7) 🏕 ⛰ 🚶 🐾

Lost Lake is a tiny lake at the base of Saloompt Peak. The 2 km (1.2 mile) trail is fairly easy, although there are a few steep pitches as it winds up the southern toe of the mountain to the small lake. Expect to take about half an hour to hike to the lake that is surrounded by rock cliffs. There is an area for tents or simply bring along a picnic and soak in the surroundings.

BELLA COOLA

"The Real B.C."

...Friendly Folks
...Rich History
...Coastal Forest
...Abundant Wildlife
...Great Fishing

and Relaxing Atmosphere...

bellacoola.ca

M. Gurr Lake Trail (Map 12/C1)

This is an easy (1 km/.6 mile) hike that offers spectacular views of the Coast Mountain ranges and fjords. The small, crystal clear lake is very cold, but some like to take a dip on a hot summer day. Others cannot wait to get away from the annoying black flies. Beyond the lake, a rough trail continues on to a viewpoint over South and North Bentinck Arms. On clear days, the view of the fjord like coast will astound even the most casual outdoors person.

Medby Rock Lookout (Map 22/B7)

Named after artist Carl Medby, who liked to come to this spot to paint, this is a difficult uphill slog along a trail that is frequently overgrown. The route is steep, and climbs steeply to the viewpoint. Give yourself at least an hour to reach the lookout, which used to be the site of a forestry lookout.

Mill Creek Valley Route (Map 21/G7)

Like many of the longer trails in the Bella Coola area, parts of this trail are prone to being overgrown, and much of the route is a rough bushwhack up a steep mountain. The trail initially starts out along an old logging road (after wading across Mill Creek), but it all but disappears, following a faint game trail. After about half an hour, if you keep within earshot of the creek, you should stumble upon a slightly more defined trail, with some old blazes. This trail leads you up to the top of a prominent headwall. Strong route finders can do this trip in a day (especially if they've done it before), but most people take a couple days to do the trip. This is a difficult route, and only for folks with strong route finding skills or a guide.

Nusatsum Mountain Route (Map 22/C7)

This route follows the trail to the Medby Rock Lookout Trail (see above), and then climbs up to the secondary summit of Nusatsum Mountain. This is a long, hard slog (give yourself at least 8 hours to get to the top, and about the same coming down) up the shoulder of the mountain to this lovely alpine summit. Is it worth it? As you search for a route up for the first couple hours past Medby, you might not think so. Once you break out into the alpine, the reward unfolds before your eyes.

Odegaard Falls Trail (Map 13/D3)

The Odegaard Falls Trail is a fairly easy, 4 km (2.4 mile) return trail that begins at the nearby Nusatsum River Recreation Site. From the parking area, the Nusatsum River flows down a steep, narrow canyon and the trail winds its way down through the beautiful hemlock, cedar, and balsam forests next to the river. After about 30 minutes, the trail meets Odegaard Creek where a bridge (or tricky log crossing if the bridge is still washed out) marks the beginning of a moderate, steady climb up to the falls. The last 300 metres (900 feet) of the trail is often muddy and slippery from the spray of the falls. The trail leads to a viewpoint of the 200 metre (600 foot) high falls.

Odegaard Loop Route (Map 13/D3)

This is a difficult six hour loop that departs the Odegaard Falls Trails and follows a blazed route to a wet meadow at the top of the falls. You'll climb at least 200 metres (600 feet), as that's how high the falls are. This is not an easy route to follow.

Salloomt Peak Route (Map 22/B7)

This is a bushwhack through the tangled vegetation that grows in the lower valleys of this verdant rainforest, leading to the exposed, rocky 1,871 metre (6,138 foot) summit of this mountain. The trail gains an astounding 1,525 metres (5,000 feet) over about 6 hours. There are some exposed sections near the end that should only be attempted by experienced mountaineers.

Saloompt Forest Interpretive Trail (Map 22/A7)

There is a cluster of four trails located between Saloompt Road and the Bella Coola River in Hagensborg. The trails aren't long (the longest, the Discovery Trail, is barely 0.5 km/0.3 miles long), and are easy to hike. They are a good introduction to hiking in the coastal rainforest of the Bella Coola Valley, through some pockets of old growth trees. One of the trails parallels the river, and is a popular nature watching spot, especially when the salmon are running. Be careful, as there are often bears in the area too.

Snooka Creek Trails (Map 22/G7)

Developed by the BC Forest Service, this trio of trails offers easy to moderate hiking, biking, and riding. The three trails total 10.9 km (6.7 miles), and can easily be hiked in an afternoon. The Snooka West Trail has the best views over the town of Bella Coola and the historic Talleo Cannery.

Snooka Creek Valley Route (Map 12/G1)

Continuing south from the Snooka Creek Trails is a difficult hike to the headwaters of Snooka Creek, in the shadow of Noohalk Mountain. The trail cuts through some lush vegetation, and, depending on when the trail was last brushed, is often overgrown. But once you reach the lakes at the head of Snooka Creek, you'll be glad you made the effort. There are three lakes located in a horseshoe valley, with towering, usually snow-capped mountains on three sides, and many ridges, peaks and summits to explore. Give yourself at least five hours to make it to the lakes or bring a pack and spend a few days exploring this alpine wonderland.

Stupendous Mountain Route (Map 22/F7)

Stupendous Mountain is the monolith that rises across the river and above the Fisheries Pool Campsite in Tweedsmuir. The prominent peak beacons to those mountaineers that see it. The route begins at the top of an overgrown logging road, through some difficult sections of slide alder and talus slopes, before reaching the open alpine above the trees. This route requires some scrambling, and should be left to experienced backcountry travellers who don't mind using their hands to climb once in a while. You'll need at least seven hours to get to the top.

Tseapseahoolz Creek Route (Map 22/B6) 🚶 📷 🚻

Another rough route where you'll have to claw your way out of the lower rainforest into a sub-alpine wonderland. Your ultimate destination is an unnamed lake at the head of the creek, surrounded by five mountain peaks. The route passes through an old growth forest along an old trapper's trail, but gets difficult when you have to cross overgrown avalanche slopes. The old trail is marked with small blazes that can be difficult to follow. There is no trailhead. Experienced route finders can pick up the trail once they enter the old growth forest. To do this, you must first cross the talus slope, which is visible from the end of the road.

Walker Island Park Trails (Map 21/G7) 🚶 🚴 🚻

Tucked up between Snootli Creek and the Bella Coola River, there is a handful of easy, short trails in Walker Island Regional Park. Most of the trails incorporate some road travel. For example, the Gazebo Loop is 3.6 km (2.2 miles) long, but only a portion of that is on actual trail. A definite highlight in the area is the big cedar trees near the parking lot and Beaver Pond.

North Chilcotin Trails

Highway 20 bisects the Chilcotin into two uneven, misshapen masses of land. South of the Highway lies an area of high elevation plateau, and open forest that slowly runs into the Coast Mountains (in the west) and the higher mountains of the South Chilcotin (in the east).

North of the highway, the Chilcotin slowly transforms into the Interior Plateau. This area has many trails and a lot of history. For the avid hiker, mountain biker or horseback rider, there is a lot of country out there to discover. It is an area without a lot of dramatic features. A rather notable exception is the twin, isolated volcanic ranges that define Itcha Ilgachuz Provincial Park. These are marvelous areas to explore, full of meandering trails and high alpine or so we're told. Most of these trails are guide outfitter trails, who try to keep their trails out of the public domain. But for self-sufficient, long distance hikers there are many historic routes that bisect the region. The Alexander MacKenzie Trail has long been 'The Trail' to explore in the area, but trails such as Lt. Palmer Route are slowly being rediscovered.

Alexander MacKenzie Trail (Maps 22, 23, 32, 33, 34, 35, 36, 44, 45)

See insert on page 28.

Alexis Creek Cross-Country Trails (Map 19/B5) 🚴 ⛷

A series of four loops totaling 8.5 km (5.2 miles) that are becoming increasingly popular with mountain bikers. You'll climb about 200 metres (650 feet) to the highest point of the system. The two most popular loops are Gorby Killer and Schmidt, but there are a number of trails that loop and interweave, making this a great area to explore.

The National Hiking Trail (Maps 21, 22, 23, 32-36, 44, 45) 🥾 ⛺ 🚶 🚻

While the Trans Canada Trail down south has been getting all the publicity, the National Hiking Trail committee has been quietly stitching together trails. They have managed to assemble a trail that is currently closer to crossing the country than the TCT. The nice thing about the NHT is it eschews following roadways, instead sticking to honest-to-goodness trails (although one large section of the BC Trail is actually a water route). Through BC, the trail follows the Goat River Trail, The Telegraph Trail, the Blackwater Wagon Road, and, of course, the Alexander Mackenzie Trail. The trail has been in the works since 1971, and the Federation of BC Mountain Clubs has been working on the BC Section since 1997. For more information, contact the Federation of BCMC (www.mountainclubs.bc.ca) or the National Hiking Trail Committee (www.nationaltrail.ca).

Blackwater Canyon Trail (Map 45/C7) 🚶 🐟 🚻

This is a short (1.7 km/1 mile), easy trail along the Blackwater River, from the Blackwater Crossing Recreation Site. There is a maze of game and fisherman trails in the area and the Collins Overland Telegraph Trail continues south. The Canyon Trail is flagged with orange markers. Take care when hiking near the 61 metre (200 feet) high cliffs of the canyon.

Blackwater Wagon Road/Panhandle Phillips Horse Trail (Maps 24/C6-33/G5) ⛺ 🚶 🐎 🚻

Starting from the Stampede Grounds in Anahim Lake, this historic route is the main access into the Itcha Mountains region of the remote park. The route crosses several roads and creeks on its way up into this wild and rugged area before eventually dropping down to the Blackwater River Valley to join up with the Alexander MacKenzie Trail.

Bobtail Bluff Trail (Map 44/F2) 🚶 🚻

Starting at the Bobtail Lake Recreation Site, this trail has a few steep pitches as it climbs to the top of the Bobtail Bluff, 370 metres (1,214 feet) above the lake. The trail is easy to follow and leads through a mixed forest to a viewpoint over the lake.

Bobtail Mountain Trail (Map 44/G1) 🚶 ⛷ 🏠 🚻

The Bobtail Mountain trail is 5 km (3 miles) in length with a change in elevation of 470 metres (1,624 feet). It meanders up to a south-facing viewpoint at the summit of Bobtail Mountain, and on to a north-facing viewpoint where a small hut has been built to provide shelter. The route is also popular with backcountry skiers in winter.

Christensen Creek Trail (Maps 24/C5-D2) ⛺ 🚶 🐎 🚻

This old wagon road can be picked up just north of the Christensen Creek Bridge and Clesspocket Ranch on the Upper Dean River Road. The route breaks away from Christensen Creek and provides the main access into the Ilgachuz Mountains around the alpine and sub-alpine of Mount Scott. Routes continue north, east and west.

Crater Lake (Map 36/C7) ⛺ 🚶 🐟

This easy 1.6 km (0.9 mile) trail is found off the Michelle-Baezaeko Road, and leads to a small, isolated lake. There is a place to pitch a tent at lakeside.

The Dome Trail (Map 20/B4) 🚶 🚻

Found in the heart of the Chilcotin Military Training area, access to this trail may or may not be possible, depending on the day, and whether anything is happening at the site. This round, almost boxy plug of volcanic rock is fairly easy to get to via a 5.5 km (3.3 mile) trail, gaining 325 metres (1,056 feet) to the top. The views of the surrounding plateau are impressive.

Eagle's Nest Marsh Trail (Map 24/B6) 🚶 🚻

From the Eagle's Nest Resort sign, an easy trail leads through a popular bird watching area. The marsh is home to a wide variety of birds, including swans, pelicans, owls and of course eagles.

Fort George Canyon Trails (Map 45/G1) 🚶 ⛷ 📷 🚻

The Fort George Canyon is located 24.5 km (15 miles) southeast of Prince George. There is a pleasant, easy 5 km (3 mile) trail through the boreal forest to the historic canyon on the Fraser River. There are interpretive signs along the trail. Huge sternwheelers used to run through this canyon, but passengers would have to disembark while the boat was cabled through the pillars of volcanic rock. In winter, there are a series of trails that are popular with cross-country skiers.

Itcha Ilgachuz Provincial Park (Maps 24, 25, 33, 34)

This is a vast wilderness area, rife with old horse trails. The easiest way into the park from the north is via a pair of seismic lines from the Michelle-Baezaeko Forest Service Road, one of which leads almost straight to Itcha Lake. The main access into the park from the south is via the Christensen Creek Trail, an old wagon road leading up Christensen Creek from Clesspocket Ranch. This wagon trail leads directly into the alpine and sub-alpine around Mount Scott, and eventually exiting the park via Carnlick Creek. Another route into the park is found along the historic Blackwater Wagon Road/Panhandle Phillips Trail (see above). This trail bisects the middle of the park and provides access to both the Itchas and Ilgachuz Ranges.

Johnston Homestead & Falls (Map 36/D7)

This is a short (400 metre) walk to a historical site and waterfall. The trail starts the at 6.3 km (3.8 mile) mark of the Marmot Lake Road.

Kappan Mountain Trail (Maps 24/A7-15/A1)

From the south end of Kappan Lake, a trail makes it way up to Kappen Mountain and beyond. The trail is also known as the Floyd Mecham Trail, after the pioneer who discovered the route.

Klinaklini Valley Trail (Maps 15/F7-6/B2)

Starting at the end of a 4wd road off Highway 20, the length of this trail depends on how far you can drive and how far you want to walk. This is a remote and rugged river valley that leads to Klinaklini Lake. It is a long haul into the lake so be prepared for an overnight trip. It is also possible to follow the route up Brussel Creek into the alpine area west of Tweedsmuir Park.

Lt. Palmer Route (Maps 23, 24, 15, 16, 17, 36/D7)

See Insert on Page 29.

MacKill Lake Trail (Map 19/A1)

This 3 km (1.8 miles) easy trail circles MacKill Lake that offers kids a chance to try their luck fishing. History buffs will find 1 km of the trail follows the remnants of the old Lt. Palmer Route.

Marmot Lake (Map 36/E6)

There is an easy, 4 km (2.4 mile) hiking trail around Marmot Lake. The trail provides good shore access for anglers.

Martin Meadow Trail (Map 27/G2)

With so much history in the area, it is nice to explore trails such as these. This one follows an old wagon trail through Loomis Meadows to Martin Meadows, east of the Nazko River. The trail starts at the 35 km mark of the Honolulu Road.

Collins Overland Telegraph Trail (Map 37/G3–44/E1)

The Telegraph Trail is part of a historically significant route that ultimately failed to establish telegraph communications with the Yukon. This route was not only a maintenance trail for the telegraph line, but also a land-based transportation route (similar to the more famous Old Cariboo Wagon Road). Today, the Telegraph Trail Preservation Society promotes the historical significance and preservation of this historic site by restoring, maintaining and promoting the trail for recreational use.

The Collins Overland Telegraph Company was chartered to construct a telegraph line from New Westminster, to the northwest. On September 14, 1865, 435 miles of line had been strung to Quesnel. Construction continued, and the trail made it past Kispiox before construction was halted by the completion of a marine telegraph cable in July 1866. The push to preserve the trail began in 1971, and a section of trail, now over 60 miles in length, has been located and restored north of Quesnel. The best section of the route, for trail enthusiasts is north of the Blackwater Road on Map 37. After crossing the Blackwater River, the route follows a series of roads northwest past Bobtail Lake towards Fraser Lake.

Maydoe Creek Trail (Maps 15/C4-14/G6)

Trails often lead to remote lakes and this is certainly the case in this book. The May Doe Creek Trail starts at the south end of Charlotte Lake and skirts the north side of the creek before breaking out into the alpine area around Whitton and Wilderness Lakes. The trails around Whitton Lake were developed by Chris Czajowski of Nuk Tessli Alpine Experience and are marked by blazes and cairns. Sections of the trails may be boggy or tricky to negotiate due to rocky terrain. In addition to exploring the alpine, there are backcountry cabins and some fine summer fishing for rainbow available. Contact Nuk Tessli Alpine Experience (see service providers) for more information.

McClinchy Creek Trail (Map 15/D5)

From the end of the logging road, a trail can be picked up on the north side of the creek. It is a long walk into the lake, and most come here to fish.

Obsidian Creek (Anahim Peak) Trail (Maps 23/G1)

Beginning south of Obsidian Creek, you will have to cross the Dean River to access this trail. The trail then crosses the creek on its way up to Anahim Peak in Tweedsmuir Park. The reward is a fantastic view of the Coastal Mountains, the Dean River Valley and the Chilcotin Plateau.

Peter Fuller Pack Trail (Maps 24/A1-C1)

Another route into the mountains of Itcha Ilgachuz Park, this trail requires crossing private property to access. Please ask permission from the folks at Kinto Ranch. The ranch and trailhead is found about 3 km off the Upper Dean Road.

Rainbow Lake Trail (Maps 33/A7)

This trail begins from a rough 4wd road system west of the Upper Dean River Road. The trail climbs past the lake into the mountains of Itcha Ilgachuz Park.

Tatla Lake Trails (Map 16/E7)

A series of loop trails between Tatla Lake and Martin Lake, totaling about 30 km (18 miles). While these trails are best known as cross-country ski trails, they are open in the summer for hiking, biking and horseback riding.

Teepee Lake Trail (Map 36/B2–E2)

This 20 km (12.2 mile) trail begins 1 km north of the Blackwater Bridge on the Nazko Road. The route mostly follows an old road. In fact, people have been known to make it all the way to the lake with 4wd vehicles, although that isn't recommended. There's an old range cabin at the lake that has been taken over by the locals, who keep the cabin well stocked. Fishing in the lake is great, and that's the reason most people come here in summer. In winter, it is a nice snowmobiling destination.

The National Hiking Trail (Maps 21, 22, 23, 32, 33, 34, 35,36. 44, 45)

See insert on page 32.

Wentworth Trail (Map 28/A2) ⛺ 🚶

The Wentworth Trail isn't a very long trail. It is only 0.5 km (0.3 miles) long and many people haul in a canoe to enjoy the tranquility of the secluded lake. There is also a place to set up a tent at lakeside.

Whitton Creek Trail (Maps 15/C4-14/G5) ⛺ 🚶 🐟

An old trappers trail can be found on the south side of Charlotte Lake. It leads up Whitton Creek to the confluence just east of Whitton Lake. The trail is very overgrown and impossible to find in many places.

Williams Lake River Trail (Map 20/G3) 🚶 🚴 🏍 ⛏

This trail is located on the east side of the Fraser River, and follows the Williams Lake River Valley. The most scenic section is the area closest to the Fraser River, while dozens of bird species can be seen along the route. The trail starts in a not so scenic industrial area of Williams Lake. The trail is 12 km (7.2 miles) long, and the first 7 km (4.2 miles) are open to vehicles.

Spruce Lakes Area

A sprawling area of big, open alpine, and kilometre upon kilometre of trails, the Spruce Lakes area has been partially protected by the establishment of the Big Creek South Chilcotin Provincial Park. Another park was created to protect the Spruce Lakes area, but that process has been halted, and the fate of this recreational paradise is up in the air. Environmentalists, conservationists, and most anybody who has actually visited this area want to see it preserved. The alpine flower bloom is considered one of the most spectacular natural phenomenons in the province.

This book covers the less developed northern reaches of the area. Although we have done our best to show and describe the trails and routes in this area, it is a remote area and many of the trails are falling into a state of disrepair. If you do plan on visiting the area, a copy of the Backroad Mapbook for Southwestern BC is needed to show road (or trail) access from the south.

Castle-Cardtable Route (Map 4/D6–F7) 🚶 ⛏

There are some old trails running through this region that can be followed, but many people just head cross-country through the open alpine that characterizes this spectacular region. Portions of the western route are quite rocky. Access is from the Mud Paradise Forest Service Road, or via an old trail that heads northwest from the Tyaughton Creek Trail. This latter route has one section that climbs 900 metres (2,925 feet) in 4 km (2.4 miles). There are no trailheads, trail markers or·signs.

Dash Hill Routes (Map 4/D4-F5) ⛺ 🚶 🐎 🚴 🏍 ⛏

A network·of old mining roads allow access to the vast alpine area on upper Dash Creek. These roads join trails/routes to Dash Hill, Dash Creek, Big Creek, Lone Valley Creek and Relay Creek. Due to snow accumulations, they are best travelled in summer and early fall. There are no trail markers or signs.

Deer Pass Trail (Map 4/C6–C7) ⛺ 🚶 🐎 ⛏

This is a 10 km (6 mile) trail, which starts just past the packers cabin at Trigger Lake. It climbs very steeply for the first 2 km (1.2 miles), eventually gaining 800 metres (2,600 feet) to Deer Pass, at the 4.5 km (2.7 mile) mark. The trail continues on to Tyaughton Creek, another 5.5 km (3.3 miles) beyond, and 600 metres (1,950 feet) below.

Eldorado Mountain Routes (Map 4/G7) 🚶 🚴 ⛏

A combination of old mining roads, trails, and alpine ridges give hikers and mountain bikers the opportunity to climb up to some spectacular viewpoints. The trail starts at Taylor Creek, about 0.75 km down the trail from the Taylor Basin Cabin (see Southwestern BC Mapbook). There are no trail markers or signs. Due to snow accumulations, they are best attempted in late summer/early fall.

Alexander MacKenzie/Nuxalk-Carrier Grease Trail (Maps 22, 23, 32, 33, 34, 35, 36, 44, 45) 🚣 ⛺ 🚶 🐎 🚴 🏍 ⛏

The name Alexander MacKenzie resonates throughout the region covered by this mapbook. The trail that bears his name is an east-west thread that ties the region together. Mackenzie was the first European to cross North America by land, reaching the Pacific in 1793. For much of his way across country, MacKenzie went by canoe, but just south of where the Blackwater River flows into the Fraser, he hopped out of his canoe, and began his trek by land. This route, originally called the Grease Trail, has been mostly preserved as it cuts across the landscape of Central BC.

Designated as the first heritage trail in British Columbia in 1985, the 420 kilometre long Alexander MacKenzie Heritage Trail is gaining international recognition among hikers. The trail includes local wagon roads, provincial highways, forest access roads, rivers, and coastal waterways. Approximately 300 km (186 miles) of this corridor is recreational trail, and about 100 km (62 miles) is well-preserved aboriginal footpath. Portions of the trail have been in use for thousands of years.

In the east, a parking lot has been developed next to the Blackwater Road, near a viewpoint overlooking the Blackwater River Canyon. This is the main trailhead, although backpackers wishing to hike the whole route will have to find their way along a complex maze of logging roads to the Kilometre 0 site on the banks of the Fraser River. This is where MacKenzie began his land route. The trail is best done in late summer or early fall and can be sampled on foot, by bike, on a horse or on an ATV. Beyond the crossing of the Euchiniko River (Map 44/C7) the route becomes very remote and should only be attempted by well prepared backpackers.

The 80 km (50 mile) stretch of the trail in Tweedsmuir Provincial Park (a difficult five to seven day stretch through some extremely remote territory) is perhaps the most scenic of the entire route. The trailhead is found on Highway 20 (Map 22/E7). In between are some fabulous views, endless fishing holes and the odd lodge to pamper yourself before heading back into the wild.

It is strongly recommended to pick up a copy of In the Steps of Alexander MacKenzie Heritage Trail guidebook. It was mapped and written by John Woodworth and Halle Flygare. Although dated, it is a tremendous planning tool that still accurately maps and describes the route.

Greasy Hill Trail (Map 4/E7) 🚶

This is the original trail between Spruce Lake and upper Tyaughton Creek. It is slowly disintegrating and isn't travelled much anymore. While the trail isn't closed, the W.D. Trail is a much preferred route.

Gun Creek Trail (Map 4/C7–A7) ⛺ 🚶 🐎 🚵 🚴 🏍 🚣 ⛏

The Gun Creek Trail starts at Jewel Bridge (see Southwestern BC mapbook) and is the main route into Spruce Lake from the south. South of Spruce Lake, the trail branches west and passes Hummingbird Lake and Trigger Lake before climbing south to Taylor Pass along the Gun Creek Valley. The section in this book doesn't see a lot of use, and while still passable, is suffering from blow down, especially between Trigger Lake and the alpine of Taylor Pass (south of our maps). This trail was once a great trail, and with a bit of work and a bit more traffic, could regain its former glory. Most people heading for the Taseko Lakes area take the Warner Pass Trail.

Little Paradise Trail (Map 4/C6–E5) 🚶 🐎 ⛏

This trail starts 27 km (16.5 miles) along the Tyaughton Creek Trail, and heads north to a pass overlooking Little Paradise Valley. It's 4 km (2.4 miles) and 500 metres (1,625 feet) up to the pass. At the pass, another route to Castle and Cardtable Mountains follows a ridge heading southeast. Beyond the pass, the trail follows Little Paradise Creek to its confluence with Relay Creek, another 8 km (4.9 miles) beyond and 600 metres (1,950 feet) below the pass. There are no trail markers or signs.

Lizard Creek Trail (Map 4/C6) 🚶 🐎 🚶
This trail gains about 100 metres (325 feet) in 3.5 km (2.1 miles) along the north bank of Lizard Creek. The trail doesn't really end here, but splits into a number of faint routes accessing Lizard Lake, Trail Ridge, Deer Pass and Mount Sheba. There are no trail markers or signs.

Mount Sheba Routes (Map 4/C7–E7) 🚶 🐎 🚶
West of Spruce Lake, a rough access route climbs up into the alpine along the ridge that Mount Sheba is on. This route does not connect with other routes that access Mount Sheba from the west. There are no trail markers or signs.

Open Heart Trail (Map 4/D7) ⛺ 🚶 🐎 🚶
This trail starts at the north end of Spruce Lake, and climbs steeply up and out of the valley, over a ridge, and down to the Gun Creek Grassland Campsite, just south of our map. The trail is 5 km (3 miles) long, and gains and loses about 500 metres (1,625 feet) of elevation.

Relay Creek Trail (Map 4/D5) ⛺ 🚶 🐎 🚵 🚶
The northern most trailhead into the Spruce Lake Trails area, the Relay Creek Trail travels 12.5 km (7.6 miles) to Big Creek. There are a number of trails that split off from the main trail.

Spruce Lake Creek Trail (Map 4/E7) ⛺ 🚶 🐎 🐟
This is a short spur of a trail along Spruce Lake Creek to Spruce Lake, from the Tyaughton Creek Trail.

Spruce Lake Trail (Map 4/D7) ⛺ 🚶 🐎 🚵 🐟
Spruce Lake is the heart of this region, and this trail to the lake starts from the 11.5 km (6.9 mile) mark of the Gun Creek Trail (junction is just south of our maps). The first kilometre climbs steeply (200 metres/700 feet), but the rest of the trail to a recreation site on the north shore of Spruce Lake is easy.

Tyaughton Creek Trail (Map 4/C6–G7) ⛺ 🚶 🐎 🚵 🚶
One of the main routes in the Spruce Lake area, this trail has two trailheads along the Paradise Creek Forest Service Road. The trail follows Tyaughton Creek and up almost to its headwaters in Elbow Pass. The trail climbs with moderate grades through the northern part of this area. The trail is about 31 km (18.9 miles) long to the pass, then it splits, with the Lorna Lake Trail heading west to Big Creek (another 3.5 km/2.1 miles). Another route leads north along Graveyard Creek to Big Creek (another 7 km/4.3 miles).

W.D. Trail (Map 4/D7) 🚶 🐎
This trail starts at Spruce Lake and heads generally north for 5 km (3 miles) to a junction with the Tyaughton Trail. Mostly used by people heading for Spruce Lake along the Tyaughton Creek Trail, or more often, as a detour around a rough crossing of Spruce Lake Creek by people hiking/riding the Tyaughton Creek Trail.

Warner Pass Trail (Map 3/G6–4/D7) ⛺ 🚶 🐎 🚵 🚵 🚶 🚶
One of the most popular trails in the area, this trail heads up from Trigger Lake, past Warner Lake, and into Warner Pass, climbing 750 metres (2,438 feet) over 10 km (6 miles). Beyond the pass, the trail continues for another 11.5 km (6.9 miles) to hook up with the end of a mining road at Battlement Creek.

South Chilcotin Trails

Tucked into the bottom of our maps, the South Chilcotin area is a land of high drama. It is an area dominated by dry, arid grasslands that are surrounded by jagged mountain peaks. This starkly beautiful region, features vast alpine meadows, and easily accessible ridges side by side with heavily forested valleys that are nearly impassable. Some of the most beautiful wildflower blooms in the world occur here every summer. And the trails. This is a land of trails. From hiking trails in the Spruce Lakes area (there's so many, it gets its own section), to converted cattle trails, from the ranges of the Tatlayoko area to the remote reaches of Chilko Lake, this land was made for walking or riding. Quite often mountain bikes and horses can access these trails too.

Bluff Lake Trail (Map 7/C3) 🚶 🚶
Officially, this is only a 1 km (0.6 mile) easy hike onto the rock bluffs that the lake gets its name from. But it is possible to make a circuit loop out of the trail by following an old road and returning along the main road.

Burkholder Trail (Map 5/D7) 🚶 🐎 🚵 🐟 🚶
From the Lac La Mare Recreation Site (see Southwestern BC mapbook), anglers use this trail to access Burkholder Lake. The trail extends into the Shulaps Range to join up with a seemingly endless trail system above Carpenter Lake. This is a great destination for hikers or horseback riders. Further north, the trail joins up with the Noaxe Lake/Quartz Mountain system (see below).

Churn Creek Trails (Maps 5 & 11) 🚶 🐎 🚵 🚵 🚶 🚵
The Churn Creek area has not seen a large amount of recreation in the past. Use has been limited predominantly to deer and sheep hunting. The custom of restricting access to private lands, which has been practiced by owners of the Empire Valley Ranch since the 1920's, has had a discouraging effect on recreation. With the creation of the Churn Creek Protected Area, this is changing. The area is divided into two sub-zones, the motorized sub-zone (a small area in the north, and a large area in the south) that is open to motorized vehicles along old roads and cart tracks. The large non-motorized zone has a number of old logging roads, ranch roads, and cattle trails that are open to hiking, biking and horseback riding. Some of the trails in the area include, the Churn Flats Trail, the Clyde Mountain Trail, the Coal Pit Trail, the Koster Lake Trail, the Little Churn Creek-Big Basin Trail, and the Sheep Point Trail.

Dante's Inferno Trail (Maps 19/G7-10/G1) 🚶 🐟 🚶
Dante's Inferno Trail leads to a canyon that is famous for how hot it gets in summer (thus the name). There is also a small hike-in lake that offers a chance to catch small rainbow trout. That is as long as you try

---

Lt. Palmer Route (Maps 23, 24, 15, 16, 17, 36/D7) 🚩 ⛺ 🚶 🐎 🚵 🚵 🚶
Stretching from the Coastal Mountains to the Fraser River near Alexandria, there is a push to restore this historical route as a National Heritage Trail. The trail begins near the Precipice in Tweedsmuir Park (Map 23/F7) and joins up with Lunass Trail, which takes it across Highway 20 north of Nimpo Lake. The trail follows the highway south for a stretch before veering east past Aktaklin Lake. The route then intermixes stretches of trail with logging roads as it continues west of Puntzi Lake. The stretch from Puntzi towards the old fur trading fort at Alexandria is not as defined, but it does pass by several lakes where camping is possible.

Although the route has been surveyed, it is not always signed or marked. This could make tracking the trail through the maze of logging roads rather challenging. It is hoped that as awareness of the trail is increased, more and more travellers will help further define the route.

in the spring and fall when the temperature is cooler. Access is along the Beaumont Road, which leads south off Highway 20.

Doc English Bluff Trail (Map 20/G7)

Doc Bluff is an interesting half dome of rock, rising above the Fraser River. From roadside, it looks rounded and forested, the side facing the river is almost sheer cliff. Access to this is off Highway 20, just as it starts climbing up to the Chilcotin Plateau. The trail is short (0.6 km/0.3 miles), but climbs steeply to the top of the bluff, passing close to the cliffs on the top. Although tempting, the caves atop the bluff are too dangerous and difficult to explore without climbing gear.

Farwell Canyon Trail (Map 11/C1)

From the last switchback south of the Farwell Canyon Bridge, a trail heads along a ridge to the sand dune above the Chilcotin. This is one of the largest moving dunes in Canada and the view of the canyon is impressive. Extreme mountain bikers have created a trail that would challenge even the hardest of hardcore riders.

Junction Sheep Range (Map 11/E2)

Tucked into the confluence of the Fraser and Chilcotin Rivers, the trail through Junction Sheep Range Provincial Park can be explored by foot. It would be a long, hot hike through open grassland. This area is better suited for mountain biking. Big, open, rolling grassland mean fast, fun riding. (Watch out for saddle spilling rocks!) As an added bonus, this area is home to the largest herd of California Bighorn sheep in North America, and chances are good you'll spot at least part of the herd. The main cart track is open to 4wd vehicles, but if you really want to get a sense of the area, it is best to leave the vehicle at the parking lot off Farwell Canyon Road, and take a bike. Honest.

Noaxe Lake/Quartz Mountain Trails (Map 5/B7)

Between Noaxe Creek Road in the west, the Swartz Lake–Poison Mountain Road in the north and the Yalakom River to the east is an area dominated by mostly open grasslands and the high alpine of the Schulaps Range. There is a rat's nest of trails, which originated as cattle trails for the Empire Valley Ranch and Gang Ranch to the north. Over the last twenty years, the ranches have stopped using this area, due to environmental pressures, and the trails are disappearing into the grassland from whence they came. Trails that still exist often start at one place, braid, split, and then end for no reason at all. Route finding through the open grassland isn't too difficult (especially with a compass or GPS unit), but don't trust the trail you're on to lead to where you want it to go. This area has a lot of recreational value, but not a lot of recreational users and the trails are starting to fade. Destinations here include Noaxe Lake, Quartz Mountain and Poison Mountain.

Perkins Peak Trail (Map 6/F2)

Perkins Peak is the first major peak heading south out of the Chilcotin and into the Coast Mountains. From the end of the 4wd accessible Miner Forest Service Road (which climbs above the tree line), this old road heads up to a lake basin near the base of the easily hikeable Perkins Peak. Park as far up the road as you are willing to drive, then saunter up to the top. From the peak, the views of the bigger mountains to the south—the Kliniklini Icefield and the Niut, Pantheon and Waddington Ranges—is amazing. To the north, the relatively flat Chilcotin stretches to the horizon.

Potato Range Crest Route (Map 8/A5–A7)

The Potato Range is not as rugged as the mountains on the other side of Tatlayoko Lake, and the area is much easier to access. A number of trails have been developed in the area, of which the Crest Route is one of the most popular. The trail begins near the north end of Tatlayoko Lake (you'll need a 4wd vehicle to get to the trailhead, otherwise, you'll have to hike the road up, adding more distance and elevation to the trip). The route ends at Bracewell's Wilderness Lodge, where you can get a ride back to your vehicle, or hike back along the road. It would

take the better part of the day to hike this scenic trail from head to toe. Allow for an overnight trip if you do not opt for the shuttle.

Potato Trail (Map 8/A5–7)

From Bracewell's Wilderness Lodge, this trail follows the Cheshi Creek Valley for a few kilometres, before climbing steeply up to the Echo Lakes, where Bracewell's maintains a cabin. From the lakes, the Potato Trail continues north, below the ridge of the Potato Range, through Groundhog basin, and to the north trailhead, a distance of 9 km (5.4 miles) from the lakes. At the north trailhead, you can hike down to Tatlayoko Lake (6 km/3.6 miles), or return along the Potato Range Crest Route (see above).

Rainbow Creek Trail (Map 2/F5)

Access to this rough, steep trail is by boat along Chilko Lake. From a cabin on the lake, the trail climbs steeply over 6.5 km (4 miles) to Dorothy Lake, where the trail joins with the Yohetta Valley Trail and the Spectrum Pass Trail. Either return the way you came in, or arrange for a (very long) shuttle in the Gunn Valley.

Red Mountain Trails (Map 5/D4)

Red Mountain is an open peak that is easily walked...no, strolled to from a number of different access spots, like off the Poison Mountain Road. While there are a number of trails in the area, many of them are former cattle trails that may not lead where you think they do. The trails are not easily distinguished because the ground is open, and easy to cross. You can ridge walk or just make your own way.

Skinner Mountain Trail (Map 8/A7)

Another in a maze of trails and routes in the Potato Range east of Tatlayoko Lake, Skinner Mountain can be done as either a loop or an out and back trip. The trail to Skinner Mountain itself departs the Potato Trail (see above) a short way from the trailhead, and climbs steeply up to Skinner Mountain. You can return the way you came, or follow the trail to a cabin at Echo Lakes, east of Skinner Mountain. From the lakes, you can follow the Potato Trail down to Cheshi Creek, and back to where you started. This trail features shorter, less intense elevation gains, and so you might prefer to hike it in reverse (counter-clockwise).

Spectrum Pass Trail (Maps 2/G5–3/A6)

The Spectrum Pass Trail leads from the outfitters cabin below the pass (see Tchaikazan Valley Trail, below), and up and over the 2,287 metre (7,500 foot) pass to hook up with the Yohetta Trail (see below) at the west end of Dorothy Lake.

Tatlayoko Lake Trail (Maps 7/G6, 8/A6)

There is very little elevation gain (about 50 metres/150 feet) along this new trail that has been developed along the east side of Tatlayoko Lake. The trail passes through a stand of old growth forest, and there are frequent views of the big mountains on the west side of the lake. It is possible to bushwhack around the south end of the lake to an old logging road that runs along the west side of the lake, to make an almost-loop of the lake.

Tchaikazan Valley Trail (Map 3/A6–B5)

From the airstrip at Fishem Lake, a rough, maintained road branches west up the Tchaikazan River. From the end of the road, a trail follows the river to an outfitters cabin below Spectrum Pass. It is possible to follow a rough route along the river to the Tchaikazan Glacier (Map 3/A7). This route is best left to mountaineers as there is a difficult creek crossing en route.

Tullin Mountain Trail (Map 8/C5)

From the north end of Chilko Lake (at the Gwa Da Ts'ih Campground), this trail travels six hours (return) to Tullin Mountain. The glacier-fed Chilko Lake offers an inspiring view from the top. There are a number of routes in the alpine above Chilko Lake, including the Tullin Ridge Route (see below).

Tullin Ridge Route (Map 8/A6)

From Echo Lakes on the Potato Trail (see above), a well-used trail follows an open ridge to Tullin Mountain, connecting with the Tullin Mountain Trail. There are a number of unmarked routes in the alpine above the gorgeous Chilko Lake.

Waterlily Trail (Map 7/C2)

From the Sapeye Lake Recreation Site, the Waterlily Trail heads north, then counter clockwise around Waterlily Lake to a rustic picnic area. The trail is 5 km (3 mile) long, although the truly adventurous can follow a rough route along Sapeye Creek into the alpine.

Yohetta Valley Trail (Maps 2/G5-3/B4)

From the South End of Tuzcha Lake, the Yohetta Valley Trail (actually, an old road) heads up into Yohetta Valley along Yohetta Creek. Vehicles are permitted up to the park boundary. The trail follows the north side of the creek to Yohetta Lake. Beyond the lake, the trail continues around the north side of Dorothy Lake, to hook up with the Rainbow Creek Trail and down to Chilko Lake. South of Dorothy Lake, the Spectrum Pass Trail connects to Tchaikazan Valley. It would be possible to make a long loop trail by joining the latter two trail systems.

Tweedsmuir Park Trails

Tweedsmuir is a land of transitions. From the low, Coastal rainforest of the Atnarko Valley, to the high, colourful alpine of the Rainbow Range, Tweedsmuir is a land of contrasts, and of great beauty. It is also a huge area.

Trails around Highway 20 are generally in good condition, although with a shrinking budget, BC Parks cannot maintain these trails to the same standards as they have been maintained historically. In the north end of Tweedsmuir there are a number of trails that are not maintained by Parks at all. Guide outfitters with lodges in a seemingly empty wilderness have created these routes. The state of these trails is not always known, and they are best left to hikers with lots of wilderness experience.

Alexander MacKenzie Trail-Tweedsmuir Park (Maps 22, 23, 32)

Designated as the first heritage trail in British Columbia in 1985, the Alexander Mackenzie Heritage Trail is gaining international recognition among hikers. The 80 km (50 mile) stretch of the trail in Tweedsmuir Provincial Park (a difficult five to seven day stretch through some extremely remote territory) is perhaps the most scenic of the entire route. The trailhead is found on Highway 20 (Map 22/E7). From here you will climb up over the Rainbow Range, through the MacKenzie Valley, past the Tanya Lakes and over the Dean River before stepping out of the park and into another vast wilderness area. Along the way, there are rustic campsites and backcountry cabins to overnight in as well as some fine fishing holes.

Blanchet Lake Route (Map 39/B1–E5)

This trail starts from the southern shore of Ootsa Lake and is best accessed from Wistaria Provincial Park, located on the north shore of Ootsa Lake (see Central BC Mapbook). To access the trail, you'll need to get across nearly 5 km (3 miles) of open water. (Canoeing across the windy lake is not recommended.) Once across, the trail leads to Glatheli Lake, Ghitezli Lake, Chief Louis Lake, Nutli Lake, and ultimately Blanchet Lake. This is a remote and rugged 50 km (30 miles) route that may or may not be marked.

Boyd Pass Connecting Trail (Map 23/A3)

From Crystal Lake, this trail connects to the Alexander Mackenzie Heritage Trail just north of Rainbow Cabin. It is a short, easy trail, considering that to hike this trail, you will first have had to walk 30 km (18.3 miles) to get to it.

Capoose Trail (Map 22/F5–23/A5)

This moderate, 28 km (17.5 mile) return trail connects the Alexander Mackenzie Heritage Trail to the Tweedsmuir Trail near Octopus Lake. The trail crosses a beautiful sub-alpine valley.

Chickamin Mountain Trail (Map 38/C5) ▲ 🖈 📷 ⏚

A boat access trail starting from the Blackwell Point Campsite leads into the alpine meadows of the Chickamin Mountain Range. The actual trail is only 3 km long (1.8 miles), but climbs steeply, gaining 600 metres (1,950 feet) to the alpine. Expect to take three hours, more if you want to wander further west or south to the actual mountain peak.

Crystal Lake Trail (Map 23/A3–B4) ▲ 🖈 🐎 🛶 ⏚

Breaking off the Octopus Lake Trail, this moderately difficult trail climbs 1,000 metres (3,280 feet) to the Rainbow Cabin and a junction with the Alexander Mackenzie Grease Trail beneath Mount McKenzie. Give yourself two days to hike this 50 km (31 mile) return trail. This is prime caribou country, and there is a good chance you will see some, especially in the alpine ridge around Crystal Lake.

Glatheli Lake Route (Map 38/F2–39/D1) ▲ 🖈 📷 🐟 ⏚

From a bay near the northeast end of Whitesail Lake, a rough route heads east across Northern Tweedsmuir Park, past Goodrich Lake, and on to Glatheli Lake. This trail is not an official BC Parks trail, and it may or may not be in hikeable condition.

Hunlen Falls Loop Trail (Map 14/D1) 🖈 🐟 ⏚

This trail starts at Turner Lake (at the end of the Turner Lake Trail, see below), and skirts the north shore of Turner Lake to a viewpoint over the impressive 260 metre high (845 feet) falls. Along the way, the trail crosses over a footbridge (a great place to fly fish), and parallels the southeast wall of Hunlen Creek Canyon. This viewpoint is potentially dangerous, so use caution. A short side trail leads to another lookout over Lonesome Lake.

Junker Lake Trail (Map 14/D1–D3) ▲ 🖈 🐟 ⏚

Looking to see the Turner Lake Chain, but don't want to canoe? This moderate trail passes by four of the six lakes in the chain, as it travels through rolling pine forests and meadows. The trail covers 21 km (13 miles) return, and winds up at a sandy beach on the northeastern shores of Junker Lake.

Kettle Pond Trail (Map 23/A7) 🖈 ⏚

A short, easy trail to a kettle pond, formed when a large chunk of ice from the last ice age melted. The trail is 1 km (0.6 miles) long with little elevation gain.

Mount MacKenzie (Map 22/G3) 🖈 ⏚

From the Rainbow Cabin (basically where the Tweedsmuir Trail, Crystal Lake Trail and Alexander Mackenzie Heritage Trail join up), Mount Mackenzie can be climbed. Although relatively easy, it is an unmarked walk through an alpine meadow that is thick with flowers at certain times of the year. From the top, panoramic views of Tweedsmuir and beyond make the side trip well worth the effort.

Musclow Lake Trail (Map 38/A7) 🖈 🐟

A short (1.5 km) trail with minimal elevation change, the Musclow Lake Trail follows Musclow Creek to the remote backcountry lake. The hike is the easy part, getting to the trailhead requires a long trip by boat.

Octopus Lake Trail (Map 23/A5–C5) ▲ 🖈 🐎 🐟 ⏚

The trail to Octopus Lake gains almost no elevation over 15 km (9 miles) one-way from the Rainbow Range Trailhead. This is an easy introduction to longer hiking. There is a tent pad and fishing for cutthroat at Octopus Lake.

Panorama Lakes Trail (Map 14/B2) ▲ 🖈 ⏚

From Molly Lake, this route follows a series of lakes (Gem, Echo), then cuts north to a junction with the Ptarmigan Lake Trail. It also hooks up with the Whistler Pass and Rosemary Pass Trails.

Precipice (Hotnarko Canyon) Trail (Map 23/D7–G6) 🖈 ⏚

A moderate hike of 12 km (7.3 miles), gaining 400 metres (1,300 feet) of elevation, the Precipice Trail is in variable condition. It follows an old telegraph trail to 150 Mile House that has been partially obliterated by slides and alder growth. That said, some sections are very distinct, and the section in Tweedsmuir Park is fairly easy to follow. The trailhead is from the Turner Lake Trailhead, at the end of the Tote Road. Beyond Precipice Creek the trail follows the historical route of Lt. Palmer heading east all the way to Alexandria on the Fraser River.

Ptarmigan Lake Trail (Map 14/D1–B1) ▲ 🖈 ⏚

West of Hunlen Falls, there is good alpine hiking to Whistler Pass along this 12 km (7.2 mile) trail. The trail breaks into the alpine and follows a series of cairns (known as stone women, after the all-girl youth crew who built them) to a campsite on Sandy Ridge, at the northeast corner of Ptarmigan Lake. The trail isn't difficult, but it is mostly uphill. Beyond Ptarmigan, the Whistler Pass and Rosemary Pass Trails offer a more challenging but enjoyable loop past Molly Lake.

Rainbow Range Trail (Map 23/C4) 🖈 🛶 ⏚

The Rainbow Range Trail is an easy trail leading into an almost surreal alpine landscape of kaleidoscope-hued mountains, interspersed with many tarns. The 16 km (10 mile) trail starts out in a Lodgepole pine forest and climbs through whitebark pine and alpine fir before breaking out in the alpine. The trail ends at a small alpine lake, but there is so much open ground to explore up here, that you could wander for days, even weeks. The sub-alpine forest in this area is home to one of BC's largest herds of mountain caribou.

Redfish Lake Trail (Map 38/G7) 🖈 🐟

The Redfish Lake Trail heads 1.6 km (1 mile) from the northern shores of Eutsuk Lake (water accessed trailhead) to a remote but popular fly-fishing lake. Bring along a canoe and enjoy this lovely backcountry paradise from the water.

Rosemary Pass Trail (Map 14/B1)

From Ptarmigan Lake (which is reached via the Ptarmigan Lake Trail, which is in turn reached from the Turner Lake Trail), this trail follows the western shores of Ptarmigan Lake, through Rosemary Pass. It connects with the Panorama Lakes Trail near Gem Lake.

Sabina Lake Route (Map 39/E1–F2)

This trail starts from the southern shore of Ootsa Lake, and is best accessed from Wistaria Provincial Park, located on the north shore of Ootsa Lake (see Central BC Mapbook). To access the trail, you'll need to get across nearly 5 km (3 miles) of open water. (Canoeing across the windy lake is not recommended.) The trail is about 16 km (10 miles) long, and passes though one of the wildest areas still left in the province.

Sand Cabin Bluff Trail (Map 39/A7)

A very short (0.5 km/0.3 mile) trail from Sand Cabin Bay to the top of a rock bluff above Eutsuk Lake. There are nice views over the Nechako Plateau and the lake from the bluff. Give yourself about half an hour to climb to the top of the 90 metre (293 foot) bluff.

Sugar Camp Trail (Map 23/D7–F7)

A historic first nations trade route, this 12 km (7.2 mile) trail starts (and ends) on the Tote Road. It is a part of the route that Lt. Palmer followed into the interior. Prior to the construction of Highway 20 in 1953, this was the lifeline between Anahim Lake and Bella Coola. Watch for the unmarked trailhead, about 100 metres (325 feet) past the Sugar Camp Creek Bridge. Similar to the Precipice Trail, this trail takes hikers out of the park through the upper Hotnarko River Valley, to the Precipice, an area bounded by miles of sheer cliffs formed by basaltic rocks.

Sunshine Lake Trail (Map 14/C4)

From the southern end of the Turner Canoe Circuit, this 2.5 km (1.5 mile) trail heads to Sunshine Lake. There is camping and good fishing at the lake. If you really wanted to, you could probably carry a canoe, but the 200 metre (650 feet) climb makes this rather difficult.

Surel Lake Trail (Map 38/A7)

A short (1.5 km/0.9 mile), easy trail in north Tweedsmuir, this trail runs from Eutsuk Lake (trailhead is boat accessible only) to Surel Lake. The views across the lake are amazing and the Surel Falls, which are passed en route, make a nice resting point.

Tetachuk River Trail (Maps 31/G1–39/G7)

This trail could be used as a portage trail, if canoeists or kayakers were foolhardy enough to be circumnavigating the Nechako Reservoir (an extreme paddling route that is not recommended for most). The Redfern Rapids form a barrier to boaters not using jet boats, and this trail is often hiked by folks to good fishing holes near the bottom of the rapids. The trail is about 5 km (3 miles) long.

Turner Lake Trail (Map 14/D1–23/B7)

This trail follows the old Tote Road along the Atnarko River, and passes through prime grizzly bear habitat on its way to Turner Lake. Hikers should allow 10 to 12 hours to reach the north end of Turner Lake, where there is a primitive campground. The trail covers 16.4 km (10 miles), and climbs nearly 1,000 metres (3,250 feet), before leveling out the last few kilometres (about a mile). At the time of this writing, the trail hadn't been cleared in the last few years, and there is a lot of blown down trees to cross over.

Tweedsmuir Trail (Map 22/G3–23/A7)

West of Tweedsmuir Provincial Park's headquarters on Highway 20 (just east of the sani-station at Mosher Creek) is the start of the trail. This trail climbs about 35 km (22 miles) to the Rainbow Cabin on the Alexander Mackenzie Heritage Trail.

Valley View Loop/Burnt Bridge Trail (Map 22/F7)

Tweedsmuir is a big park, full of big hikes. The Burnt Bridge Trail is a refreshing alternative to all that. This is a short, fairly easy day hike (it does climb a bit but will take a mere two hours to complete) as it heads north from the Alexander Mackenzie Heritage Trailhead along Burnt Bridge Creek to a small suspension bridge. The trail then loops back to the parking area. There is a great viewpoint over the Bella Coola Valley.

Whistler Pass/Molly Lake Trail (Map 14/B1)

From Ptarmigan Lake (which is reached via the Ptarmigan Lake Trail, see below), this trail heads up through Whistler Pass to Molly Lake. The trail hooks up with the Panorama Lakes Trail and forms a 11 km (6.6 mile) circuit back to Ptarmigan Lake via Rosemary Pass (see above).

Zinc Bay Mining Trail (Map 38/A5)

From Zinc Bay on Eutsuk Lake another water access only trail is found. This 4 km (2.4 mile) trail heads up from Zinc Bay along an old mining road, climbing 1,300 metres (4,225 feet) up the north side of the Chickamin Range.

Wilderness Camping

The BC Forest Service has historically maintained a series of campgrounds across this province. These sites range from rustic backcountry sites with few if any amenities to well developed sites complete with a campground host, picnic tables and pit toilets. Commonly referred to as Rec Sites, they have formed the backbone of outdoor recreation throughout the backroads of British Columbia.

We say historically, because with the whole BC Forest Recreational infrastructure in a state of flux, the future of many of these recreation sites is in question. The government has determined that managing recreation sites is no longer a core priority of the Ministry of Forests. To makes matters worse, the ministry is no longer maintaining many of the Forest Service Roads. All of this could result in sites being closed or privatized, or simply not accessible to people without an ATV or a 4wd vehicle.

While at the time of the writing (spring 2003) the information was accurate, things may have changed by the time you read these words. The government is hoping to have everything in place by the spring of 2004, but for now, most of the sites are user maintained, so pack out what you pack in, and treat these sites with respect. If we prove that these sites can remain clean and well kept, it will go a long way towards keeping this invaluable resource.

We have divided the Forest Service Recreation Sites into the current Forest Service Districts. This will allow you to contact the appropriate Forest Service Office (contact numbers in back of book) if you want to learn more about the current status or access into a particular site. We have also included information on a few other campsites or recreation areas throughout the region.

Central Coast (Mid Coast) Forest District

Formerly based out of Bella Coola, the Mid Coast Forest District has been closed. This area covers the region west of Tweedsmuir Provincial Park. It is a stunningly beautiful area that has few roads or facilities. Adding to the natural beauty is the fact few visitors to the area venture far from the highway.

Blue Jay Lake Recreation Site (Map 12/C1)

Blue Jay Lake is found high in the Coast Mountains, 26 km (15.9 miles) southwest of Bella Coola. Access is via a steep, sometimes rough forestry service road. The last few kilometres are 4wd accessible only. There are five campsites on the shores of the lake and a scenic 2 km trail leading to nearby Gray Jay Lake. While in the area, be sure to walk the M. Gurr Lake Trail. The view of the Coast Mountains and fjords is spectacular.

Clayton Falls Recreation Area (Map 21/E7)

Found at the end of the road west of the town of Bella Coola, the dam on Clayton Falls Creek is a popular picnic area. People can watch the harbour activity or explore the area around the dam.

Larso Bay (Map 12/D3)

The road into this informal camping area is deactivated and not really recommended to vehicles, but the site can be accessed by boat or ATV. The bay provides some protection for anglers and boaters on the South Bentinck Arm.

McCall Flats Recreation Site (Map 22/F7)

The access road to this site is located five minutes inside Tweedsmuir Park's western boundary, although the site itself is across the Bella Coola River and back outside the park boundary. This site is a popular destination for bears, both grizzly and black, and the occasional angler or camper. Most locals avoid the flats because of the aforementioned bruins. There are five sites next to the river.

Nusatsum River Recreation Site (Map 13/D2)

Located just 500 metres up the Nusatsum Forest Service Road from the Odegaard Falls Site, there are two picnic tables and a couple tenting sites. The site itself is very nice as the Nusatsum River flows down a steep, narrow canyon. Most visitors will follow the 2 km hike from here to a viewpoint at the foot of the falls. The trail winds its way through a beautiful hemlock, cedar, and balsam forest but can be slippery when wet.

Odegaard Falls Recreation Site (Map 13/D2)

Odegaard is a spectacular falls that cascades into the Nusatsum Valley. Access to the site is via a 25 km (15.5 mile) forestry road that may or may not be accessible by 2wd vehicle, depending on the time of year. There are three campsites, and a great view of the falls from the parking lot.

Cariboo Forest District

The Cariboo Forest District is a large district over large tracts of land on both sides of the Fraser River. Most of this mapbook concentrates on the stretches west of the Fraser River all the way to Tweedsmuir Provincial Park. This is the core area of the Chilcotin, with fabulous fishing lakes, good hunting and a laidback frontier attitude.

Alexis Lakes Recreation Site (Map 18/E2)

A semi-open site on the shores of the lake, this quiet, family-friendly site has five units, a cartop boat launch and a small beach for swimming. Access is found off the 2wd Alexis Lakes Road.

Batnuni Lake East Recreation Site (Map 43/G6)

On the eastern shores of Batnuni Lake, this 15 unit site is a popular summer destination. There is a boat launch and good fishing from the shore.

Batnuni Lake West Recreation Site (Map 43/F6)

This is a 12 unit site on Batnuni Lake with a boat launch to access the lake. Access to the site is fairly steep, and should not be attempted with larger RVs or trailers.

Becher Pond Recreation Site (Map 20/C7)

Becher Pond is primarily used as a day-use area by travellers along Highway 20. The site is located just west of Riske Creek and offers picnic tables. The pond is a good place for kids to test their luck fishing.

Big Lake Recreation Site (Map 9/B6)

Big lake, small site. There is only space for four units at this site, which is fairly popular in summer with anglers.

Big Stick Lake Recreation Site (Map 15/F6)

There are three campsites at Big Stick Lake. The site is more popular with hunters than with anglers.

Blue Lake Recreation Sites (Map 20/G1)

Located off the signed Blue Lake Road, this recreation site is easily accessible from Highway 97 north of Williams Lake. There are actually two separate recreation sites as well as a popular resort on the lake. The northern site is a day-use only area, offering picnic tables and a nice swimming area. The western site is better suited for camping.

Bluff Lake Recreation Site (Map 7/C2)

While the road past Horn Lake seems to terminate at a private residence, it actually skirts right around the property and on to the site. This site is almost exclusively a day-use site, and is basically just a boat launch onto a pretty lake. However, there is space for about one vehicle to set up camp here. There are no facilities so campers must be self-sufficient.

Boat Lake Recreation Site (Map 44/A7)

Another in a series of lakes strung out along the Euchinko River. The site features a mix of sites in an open meadow or in the forest at edge of the lake. Fishing is popular in both the lake and the river.

Boot Lake Recreation Site (Map 37/A1)

A small site set in the forest next to Boot Lake. There is a cartop boat launch and good access into this RV accessible campsite.

Bushie Lake Recreation Site (Map 29/F5)

Also known as Valerie Lake, the Bushie Lake Recreation Site is accessible by a 4wd spur road leading south from Hill Road. In addition to a few picnic tables, there is a boat launch providing anglers good access to the lake.

Charlotte Lake Recreation Site (Map 15/D4)

Charlotte Lake is a big lake that provides good swimming and canoeing in the summer. Fishing for the large trout that inhabit the lake is better in the spring and fall, but that does not deter visitors from testing their luck throughout the open water season. The nine unit campsite is easily accessed (well signed) from Highway 20. As a result, campsites are at a premium on summer weekends.

Chaunigan Lake Recreation Site (Map 8/G5)

There are six campsites and a cartop boat launch at this often windy lake. The forest service site is found on the west side of the lake, while a lodge is found on the east side of the lake. Windsurfing is popular here.

Chilko-Taseko Junction Recreation Site (Map 18/C6)

This site is primarily used as a put-in or take-out for kayakers and rafters on the Chilko River. Anglers and hunters also use the open, grassy site above the confluence of the two rivers.

Choelquoit Lake Recreation Site (Map 8/D3)

Better known as a day-use destination, there is space for three vehicle units behind the sand dunes at the east end of the lake. There is also space for informal camping in the area. A sandy beach, lots of Chilcotin sun plus a phenomenal view of the Niut Range in the background make this a great place to wile away a summer day.

Clear Lake Campsite (Map 5/C1)

Clear Lake is a small trail access lake found just south of the Churn Creek Protected Area. Similar to most of the small lakes and swamps along the Little Churn Creek-Big Basin Trail, there is a rustic backcountry camping area that has been established by previous visitors.

Clearwater Lake Recreation Site (Map 15/G6)

Found alongside the graveled section of Highway 20, this small site offers space for only two parties. It is found in an open spruce forest and also sports a cartop boat launch.

Cochin Lake Recreation Site (Maps 7/G2, 8/A2)

There are five campsites amid the open pine and aspen forest on the shores of the lake. Unfortunately, the forest is getting more and more open all the time since folks have been knocking down trees for firewood. Please don't! Although the site is starting to look a little scruffy, it remains fairly popular with anglers chasing the large trout that Cochin Lake is known for.

Crater Lake Recreation Site (Map 36/C7)

It's a 1.6 km (0.9 mile) hike into Crater Lake, a small lake off Baezaeko Road. The parking lot at the head of the trail is pretty small, and most people who visit the lake are just out for a hike, or out fishing. There is space to set up a tent near the lake, although the site is usually used for day-use only.

Cuisson Lake Recreation Site (Map 29/F6)

North of McCleese Lake, Cuisson Lake can be reached via the Gibraltar Mine Road. The forest service site is set amid the trees on the southern shore of the popular fishing lake. Picnic tables and a cartop boat launch are available at the lakeside site.

Davidson Bridge Recreation Site (Map 9/C6)

There are two campsites at this site, which is a popular launching point for rafters and kayakers heading out onto the Taseko River. Anglers also use the site. There is good road access and space enough for RVs here.

Dean River Recreation Site (Map 24/D7)

A historical plaque tells visitors of the rich history of the wild Chilcotin. The forest service site is actually found north of the historical site and offers three well spaced campsites along the river. The meandering river is a nice place to canoe. We are sure anglers coming to BC will have heard of the potential in the Dean.

Eagle Lake Recreation Site (Maps 7/G1, 8/A1)

Although the lake is not far from the highway, this site is not very busy. Perhaps it is the open meadow setting, which can get rather hot in the summer. Maybe it is the fluctuating water levels that make boat access difficult. No matter the reason, visitors should find space to camp and good fishing for trout and kokanee.

Eliguk Lake East Recreation Site (Map 33/B5)

A small tenting area is found in the Hay Meadows on the east end of Eliguk Lake. It is a long hike into the lake (about 8 days along the Alexander Mackenzie Heritage Trail from the Tweedsmuir Trailhead). So don't expect too much company. There is a resort on the west end of the lake that has most of its visitors fly in.

Fir Lake Recreation Site (Map 19/G2)

Although the 4 km (2.4 mile) access road is a little rough, RVs will find plenty of room at this ten unit, semi-open site. The lake is known as a great fly fishing destination and there is a hiking trail around the lake for all to enjoy. In fall, this site is popular with hunters.

Fish Lake Recreation Site (Map 9/D7)

Not surprising, the most popular activity at this lake is fishing. Access to the lake is via a 4wd road (or even worse if the road is wet). The small site offers room for five camping units and a cartop boat launch. Anvil Mountain makes a beautiful backdrop to the campsite.

Fishpot Lake Recreation Site (Map 36/B6)

There is a small open site with space for five vehicle units on the shores of Fishpot Lake. The road in is steep, but manageable by 2wd vehicle. The gravel boat launch is popular with anglers, while the surrounding area sees a fair bit of hunting activity in the fall.

Fletcher Lake Recreation Site (Map 10/D2)

A rough boat launch has been built at this open, grassy site with space for six camping units. The site is usually busy since the roads from Farwell Canyon and Hanceville are both good and there are some large trout in the lake.

Hanham Lake Recreation Site (Map 44/A7)

This small, open site is found at the end of a narrow, winding access road that is not RV friendly. There is good fly fishing along the Euchiniko River, which flows into and out of the lake.

Honolulu Recreation Site (Map 27/F1)

It's an exotic name, but don't expect a jungle full of orchids dripping dew here. This 10 vehicle unit site located on the Nazko River is all about dry arid, Chilcotin–style summer. The semi-open area is accessed off the Honolulu Road (2wd).

Horn Lake Recreation Site (Map 7/C2)

The largest (and arguably nicest) forest service site in the Chilcotin, Horn Lake sports 14 park-like campsites. Each site is well spaced and all are spread along the waterfront. Even better, despite easy access to the site, it is remote enough that the campsite is rarely full. The lake is a popular fishing lake and is set in a beautiful area that begs to be discovered by the intrepid explorer.

Hotnarko Lake Recreation Site (Map 23/G6)

This remote lake is accessible along a series of old roads to the west of Anahim Lake. The roads have been blocked and as a result the three unit campsite makes a peaceful tenting area for people willing to hike or bike in. Anglers are well advised to haul in a canoe or small boat as shore fishing is difficult and the lake is too windy for float tubes.

Kappan Lake Recreation Site (Map 24/A7)

This is a very busy site on a popular rainbow fishing lake. The site is south of Anahim Lake on the Kappan Lake Road. Access to the site is very easy, as the Kappan Lake Main is in arguably better shape than the gravel portion of Highway 20.

Kappan Lake West Recreation Site (Map 24/A7)

Unlike the other site on Kappan Lake, access into this site is difficult, and best accomplished with a 4wd vehicle or by the most patient of 2wd drivers. Even then, good weather, high clearance and a great deal of luck is needed. We gave up after the first kilometre of avoiding puddles deep enough to fish in and basketball-sized boulders, with no lake in sight. Those who make it to the site will find space for three groups, a cartop boat launch, and usually nobody else.

Kevin Lake Recreation Site (Map 44/B5)

A small secluded site with a poor access road (4wd only), help make this a good fishing lake. The site sees few visitors and is a quintessential user-maintained area. Please pack out any garbage you bring or see.

Kilometre 64 Recreation Site (Map 44/C7)

Chances are most people will be able to find this forest service site. It is a small site located where on the Batnuni Road? In addition to fishing or paddling on the river, visitors often like to explore a bit of history along the Alexander Mackenzie Heritage Trail.

Kilometre Zero Recreation Site (Map 45/F7)

Marking the beginning of the Alexander Mackenzie Heritage Trail, this small site is set in the forest on the banks of the Fraser River. Access to the site can be frustrating as there is a maze of logging roads in the area.

MacKill Lake Recreation Site (Map 19/A1)

Found along the historic Lieutenant Palmer Route, this walk-in site is accessed on a short 1 km trail. It isn't unreasonable to bring a canoe along with you. The stocked lake is designated as a children's fishery, making it an ideal family getaway. There is room for five tenting parties.

Marmot Lake Campsite (Map 36/E6)

This is actually a 33 site campground operated by the Nazko Community Association and managed by an on site caretaker. There is a hiking trail around the lake, a boat launch, and a swimming beach area. There is a fee to camp here.

McIntyre Lake Recreation Site (Map 20/F7)

Set in a small open area next to the lake, this forest service site is easily reached via the Meldrum Creek Road (1100 Road). This is a good camping destination as the lake is not known for its fishing.

Miner Lake Recreation Site (Map 6/G1)

This small, remote site doesn't see much use during most of the year, except for hunting season. The lake is also a fine fishing and canoeing destination.

One Eye Lake Recreation Site (Map 16/A7)

Due to the good access from Highway 20, this seven unit site is fairly busy throughout the year. Most of the use comes from anglers chasing rainbow and dolly varden.

Palmer Lake Recreation Site (Map 28/A7)

A popular fishing destination with space for six vehicle units. The last 6 km (3.6 miles) into the lake are very rough and vehicles with trailers or RVs will find it all but impossible to access this site. The lake can be windy at times.

Pelican Lake Recreation Site (Map 44/D7)

Easily accessed on the Pelican Lake Forest Service Road, this is a popular, RV friendly site. The forested area helps keep the summer heat out, while the lake is a fine fishing and boating destination.

Pinto Lake Recreation Site (Map 16/G7)

There is space for two camping units on the shores of this small lake, but the site is mostly used as a picnic spot. There are no fish in the lake.

Poison Lake Recreation Site (Map 24/A3)

There is space enough for six groups at this site, just north of Anahim Lake on the Upper Dean River Road. Despite the name, the lake is known for its good fishing.

Puntzi Lake Recreation Site (Map 17/E3)

Puntzi Lake is a popular destination for anglers, but most of the visitors prefer to stay at one of the many resorts on the lake. This means this five unit site, which is set in an open area next to the lake, is often quiet.

Pyper Lake Recreation Site (Map 17/D6)

There are three picnic tables in a clearing at the east end of the lake, which offers a great view of the Coast Mountains when looking west down the lake. The site is a few minutes off Highway 20, and is a popular swimming hole. There is a cartop boat launch used by anglers and recreational canoeists. The singed area on the fringe of this site is the result of a careless camper letting their campfire get away from them. This is the sort of activity that can jeopardize this wonderful resource. Please be careful!

Raven Lake Recreation Site (Map 19/F5)

A large site on the forested shores of Raven Lake, this recreation site is accessible to RVs along a main haul logging road. There are a dozen picnic tables strung out between the shores of the lake and the 3600 Road as well as space for groups in the open area. Anglers will find a rough boat launch but should be aware of the boating restrictions on the lake. While some of the sites are very nice, there isn't much space between the lake and the road. On weekdays, the logging trucks start

to thunder by at four o-clock in the morning. The lake is a popular ice fishing spot.

Sapeye Lake Recreation Site (Map 7/C2)

There are eight units at this pretty site, found above the road at the base of Horn Bluff. The access road is in good condition, but very narrow, and trailers are not recommended. The lake is a good fly fishing and canoeing destination.

Scum Lake Recreation Site (Map 9/D2)

Pleasant sounding place to visit, isn't it? While the lake doesn't live down its name, it isn't the most popular destination. The last 10 km (6 miles) of the road into the two-unit site is fairly rough. There is a cartop boat launch, but fishing is spotty. Scum Lake is also part of the Eleven Sisters chain of lakes, which can be strung together as part of a rustic canoe route.

Snag Lake Recreation Site (Map 43/G6)

Snag Lake is a small lake just east of Batnuni Lake. The lake outflow is a popular place to fish and a recreation site has been established here. The small lake warms up enough to swim in during summer.

Snaking River Recreation Site (Map 36/E4)

At this point, the once wild Snaking River mellows to a gentle, warm river that is a great place to canoe or swim in. The forest service site offers space for ten units in a treed area on the banks of the river.

Tatla Lake Recreation Site (Map 16/G7)

Located in an open aspen forest on the slopes above Tatla Lake, this scenic spot is popular with kokanee anglers. The gravel boat launch is a bit steep, and might give some vehicles trouble.

Tatlayoko Lake Recreation Site (Maps 7/G5, 8/A4)

Set alongside a turquoise lake in a mature stand of massive fir trees across from a dramatic mountain ridge, this is a wonderful camping spot. There is a boat launch, but be warned that the lake is subject to frequent high winds. The five large, well-spaced sites are close enough to the lake to see through the trees, but far enough back so that the main force of the wind frustrates itself on the trees.

Till Lake Recreation Site (Map 20/F5)

You can find this large forest service site via a rough 2wd road that branches west off the Meldrum Creek Road (1100 Road). This site sits along the north end of the lake amid a stand of trees. Swimming and fishing are the primary activities at the lake.

Titetown Crossing Recreation Site (Map 44/B7)

A small tenting site along the Alexander Mackenzie Trail, the site is just across the narrows from the Batnuni Lake Road.

Tsuniah Lake Recreation Site (Map 8/F6)

Depending on the time of year and the make of vehicle you drive, you may or may not be able to make it to this site with a 2wd vehicle. If you do make it, you will find excellent fishing and a cartop launch. You may also find one of the eight units here free, but it is a popular destination.

Twan Lake Recreation Site (Map 29/B7)

The rough access along the 0-3 Road ensures few visitors and a peaceful outdoor getaway. There are several campsites, complete with picnic tables, as well as a cartop boat launch at the lakeside forest service site.

Twin Lakes Recreation Site (Map 37/F2)

The campsites are set in the thick forest on the shores above the northern lake. Unfortunately, there are steep banks between you and the lake.

Two Lake Recreation Site (Map 18/E2)

A very small (two unit) site in a sandy, semi-open area next to the lake, this site is a popular fishing spot throughout the year. In the fall, hunters are the main visitors to the area and ice fishing is common in the winter. Access is found off the 2wd Alexis Lakes Road.

Tzenzaicut Lake Recreation Site (Map 28/F3)

Tzenzaicut Lake is a great fishing lake, and this recreation site sees a lot of use from anglers. It is a large, treed site that can be used by small groups. There is a gravel boat launch, a gravel beach, and a good access road into the site.

Vedan Lake Recreation Site (Map 9/A6)

There is space enough for six units at this site, which also features a nice gravel boat launch. The lake is quite windy, so canoeing is not recommended.

West Road River Recreation Site (Map 36/E3)

Strangely enough, locals call the river the Blackwater River, not the West Road. Visitors to this site will see why. The site sees a lot of use by groups canoeing the Snaking and Blackwater Rivers as well as a few anglers and hunters. It is a tenting only site.

Wentworth Lake Recreation Site (Map 28/A2)

Access can be dicey to this site, along a 4wd road. Check with the Ministry of Forests for current conditions. If you can manage the drive, you will still have to hike 800 metres to the tenting site on Wentworth Lake. However, the spot is very nice, and the poor access assures you that if you can make it, you'll probably have the site to yourself.

Lillooet Forest District

The Lillooet Forest District is another district that will have been relocated by the time this book is published (most likely to Merritt). Regardless, recreationists will find these Forest Service Sites scattered in the southeast section of the maps. Most of the activity in this area is focused around the fantastic Spruce Lake Trail system and some very remote lakes.

Hummingbird Lake (Map 4/C7)

Little more than a clearing next to a backcountry lake, this secluded site makes a fine hike-in destination.

Mud Lake North Recreation Site (Map 5/A5)

Despite the 4wd access, the Mud Lakes are a popular destination for 4wd enthusiasts and anglers. There is a pair of small, open sites at the north end of Upper Mud Lake. It is possible to launch a small boat or canoe onto the lake.

Mud Lake South Recreation Site (Map 5/A5)

A single camping unit is found on Lower Mud Lake, which is only accessible by a 4wd vehicle. Off-road enthusiasts (motorbikes and ATVs) frequent the area.

Relay Ford Recreation Site (Map 4/G7)

Access to the Relay Ford site is not always possible along the rough 4wd road. If it is accessible, this single site on the shores of Relay Creek is most often used as a base for trips into the Spruce Lakes area. The site also attracts anglers and gold panners.

Schraeder Lake Recreation Site (Map 5/G4)

The small, semi-open site on the shores of Schraeder Lake has space for two vehicle units. Fishing is a popular pastime and the site sports a cartop boat launch. Hunters also frequent the area in fall.

South French Bar Creek Recreation Site (Map 5/G5)

Located 1 km downstream of South French Bar Creek Bridge, this small site has space for three vehicle units. It sees heavy use in the fall, during the hunting season.

Spruce Lake East and North Recreation Sites (Map 4/E7)

These sites are used by people exploring the Spruce Lake Trails or testing their luck in one of the better fishing lakes in the province. Both sites are small, and most people without horses prefer the northern site.

Swartz Lake Recreation Site (Map 5/A5)

There is a single unit at the north end of Swartz Lake. Access is by 4wd, and the area is a popular destination for 4wd enthusiasts as well as people on motorbikes or ATVs.

Trigger Lake (Map 4/C7) ▲ 🚶 🐎 🚴 🛶 🐟

Found just northwest of Hummingbird Lake, Trigger Lake is another trail access only lake. Visitors will find signs of previous campsites and a trappers cabin in the area.

Tyaughton Creek Recreation Site (Map 4/G7)
▲ 🚶 🐎 🐟

There is space for three vehicle units at this 2wd accessible site on Tyaughton Creek. This is about as far as folks with 2wd vehicles are assured to make it when heading towards Eldorado Mountain or Big Creek Provincial Park. It is also used as a starting area for trips into the Spruce Lake area.

Upper Relay Creek (Map 4/E5) ▲ 🚶 🐎 🐟

Although you may be able to drive all the way into this informal camping area, most visitors come in by foot or on horse. It is found at the north end of the Spruce Lake Trail system, which is much less developed and used than the trails in the south.

Prince George Forest District

Although only covering the northeast portion of this book, this is an outdoor recreation hotbed. There is an abundance of forest service sites ranging from remote backcountry tenting areas to easy to access RV friendly campsites.

Barton Lake Recreation Site (Map 44/G4)
🏕 🛶 🐟 🚻 🖼

Set in the forest beside a scenic lake, these eight small sites make a fine camping destination. There is good 2wd access for people wishing to bring in small RVs as well as an informal camping area a bit further south. The chilling call of the Loon, the fine fishing and abundance of wildlife help make this a popular place to visit.

Blackwater Crossing Recreation Site (Map 45/C7)
▲ 🚶 🐎 🛶 🐟

Blackwater Crossing is a 10 unit site on the shores of the Blackwater River. The treed site is on the north side of the river, and is RV accessible. The historic Alexander Mackenzie Trail crosses through and there are walking trails along the river in both directions.

Bobtail Lake Recreation Site (Map 44/F2)
🏕 🏕 🛶 🚶 🛶 🛶 🛶 🐟

Located on the Old Telegraph Trail route to Quesnel, this is a popular site, with twenty camping spots across two separate areas on the east side of Bobtail (Naltesby) Lake. The sites found on the scenic peninsula fill up quickly. There is a cartop boat launch and the sites are RV friendly.

Clear Lake Recreation Site (Map 45/D1)
▲ 🏕 🛶 🛶 🐟 🖼

Found on a 2wd secondary road, this forest service site offers room for six vehicle units in a semi-open area. Similar to most sites in the area, the activities are usually based around the lake.

Cleswuncut Lake Recreation Site (Map 45/C7)
🏕 🛶 🛶 🐟

This small site is located next to the Blackwater Road south of Prince George. It is a small site with room for only two units as well as a cartop boat launch.

Lintz Lake Recreation Site (Map 44/D5) ▲ 🛶 🛶 🐟 🖼

Lintz Lake is a small lake, just off the Pelican Lake Road. The lake is well stocked with rainbow trout. There are twelve units and a gravel boat launch at this forest service site, which is located on the north side of the lake.

MacKenzie Lake West and North Recreation Sites (Map 45/E3)
▲ 🛶 🐟 🖼

There are forest service sites at this pair of small lakes just off the Blackwater Road. Both sites are small, sharing seven camping spots between the two. It is also possible to hand launch cartop boats at both lakes.

Meadow Lake Recreation Site (Map 44/E5)
▲ 🛶 🛶 🐟 🖼

Although fishing is the main activity on this lake, don't expect to find great success. But if you are looking for a small out of the way campsite, this is the place to come. There are five treed sites at the end of a narrow and winding access road. There is also a cartop boat launch.

Punchaw Lake Recreation Site (Map 45/D5)
▲ 🛶 🛶 🐟

Suitable for individual or group camping, the RV accessible site is a popular destination for anglers. There are ten units in a semi-open area on the west side of the lake.

Shesta Lake Recreation Sites (Map 45/E2)
🏕 🏕 🛶 🛶 🐟 🖼

Built on an old open mill site on the north end of the lake, there are ten RV accessible camping spots and a cartop boat launch at the forest service site. There is also a day-use site at the south end of the lake.

Tagai Lake Recreation Site (Map 44/D5) ▲ 🛶 🛶 🐟 🖼

Access into this forest service site can be difficult when wet. During the drier times, the twelve campsites on the east side of lake see plenty of activity from anglers. There is a cartop boat launch onto the lake.

Tory Lake Recreation Site (Map 44/G4) ▲ 🐟 🖼

At the 41 km mark of the Pelican Forest Service Road, this small site can be a little loud when logging trucks are hauling. The three sites are set in an open area overlooking the small lake to the south. It is possible to hand launch canoes or small boats onto the lake.

Vanderhoof Forest District

This mapbook touches on the southern reaches of the Vanderhoof Forest District. This area is popular with anglers and hunters looking for a place to get away from it all.

Arthur Lake Recreation Site (Map 43/A3)

Arthur Lake is a small lake to the west of Finger Lake. The forest service site is even smaller, with space for only one group.

Brewster Lake Recreation Site (Map 42/F5)

There's space for two vehicle units at this small site on the shores of Brewster Lake. As you might expect, fishing is the prime pursuit here.

Cheslatta River Recreation Site (Map 42/A1)

Located 1.5 km upstream from Cheslatta Falls, most of the campers who stay at this eight vehicle unit site make the hike to the falls along a good trail along the banks of the river.

Chutanli Lake Recreation Site (Maps 42/G6; 43/A7)

Chutanli means, "where the trout swim under the spruce trees" in the language of the Carrier people. Not surprisingly, there is good fishing in the lake. There are twelve units at this site as well as a boat launch onto the lake. An old prospectors cabin is found in the area, which was built on an ancient campsite used by the Kluskus aboriginal people.

Cicuta (Rum Cache) Lake Recreation Site (Map 41/G2)

Cicuta or Rum Cache Lake is a popular fly fishing lake with trophy size trout. Surrounded by high bluffs, there are six campsites and a cartop boat launch at this pretty site. Please observe posted angling restrictions.

Cutoff Creek Recreation Site (Map 42/B1)

There are five camping spots on this tree covered flat overlooking the Nechako River. The site makes a good take-out spot for canoe day trips from below Cheslatta Falls. RVs can access this site.

Eulatazella (Graveyard) Lake Recreation Site (Map 44/D1)

There is space enough for three groups at this site, which overlooks Eulatazella (Graveyard) Lake. A gravel boat launch and good road access make this a popular place for anglers with bigger boats and trailers.

Fish Lake Recreation Site (Map 42/A2)

Located on the shores of Fish Lake, this site is found 3 km (1.8 miles) from Kenney Dam. Access is good enough to allow RVs to access the four popular campsites. There is a boat launch onto the lake.

Frank Lake Recreation Site (Map 43/E1)

Frank Lake is a small lake located in the Nulki Hills. There is space for five vehicle units at the forest service site.

Grizzly Lake Recreation Site (Map 44/D2)

Grizzly Lake is a popular fishing lake and this forest service site sports a cartop boat launch. There is room for six vehicle units.

Hobson Lake Recreation Site (Map 42/C2)

A narrow, winding road leads to this lake named after cowboy author Rich Hobson. There is a small cartop boat launch, suitable for small boats or canoes only. Please observe posted special angling restrictions.

Home Lake Recreation Site (Map 43/A1)

There is an A-frame cabin on the west end of Home Lake, which marks the end of the Home Lake Trail (although an unmaintained route continues west). The cabin is available for use by hikers and backcountry skiers; there is a sign-in at trailhead. If the cabin is full, there is a pair of tent pads.

Knewstubb Lake Recreation Site (Map 42/A2)

Overlooking the Knewstubb Lake portion of the Nechako Reservoir, this eight vehicle unit site is located just east of Kenney Dam. It is an ideal base for day trips in the area. Access into the area is on a good 2wd road.

Kuyakuz Lake Recreation Site (Map 34/E2)

The name of this lake means, "fish come here often." Not surprisingly, the seven unit campsite sees heavy use from anglers.

Suscha Lake Recreation Site (Maps 34/G1, 35/A1)

In the language of the Carrier First Nations, the name of this lake means "and big black bears, too." We think this is warning enough. The forest service site is located in an open pine forest, with space for five groups. Just north of the camping area is a boat launch and picnic area.

Tanli Lake Recreation Site (Map 42/G7; 43/A7)

There is a silviculture camp on this small lake. The camp is open to the public when not required by reforestation crews who are usually only here in the spring and early summer.

Top Lake South Recreation Site (Map 33/G1)

This is a small, two unit site on a small roadside lake located in a low pass in the Fawnie Range. The site is just off the Kluskus-Ootsa Forest Road and access is usually quite good.

Wildlife Viewing

The remote nature of the Chilcotin Plateau makes this an ideal place to discover one of British Columbia's greatest treasures- wildlife. Unique to this region is the rare White Pelican and wild horses. The pelican is a large bird that can be found feeding around many small lakes and even has its own park. There are also many other birds and large animals as well as an impressive number of California Bighorn Sheep in the area.

In order to improve your chances of spotting birds and animals, wear natural colours and unscented lotions. Bring along binoculars or scopes so you can observe from a distance and move slowly but steadily. Keep pets on a leash, or better yet, leave them at home, as they will only decrease your chances to spot wildlife. Early mornings and late evenings are usually the best times to see most birds and animals.

Never approach an animal directly and for heaven's sake, do not try and bring animals to you by offering them food. Animals can become conditioned to handouts, which may put both of you, into harm's way. Rather, figure out what natural foods they prefer, and situate yourself near where these animals will feed.

What follows isn't a complete list of where you can see animals and birds, but it is a fairly good start. Some of the sites below cater mostly to birders, while other sites feature large mammals like deer and bighorn sheep. Still other sites focus on fish. All of them are worth checking out.

Alkali Lake–Reidemann Wildlife Sanctuary (Map 11/G2)

Like many lakes in the Chilcotin, Alkali is a feeding spot for the American White Pelican. The Reidemann Wildlife Sanctuary protects these feeding grounds and is a good bird watching spot for other birds, including the Long-billed Curlew (in spring) and the Tundra Swan (in spring and fall). In the summer, watch for loons, teals, and Barrow's Goldeneye.

Anahim Lake (Map 24/B5)

Anahim Lake is used by the endangered American White Pelican as a feeding ground. The lake is also home to many species of waterfowl, like Red-necked Grebe, Wood Ducks, and Green and Blue-winged Teals. In spring and summer, watch for Muskrat and River Otters, especially in the narrows between Anahim and Little Anahim Lakes.

Bella Coola Estuary (Map 21/E7)

Where the Bella Coola River flows into the North Bentinck Arm is a great spot for birding. The estuary is used by migrating waterfowl, as well as a wintering location for many species. You may see Trumpeter Swans, Canadian Geese, Mallards, American Wigeons, Barrow's Goldeneye, Bufflehead and the Common Merganser.

Brittany Triangle (Maps 2, 3, 8, 9, 18)

The Chilcotin is only one of two places in Canada where wild horses can still be seen. As many as 200 wild horses roam the 155,000 hectare area defined by the Chilco River to the west and the Taseko River to the east. The horses are believed to be descendants of the the mustangs that spread into BC's Cariboo and Chilcotin region in the mid-1700s.

Chilanko Marsh Wildlife Management Area (Map 17/D5)

Located just off Highway 20, the Chilanko Marsh is stretched out along a rather rough, 2wd accessible road. The area is best known for its waterfall, and if you go in summer, you may see Green-winged, Blue-winged and Cinnamon Teals, the Northern Shoveler, Canvasbacks, Redheads, Ring-necked Ducks, Bufflehead and Ruddy Ducks. You may also see shore birds, beaver or muskrat. In the winter, Moose feed in the area.

Chilcotin Lake (Map 17/F1)

A picturesque lake that forms the headwaters of the Chilcotin River, this lake is a popular bird watching destination. Like many lakes in the area, it is used as a feeding spot in May to August for American White Pelicans. Birds include waterfowl, Osprey, Bald Eagles, Belted Kingfisher, Grouse, woodpeckers, hummingbirds, swallows and a wide range of songbirds.

Chilko River (Map 8/E4)

Where Chilko Lake turns into the Chilko River is a great place to watch Steelhead spawn in May. This is one of the largest steelhead spawning areas in the province.

Chilcotin Marshes (Map 17/G1)

Found between Chezacut Road and the Chilcotin River, this lush wetland habitat is home to many nesting birds. The best time to view is from spring to fall. Known species include Grebes, Teals, Greater Yellowlegs, Spotted Sandpiper, Yellow-headed Blackbird, Red-breasted Nuthatch and Northern Flicker. In winter, this is prime moose habitat. There is a 1.5 km (0.9 mile) trail leading to the marshes.

Deer Park Wildlife Reserve (Map 11/A-C1)

The high country on the north side of the Chilcotin River is famous for its California Bighorn Sheep. It is also home to Mule Deer and coyotes, as well as many smaller land mammals. This area contains both private and Crown Land and visitors are asked to remain on the road corridors to avoid trespassing.

Eagle's Nest Marsh (Map 24/B6)

This viewing area is signed from the highway and starts near the Eagle's Nest Resort Sign. A gentle trail leads through the marsh, which is a good bird watching area. Birders can expect to see Trumpeter Swans, American White Pelicans, Eagles & Ospreys nests, Sandhill Cranes, Great Horned Owls and more.

Farwell Canyon (Map 11/C1)

Farwell Canyon is a spectacular area of hoodoos and sand dunes along the Chilcotin River. It is also home to California Bighorn Sheep.

Itcha Ilgachuz Provincial Park (Maps 24, 25, 33, 34)

This large provincial park (110,000 hectares) preserves a diverse variety of habitat and landscape, including volcanic landforms, alpine environments, and forested areas scattered with wetlands. The park is in

the rain shadow of the Coast Mountains, and supports a high diversity of plant and animal species. California Bighorn Sheep live here year round, primarily in the Ilgachuz Range. Moose may be observed from May to September and Woodland Caribou from June to December. Access to the park is along maintained, but long riding trails.

Junction Sheep Range Provincial Park (Map 11/E2)

A dry, arid landscape of rolling grasslands and deep gullies, the Junction Sheep Range Provincial Park is a stark, beautiful place. The area is home to many species of animals not normally found in the province, but is best known for its herd of California Bighorn Sheep, which is the largest in North America.

Pollywog Marshes (Map 16/G7)

A variety of wildlife has been observed at the marshes, including birds (Green and Blue-winged Teals, Mallards, Lesser Scaup, Barrow's Gold-eneye, Bufflehead and Ruddy Ducks) and small mammals (like beavers). The site is easily accessible off Highway 20 from the Pollywog Lake Rest Area.

Puntzi Marshes (Map 17/F4)

Just north of the Chilanko Marshes (see above), these marshes contain similar species of waterfowl and shore birds, including Horned Grebe, Green-winged, Blue-winged and Cinnamon Teals, Northern Pintail, Northern Shoveler, Redhead, Ring-necked Ducks, Northern Harrier and American Kestrel, Northern Flicker, swallows, Yellow-headed Blackbird and Eastern Kingbird. The marshes are about 3 km (1.2 miles) northeast of Chilanko Forks.

Snootli Creek Hatchery (Map 21/G7)

Established to enhance Chum (seen in July and August) and Chinook (seen in August and September) salmon in the Bella Coola system, visitors can also see Steelhead (in May) and Pink salmon (in August and September). The facility is 4 km (2.4 miles) west of Hagensborg.

Tatla Lake Marshes (Map 16/F7–17/C6)

These marshes stretch along the southern shores of Tatla Lake just north of Highway 20. As a result, access to this area is good. Watch for nesting waterfowl, snipe and songbirds, including a couple species of blackbird.

Ts'y-los Provincial Park (Maps 2, 3, 8)

A huge park in the southwestern Chilcotin, bordered by the rugged peaks of the Coast Mountains to the west and the dry Interior Plateau to the east, this park is home to a diversity of landscapes and habitat. Wildlife species include Black Bear, Mule Deer, Moose, Mountain Goat and American Beaver. Ecologically sensitive animal populations found in the area include California Bighorn Sheep, Fisher, Wolverine, Bald Eagle and amphibian species. The adjacent lands are also important habitat for Vaux's Swift, Peregrine Falcon and Townsend's Big-eared Bat. Access is via rough 2wd accessible logging roads.

Tweedsmuir Provincial Park (Maps 13, 14, 22, 23, 30–32, 38, 39)

As the largest park in British Columbia, Tweedsmuir is host to an amazing range of birds and animals too large to list here. Part of this is due to the fact that the park links the lush coastal environment with the dry, high elevation interior plateau. The park itself is centred around the rugged Coast Mountains. Another reason is the fact that much of the terrain of Tweedsmuir is all but inaccessible to humans. In fact, the northern reaches of the park rarely see any human activity other than big game outfitters in search of moose or caribou. Below we have described a few of the more easily accessed wildlife viewing areas:

Tweedsmuir South Provincial Park–Fisheries Pool (Map 22/G7) is a popular angling spot and avid wildlife watchers can watch various species of salmon and Steelhead spawn in these waters.

Tweedsmuir South Provincial Park–Lonesome Lake (Map 14/E2) is accessed by foot from the end of the Tote Road. Trumpeter Swans are visible on the lake from October to mid-April.

Tweedsmuir South Provincial Park–Rainbow Nature Conservancy Area (Maps 22, 23) is a huge section of Tweedsmuir that is designated as a Nature Conservancy Area to protect the Woodland Caribou. It is home to one of BC's largest herds of caribou. Look for these impressive animals can be seen in the sub-alpine forests of the area year round.

Tweedsmuir South Provincial Park–Turner Lake (Map 14/D2) is only accessible by floatplane, or a long hike in (and up) from the end of the Tote Road. Parts of the lake remain ice-free year-round, and Trumpeter Swans over-winter here.

Winter Recreation

The Chilcotin is big, wide and open. Where can you go snowmobiling? Where can't you go snowmobiling? Pretty well the only areas where snowmobiling is off limits is ecological reserves, private property, and most provincial parks.

The problem with that is it makes it difficult to describe where to go. We have outlined a few places where you can go snowmobiling or cross-country skiing, but know that this is just the tip of a very large iceberg. Ski touring is extremely popular in late winter, with some of the more adventurous traversing up and over the Coast Mountains from Tatlayoko Lake and into the Highway 99 area (see Southwestern BC Mapbook). Trips like these are best left to those with lots of ski touring experience.

Below you will find a few areas that have established facilities or trails. For the snowshoer and backcountry skier, many of the trails described in the multi-use trail section would make fine destinations. In fact, skiers explore all the long distant trails such as the Alexander MacKenzie Heritage Trail, the Collins Overland Telegraph Trail and the Lt. Palmer Route in the winter. Then there are the endless road systems found on the maps. Only a few of the mainlines are ploughed. The rest would make a wonderful playground for snowmobiles, skiers and even those on snowshoes.

Alexis Creek Cross-Country Ski Trails (Map 19/B5)

There are four looping trails, totaling 8.5 km (5.2 miles) near Alexis Creek. You'll climb about 200 metres (650 feet) to the highest point of the system. These trails are usually track set and cleared by volunteers of the community. If you want to venture up here on snowshoes, please stay off the tracks.

Bobtail Mountain Trail (Map 44/G1)

The Bobtail Mountain trail is 5 km (3 miles) in length with a change in elevation of 470 metres (1,624 feet). The trek requires climbing some steep pitches but once on top the reward is seemingly endless powder to ski. A rustic cabin is available for use at the top. Call the Prince George Travel Infocentre at 1-800-663-6000 to make reservations for the cabin.

Fort George Canyon Ski Trails (Map 45/G1)

In winter, there are a series of moderate trails that are popular with cross-country skiers. The main trail leads 5 km (3 mile) to the historic canyon on the Fraser River.

Goldbridge Snowmobile Area (Map 23/C4)

The town of Goldbridge is actually found south of this mapbook, but popular snowmobile destinations include the Spruce Lake and Taseko Lakes area. Snowmobilers often follow the Gun Creek Trail and Warner Pass Trail up and over the pass and into the Taseko River Valley.

Home Lake Trail (Map 43/B1)

A cabin on Home Lake makes this a popular winter destination with backcountry skiers and snowmobilers. The trail into the lake is about 12 km return but it is possible to continue onto Paddle Lake or beyond. The cabin is available on a first come first serve basis (check the registration book at the trailhead).

Itcha Ilgachuz Provincial Park (Maps 24/D2, 33/C7)

The local snowmobile club maintains a pair of cabins in the Itcha Ilgachuz, which can be used by any and all willing to make the trip into this wilderness park. This is big, wide-open country with lots of trails and alpine areas. Due to the distances involved, backcountry skiing and snowshoeing is not a popular activity here. Part of the park is zoned as an Ecological Management Zone, and snowmobiling is not allowed in this area. Also, snowmobiling is prohibited before December 15, and after April 30.

Jay Lakes Snowmobile Area (Map 12/C1)

While Bella Coola itself receives snow infrequently, the mountains above Bella Coola are often snowed under until early summer. The winter storms that bring rain to the valley bring snow, and lots of it, to the high country. The Jay Lakes area is a popular local area for snowmobiling. There's lots of sub-alpine and alpine riding.

Rainbow Range Snowmobile Area (Map 23/C4)

This is the only chunk of Tweedsmuir Park that is open to snowmobiling, but boy, is it a great area. It covers the high country of Heckman Pass and parts of the Rainbow Range. The parking area is found off Highway 20 along the infamous Hill.

Spruce Lake Area (Map 4/D7)

The sprawling trail network that makes a wonderful horseback riding and hiking destination in the summer turns into a backcountry ski/snowshoe paradise in winter. None of the trails are groomed, but snowmobiles do follow a few of the trails, including the Gun Creek and Warner Pass Trails. This means breaking snow a lot easier. The other major creek valleys (Tyaughton and Relay) are also easier to ski as they gently climb towards the mountains. Taylor Basin (see Southwestern BC Mapbook) is another popular destination since there is a cabin at the pass.

Tatla Lake Trails (Map 16/E7)

A series of loop trails between Tatla Lake and Martin Lake. The longest trail, the Race Route Circuit, is an easy 17.2 km (10.5 miles). The rest of the trails range from easy to intermediate and are shorter. If you want to venture up here on snowshoes, please stay off the track set trails.

Tweedsmuir Park Ski Trails (Map 3/G6-4/D7)

Most of the winter recreation in this big park occurs around Heckman Pass. There are a series of cross-country ski trails found around 'The Hill' on Highway 20.

Warner Pass Trail (Map 3/G6-4/D7)

Part of the Spruce Lake Trail system, mountain riders are free to roam the high alpine of this sprawling area. Touring riders tend to stick to this trail, which climbs from Trigger Lake, past Warner Lake, and to the 750 metre high (2438 feet) Warner Pass. Beyond the pass, the trail continues for another 11.5 km (6.9 miles) to hook up with the end of a mining road at Battlement Creek, which can in turn be followed past (or onto, if the ice is thick enough) the Taseko Lakes.

West Lake Cross-Country Ski Trails (Map 45/G1)

Found south of Prince George via the Blackwater Road, West Lake Park offers a series of easy cross-country ski trails. All levels of skiers can enjoy the trails and there is a sheltered picnic area in the park. Snowshoers are asked to stay off the pre-set ski tracks.

Chilcotin Mapkey

Overlap of Maps (adjusted for north)

To Vanderhoof

To Prince George

See Central BC Mapbook

38	39	40	41	42	43	44	45	
30	31	32	33	34	35	36	37	
21	22	23	24	25	26	27	28	29
12	13	14	15	16	17	18	9	20
			6	7	8	9	10	11
			1	2	3	4	5	

To Prince George

Quesnel

Alexandria

Macalister

Williams Lake

To 100 Mile House

See Caiboo Mapbook

Mount Waddington

See Southwestern BC Mapbook

Projection
North American Datum 1983
Transverse Mercator Projection
Coordinate Conversion NAD83
(WGS84) to NAD27

Individual Map Scale Bar
Scale 1:150,000 or 1cm = 1.5km

1.5km   0km   3km

1 km = 0.6214 mi.

Legend for the Maps

Recreational Activities:

Anchorage .... ⚓
Boat Launch ....
Beach ....
Campsite / Limited Facilities ....
Campsite / Trailer Park ....
Campsite (trail / water access only) ... △
Canoe Access Put-in / Take-out ...
Cross Country Skiing ....
Diving ....
Downhill Skiing ....
Golf Course ....
Hang-gliding ....
Horseback Riding ....
Mountain Biking ....
Motorbiking / ATV ....
Paddling (canoe-kayak) ....
Picnic Site ....
Portage ....
Rock Climbing ....
Snowmobiling ....
Snowshoeing ....

Miscellaneous:

Airport / Airstrip .... ✈
Beach ....
Beacon .... ☀
Cabin / Lodge / Resort ....
Ferries ....
Fishing BC Lake ....
Float Plane ....
Forestry Lookout (abandoned) .....
Gate .... =
Highways .... 🛡
  Trans-Canada ....
Interchange .... ◇
Lighthouse ....
Marsh ....
Microwave Tower .... ⚡
Mine Site (abandoned) .... ✕
Parking .... Ⓟ
Pictograph ....
Point of Interest .... ★
Portage (metres) .... P 50
Ranger Station ....
Town Village, etc .... ●
Travel Information .... ⑦
Viewpoint ....
Waterfalls ....
Winery ....

Line Definition:

Highways ....
Paved Secondary Roads ....
Forest Service / Main Roads ......
Active Logging Roads (2wd) ....
Logging Roads (2wd / 4wd) ....
Long Distance Trail ....
Unclassified / 4wd Roads ....
Deactivated Roads ....
Trail / Old Roads ....
Routes (Undeveloped Trails) ......
Snowmobile Trails ....
Paddling Routes ....
Powerlines ....
Pipelines ....
Railways ....
Wildlife Management Units ....

Provincial Park

Recreation Area / Ecological Area

City

Restricted Area / Private Property

Glaciers / Swamps

Indian Reserve

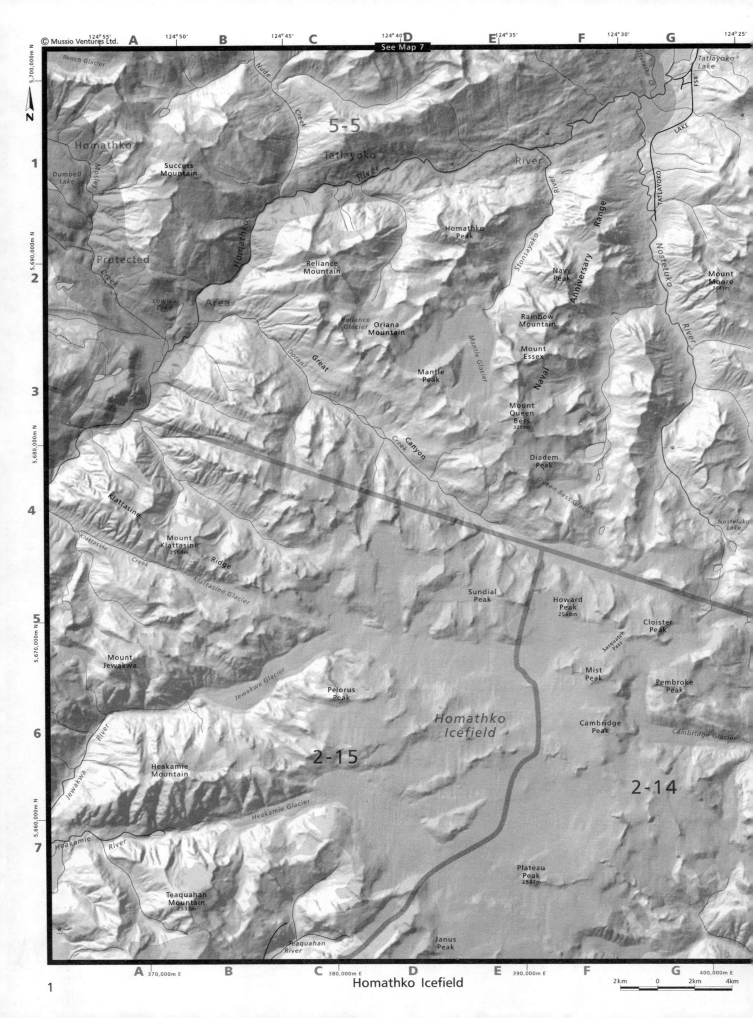

N

124° 55'   124° 50'   124° 45'   124° 40'   124° 35'   124° 30'   124° 25'

A   B   C   D   E   F   G

Bench Glacier

5,700,000m N

Homathko

5-5

Tatlayoko

Tatlayoko
Lake

FSR

Dumbell
Lake

Success
Mountain

Nude

Creek

River

River

River

Ottarasko Cr

TATLAYOKO

LAKE

1

Mosley

Homathko

Homathko
Peak

Stonsayako River

Navy
Peak

Anniversary Range

Nostetuko

Mount
Moore
3041m

5,690,000m N

Protected

Creek

Reliance
Mountain

Rainbow
Mountain

Mount
Essex

2

Lowwa
Lake

Area

Reliance
Glacier

Oriana
Mountain

Mantle Glacier

Naval

River

5,680,000m N

Doran

Great

Mantle
Peak

Mount
Queen
Bess
3289m

3

Canyon

Creek

Diadem
Peak

Queen Bess Glacier

Klattasine

Nosteluko
Lake

4

Klattasine

Creek

Mount
Klattasine
2564m

Ridge

Klattasine Glacier

Sundial
Peak

Howard
Peak
2588m

Cloister
Peak

5,670,000m N

5

Mount
Jewakwa

Jewakwa Glacier

Pelorus
Peak

Mist
Peak

Sasquatch Pass

Pembroke
Peak

Homathko
Icefield

Cambridge
Peak

Cambridge Glacier

6

River

2-15

Heakamie
Mountain

2-14

5,660,000m N

Jewakwa

Heakamie Glacier

7

Heakamie

River

Teaquahan
Mountain
2533m

Plateau
Peak
2543m

Teaquahan
River

Janus
Peak

A   B   C   D   E   F   G

370,000m E   380,000m E   390,000m E   400,000m E

2km   0   2km   4km

Homathko Icefield

1

© Mussio Ventures Ltd.

A 124° 20′ B 124° 15′ C 124° 10′ D 124° 05′ E 124° 00′ F 123° 55′ G

5-4

N

51° 25′

Mount
Tatlow
(Ts'yl-os)
3061m

1

Troloos Cr.

CHILKO Lk FSR

Garden
Indian
Reserve

Creek

Nemaia

Robertson Rd

Chilko Lake
Indian
Reserve

VALLEY

5-5

Stikelan Pass

Ch'a Biny
Big Lagoon

Stikelan
Pt

NEMAIAH

Lezbye Indian
Reserve

Nu Chugh
Beniz
Campsite

51° 20′

2

Mount
Howard
Stowe

Duff
Island

Bald Eagle?

Chilko

Canoe
Pt

Mount
Whitton

Liberated

Girdwood
Lake

Girdwood
Creek

Group

Lake

Ts'yl-os

Tredcroft
Glacier

Tredcroft

Gullboy Cr

Boatswain
Mtn

51° 15′

3

Mount
Dartmouth

Capital
Group

Provincial

Mount
Olson

See Map 3

Consort
Peak

Austen Glacier

Torch Creek

Nine Mile Creek

Franklin Arm (Tud tl'az)

Bateman
Pt

Mount
Kern

Yohetta
Lake
(Yuyadtah
Biny)

Trail

private cabin

5-5

Deschamps

Impasse Ridge

Good Hope Creek

Glasgow Creek

Glasgow
Lakes

Mount
Goddard
2470m

Rainbow
Cabin

(Tsitalh7ad
Biny)

Dorothy Lake

Volente Lake

Park

51° 15′

4

2-14

Dawn Treader
Mtn
3074m

Kese
Mtn
3060m

Burnt
Island

Rainbow
Creek
Trail

Spectrum

Rainbow Creek

Spectrum
Pass

Trail

51° 10′

5

Good Hope
Mtn
3245m

Mount
Duram
2774m

Pluvius
Peak
2883m

Glasgow
Mtn
2528m

Merriam
Mtn
3078m

Mutiny
Bay

Spectrum
Pass

Farrow Creek

Five Brothers Peaks

Farrow
Glacier

5-4

51° 05′

6

Boulanger Creek

Mount
Marston
2726m

Mount
Farrow
2896m

Southgate River

Otranto
Mountain
2714m

Goddard Glacier

Canopus
Glacier

Leipzig
Mtn
2715m

Coronel
Mtn
2668m

Norrington Cr.

Spyglass
Peak

Altruist
Lake

Altruist
Mountain

Moose
Mountain

Miserable
Glacier

Cradock
Mtn
2825m

Mount
Canopus
2743m

Wednesday
Mtn
2941m

Dresden
Mtn
2656m

Chilko
Mountain
2705m

Edmond Creek

Friendly
Glacier

Rim
Mountain

7

Scharnhorst
Mtn
2588m

Cradock
Glacier

2-14

Bishop River
Prov Park

Norrington
Glacier

Cyr Creek

Remote Creek

Rim
Glacier

51° 00′

Durham Creek

A B C D E F G

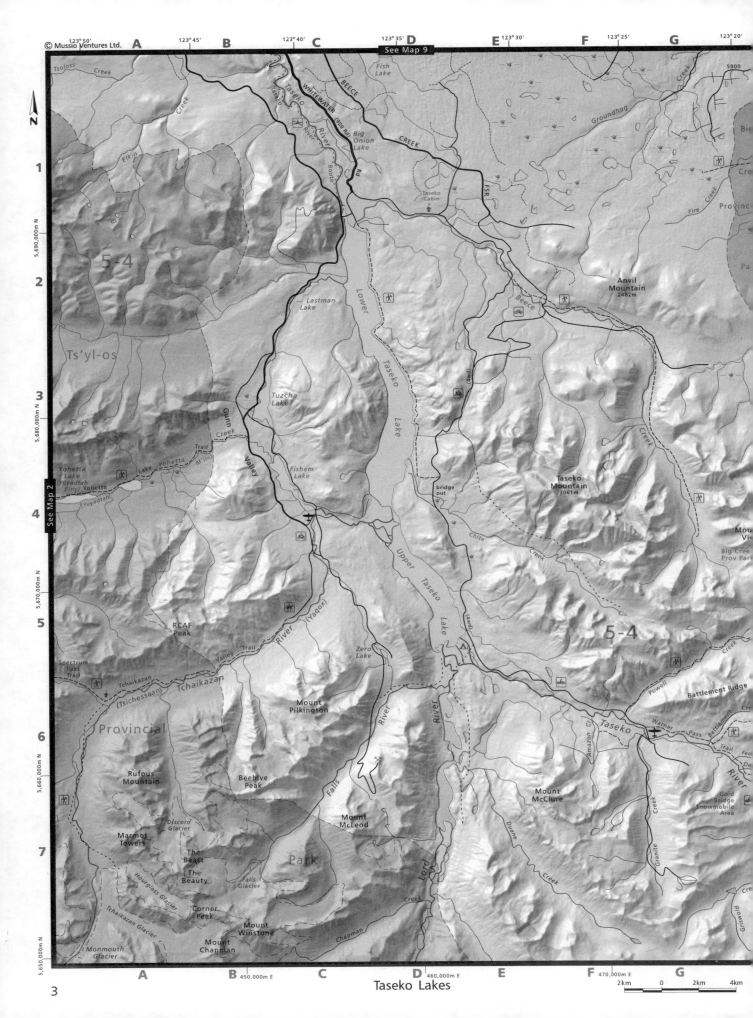

See Map 9

Taseko Lakes

3

2km   0   2km   4km

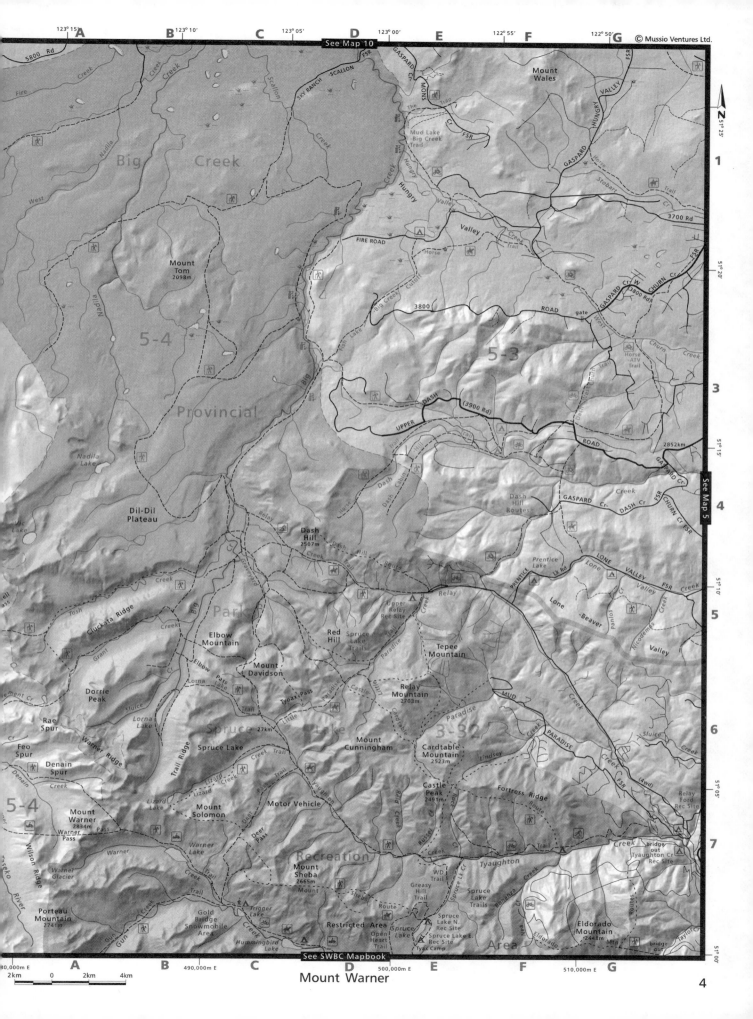

© Mussio Ventures Ltd.

Mount Wales

Big Creek

Mount Tom
2098m

5-4

Provincial

Nadila Lake

Dil-Dil Plateau

Vic Lake

Cluckata Ridge

Dorrie Peak

Rae Spur

Feo Spur

Denain Spur

5-4

Mount Warner
2834m
Warner Pass

Warner Glacier

Porteau Mountain
2741m

Taseko River

Wilson Ridge

Dash Hill
2507m

Park

Elbow Mountain

Mount Davidson

Trail Ridge

Lorna Lake

Spruce Lake

Lizard Lake

Mount Solomon

Motor Vehicle

Warner Lake

Deer Pass

Mount Sheba
2665m

Gold Bridge Snowmobile Area

Trigger Lake

Hummingbird Lake

Recreation

Red Hill

Spruce Lake Trails

Tepee Mountain

Relay Mountain
2703m

Mount Cunningham

Cardtable Mountain
2523m

Castle Peak
2491m

Fortress Ridge

3-32

MUD

PARADISE

Relay Ford Rec Site

Sluice Creek

Eldorado Mountain
2448m

Spruce Lake Trails

Greasy Hill Trail

Tyaughton

WD Trail

Spruce Lake N. Rec Site

Spruce Lake E. Rec Site

Tyax Camp

Restricted Area

Open Heart Trail

Spruce Lake

Area

bridge out
Tyaughton Cr Rec Site

bridge out

Prentice Lake

LONE VALLEY

Lone Beaver Valley

Nicodemis Valley

Hungry Valley

Gaspard

Horse Trail

3700 Rd

FIRE ROAD

Horse Trail

3800

ROAD

gate

3800 Rd

Horse ATV Trail

UPPER DASH

(3900 Rd)

ROAD

2852km

GASPARD Cr.

DASH Cr

CHURN Cr FSR

Dash Hill Routes

5-3

Churn Creek

Gaspard Cr W

CHURN Cr

5°25'
5°20'
5°15'
5°10'
5°05'
5°00'

1
3
4
5
6
7

See Map 5

123° 15'   123° 10'   123° 05'   123° 00'   122° 55'   122° 50'

A   B   C   D   E   F   G

480,000m E   490,000m E   500,000m E   510,000m E

2km 0 2km 4km

© Mussio Ventures Ltd.

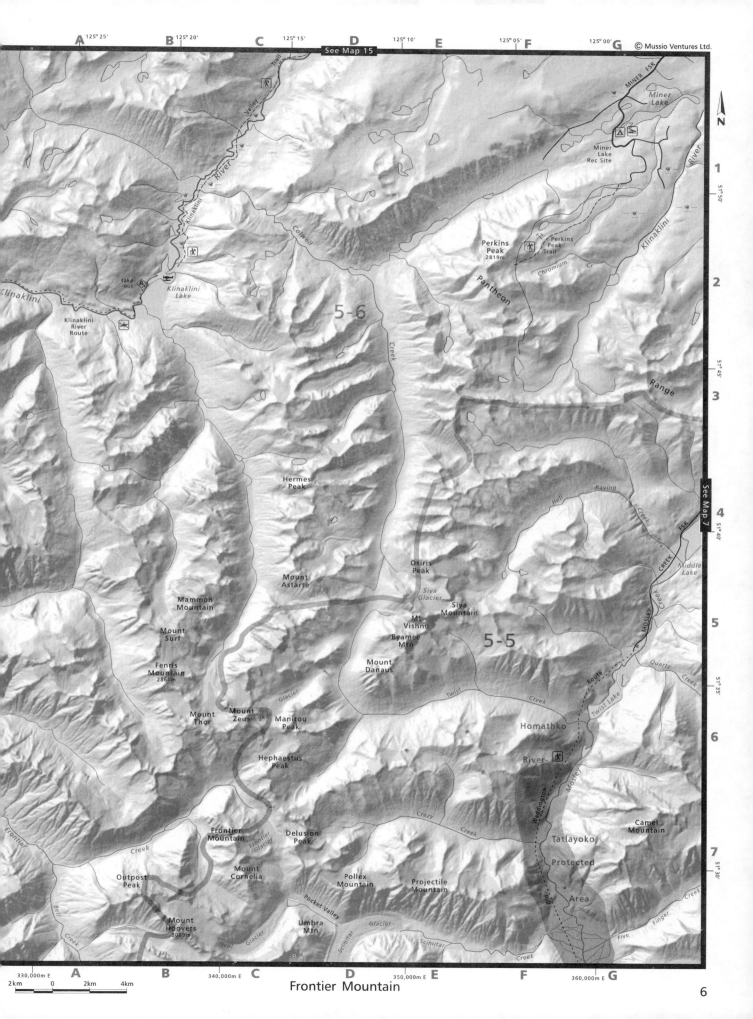

© Mussio Ventures Ltd.

N

MINER FSR

Miner
Lake

Miner
Lake
Rec Site

Klinaklini

River

1

51° 50'

Klinaklini

River

Valley
Trail

Colwell

Perkins
Peak
2819m

Perkins
Peak
Trail

Chromium   Cr

Pantheon

2

51° 45'

take
-out

Klinaklini
Lake

5-6

Creek

Range

3

Klinaklini
River
Route

Klinaklini

Hermes
Peak

Raving

Hell

Creek

See Map 7

4

51° 40'

FSR

CREEK

Mount
Astarte

Osiris
Peak

Siva
Glacier

Siva
Mountain

Middle
Lake

Mammon
Mountain

M1
Vishnu

5-5

Mosley

Creek

5

51° 35'

Mount
Surf

Byamee
Mtn

Mount
Danaus

Twist   Creek

Creek

Quartz   Creek

Fenris
Mountain
2860m

Glacier

Route

Twist Lake

Mount
Thor

Mount
Zeus

Manitou
Peak

Homathko

6

Hephaestus
Peak

River-

Weddington

Mosley

Frontier

Creek

Frontier
Mountain

Frontier
Glacier

Delusion
Peak

Crazy   Creek

Camel
Mountain

Tatlayoko

7

51° 30'

Outpost
Peak

Mount
Cornelia

Pollex
Mountain

Projectile
Mountain

Protected

Area

Bell

Creek

Mount
Hoovers
3089m

Pocket Valley

Umbra
Mtn

Oval   Glacier

Scimitar   Glacier

Scimitar   Creek

Five   Finger   Creek

2km   0   2km   4km

Frontier Mountain

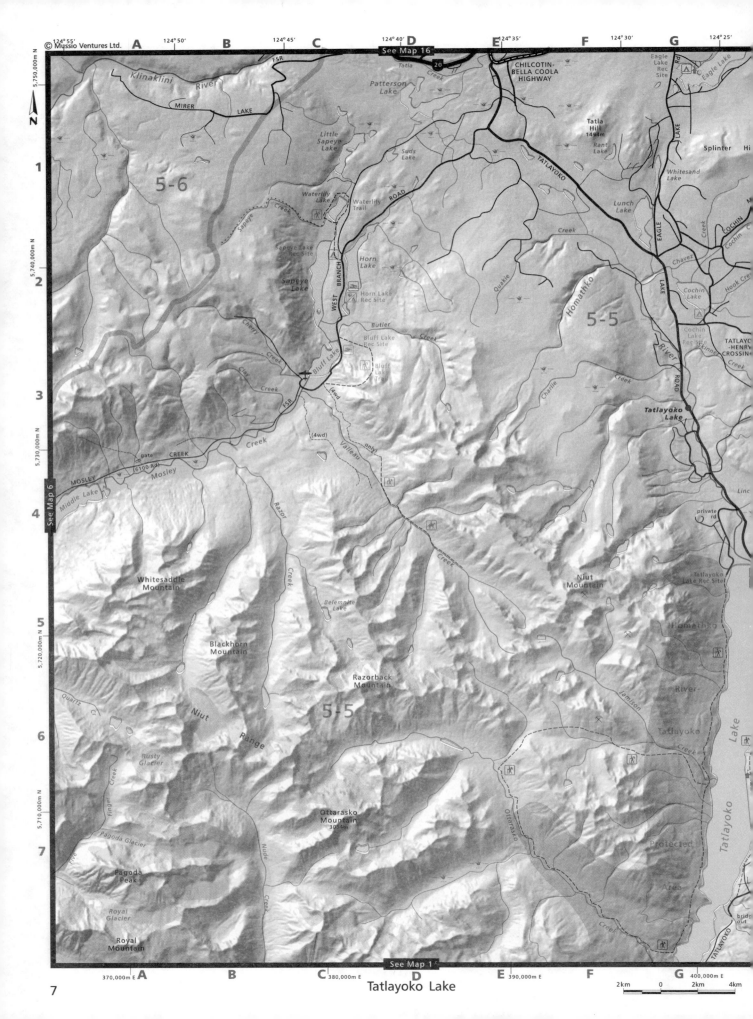

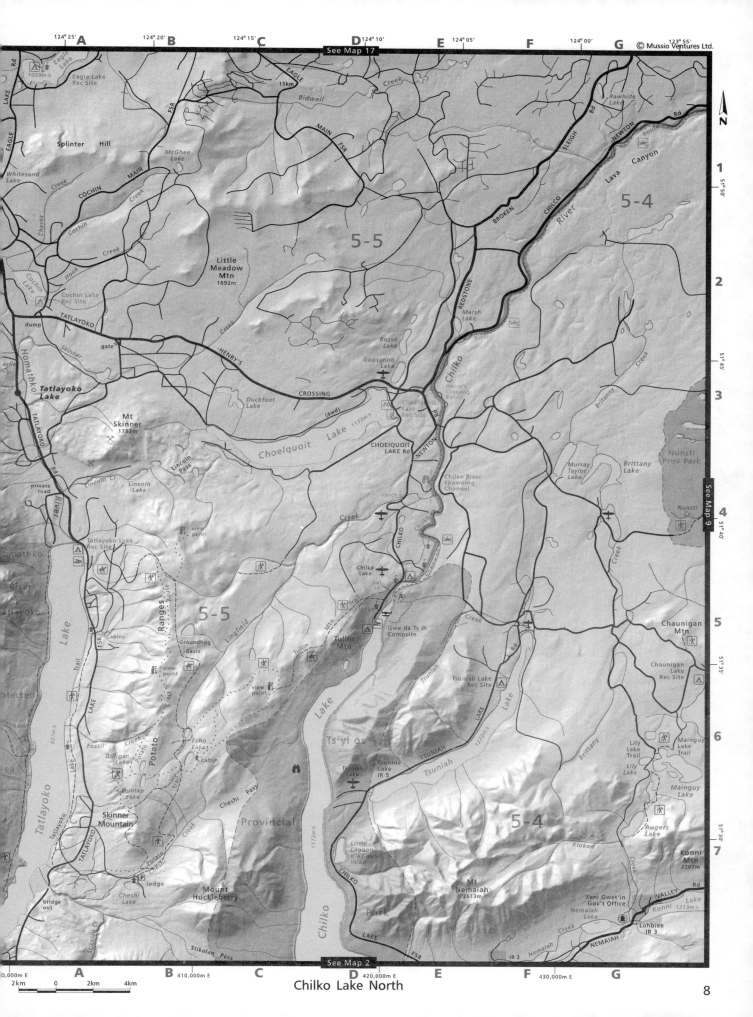

Chilko Lake North

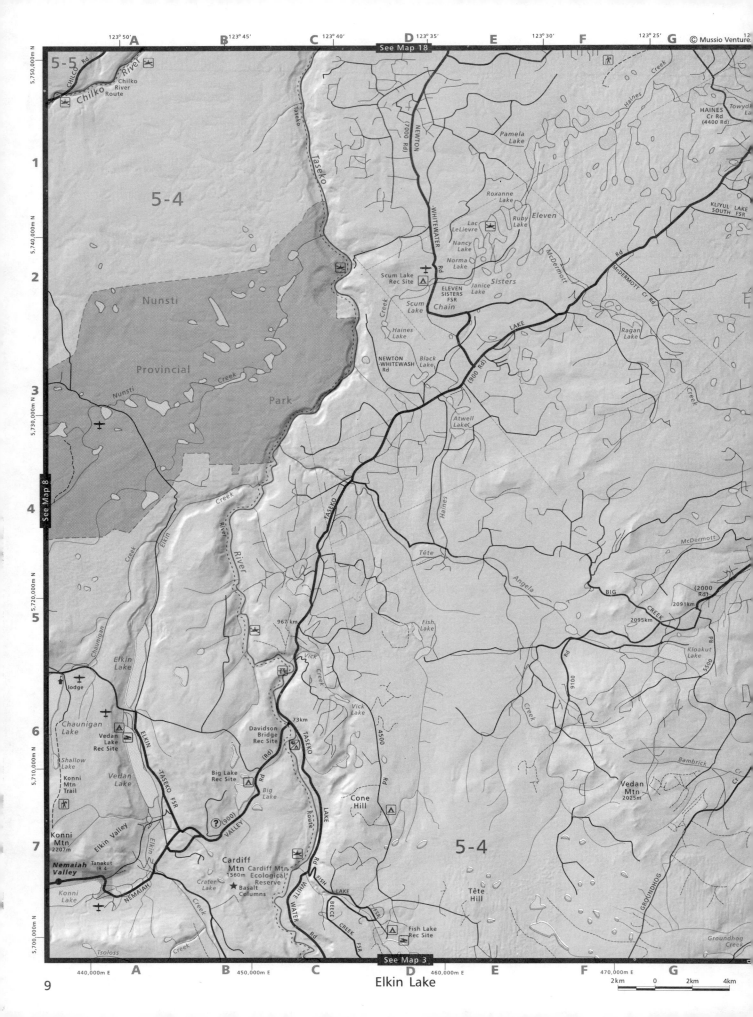

123° 50' A   123° 45' B   123° 40' C   123° 35' D   E   123° 30' F   123° 25' G

5-4

Chilko River
Chilko River Route

Nunsti

Provincial

Park

Nunsti

Creek

Elkin

River

Creek

Chaunigan

Creek

Elkin

Lake

lodge

Chaunigan
Lake

Vedan Lake
Rec Site

Shallow
Lake

Konni
Mtn
Trail

Vedan
Lake

Konni
Mtn
2207m

Elkin Valley

Tanakut
IR 4

Nemaiah
Valley

Konni
Lake

NEMAIAH

Tsoloss

Creek

Taseko

Taseko

Taseko

Creek

ELKIN

TASEKO FSR

Elkin

VALLEY

Rd

(900)

Davidson
Bridge
Rec Site

(Rd)

Big Lake
Rec Site

Big
Lake

Cardiff
Mtn
1560m

Cardiff Mtn
Ecological
Reserve

Crater
Lake

Basalt
Columns

967 km

Vick
Creek

73km

TASEKO

LAKE

Rd

WHITE WATER

Rd

FISH

LAKE

BEECE

CREEK

FSR

See Map 3

NEWTON

(7000 Rd)

WHITEWATER

Rd

Scum Lake
Rec Site

Scum
Lake

NEWTON
WHITEWASH
Rd

Haines
Lake

Black
Lake

ELEVEN
SISTERS
FSR

LAKE

(900 Rd)

Atwell
Lake

Haines

Creek

Pamela
Lake

Roxanne
Lake

Lac
LeLievre

Nancy
Lake

Norma
Lake

Janice Lake

Eleven

Ruby
Lake

Sisters

Chain

McDermott

Creek

Ragan
Lake

KLIYUL LAKE
SOUTH FSR

HAINES
Cr Rd
(4400 Rd)

Towyd
La

McDERMOTT Cr Rd

Rd

McDermott

Téte

Angela

Creek

Fish
Lake

Vick
Lake

Cone
Hill

4500

Rd

9100

Rd

Creek

BIG   CREEK

2091km

2095km

Kloakut
Lake

5500

Vedan
Mtn
2025m

Bambrick

GROUNDHOG

Cr

5-4

Tête
Hill

Fish Lake
Rec Site

Groundhog
Creek

5,750,000m N

1

5,740,000m N

2

5,730,000m N

3

See Map 8

4

5,720,000m N

5

5,710,000m N

6

7

5,700,000m N

440,000m E A   B 450,000m E   C   D 460,000m E   E   F 470,000m E   G

9

Elkin Lake

2km 0 2km 4km

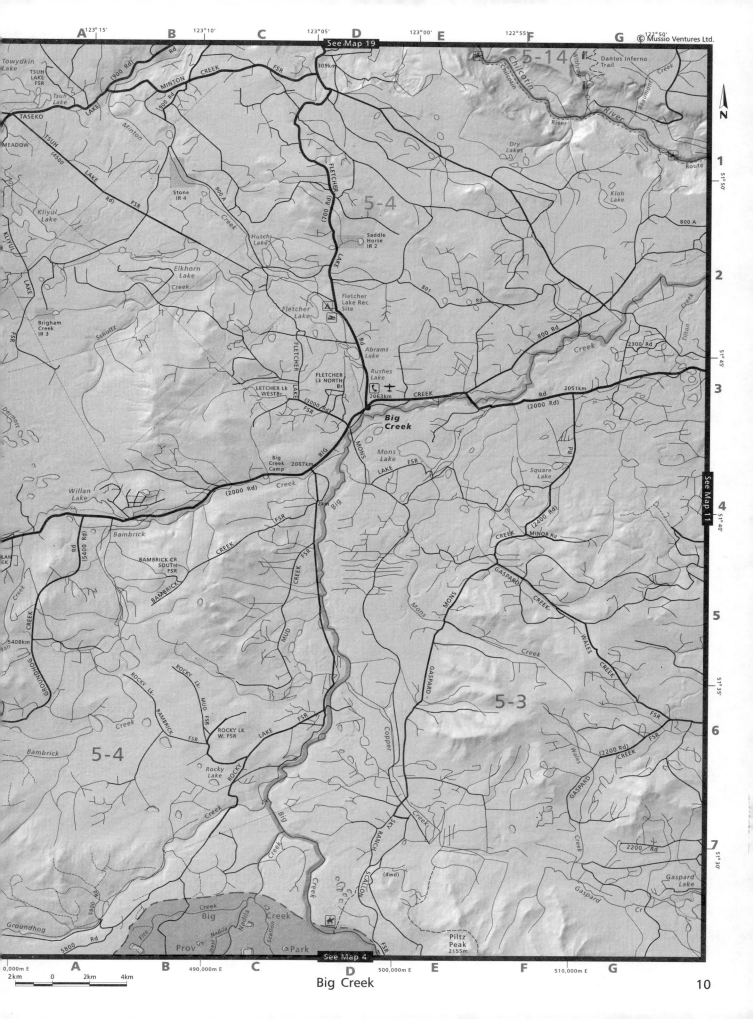

© Mussio Ventures Ltd.

5-14

Dantes Inferno Trail

Chilcotin

River

Route

1

51°50'

Kloh Lake

800 A

2

51°45'

5-4

Saddle Horse IR 2

Fletcher Lake Rec Site

Abrams Lake

Rushes Lake

Dry Lakes

Creek

2300 Rd

Tilton

800 Rd

2051km

Rd (2000 Rd)

3

51°45'

Big Creek

Mons Lake

Square Lake

Big Creek Camp 2067km

(2000 Rd)

2km

See Map 11

4

51°40'

MINOR Rd

2400 Rd

GASPARD

CREEK

WALES CREEK

5

51°35'

5-3

GASPARD

Copper

Wales

FSR

(2200 Rd) CREEK

6

51°35'

GASPARD

2200 Rd

7

51°30'

Piltz Peak 2155m

Gaspard Lake

Gaspard Cr

Bambrick

5-4

Rocky Lake

MUD FSR

ROCKY LK W. FSR

ROCKY

Big

Creek

MUD

LAKE

Groundhog

5800 Rd

Big

Nadila Creek

Scallion Creek

Prov

Park

Big Creek

Towydkin Lake

TSUH LAKE FSR

Tsuh Lake

MEADOW

TASEKO

TSUH LAKE (4500 Rd)

Kliyul Lake

KUYUL

Minton

309km

MINTON CREEK Rd

(1900 Rd)

1900 Rd

Stone IR 4

800 A

Creek

Hutch Lake

Elkhorn Lake

Creek

Brigham Creek IR 3

Schultz

FSR

Dermott Creek

Fletcher Lake

FLETCHER LAKE (1700 Rd)

FLETCHER Lk NORTH Br

LETCHER Lk WESTBr

FSR (3000 Rd)

Rd

2063km

BIG

2067km

(2000 Rd) Creek

FSR

Willan Lake

Bambrick

Rd (5400 Rd)

BAMBRICK CR SOUTH FSR

BAMBRICK

CREEK

Creek

GROUNDHOG

Rd

5408km

5400 Rd

ROCKY Lk.

ROCKY

BAMBRICK

Creek

Bambrick

Rd

5900

5800 Rd

Groundhog

Big

FletchCr

Nadila

MONS LAKE FSR

FSR

Mons

Copper

Creek

SIX RANCH (4wd)

SCALLION FSR

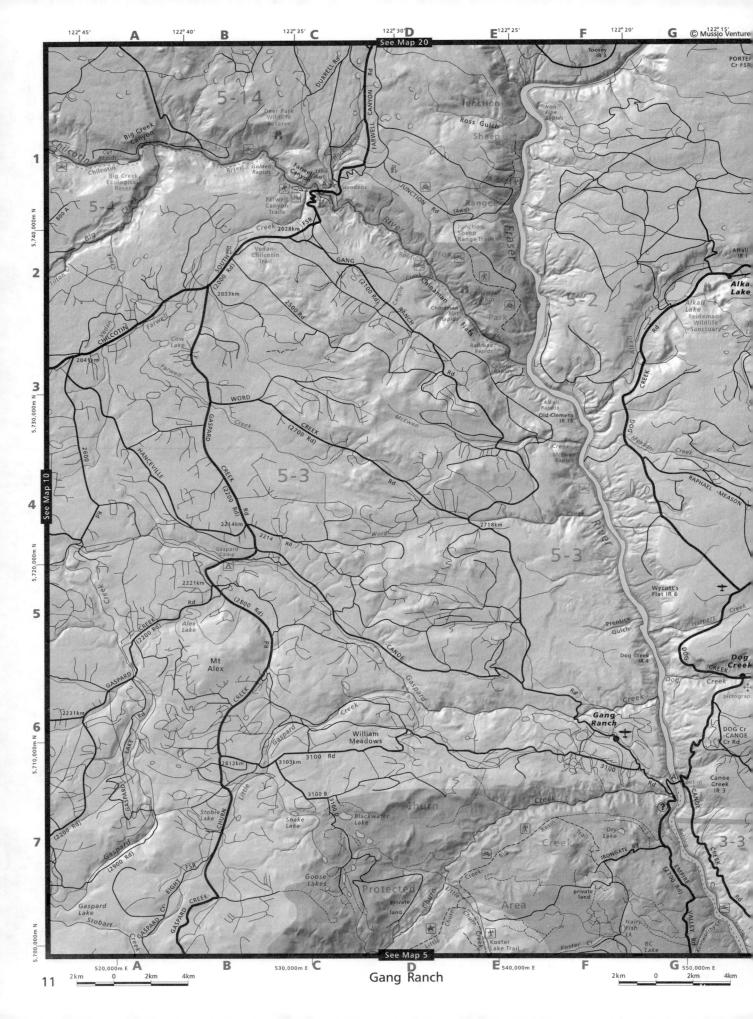

122° 45'　A　122° 40'　B　122° 35'　C　122° 30'　D　122° 25'　E　122° 20'　F　G　122° 15'
© Mussio Venture

5-14

Big Creek Canyon
Deer Park Wildlife Reserve

Chilcotin
Cut Rapids
Chilcotin
Big Creek Ecological Reserve

5-4

800 A

Tilton

River
Golden Rapids
Farwell Canyon Lookout
Farwell Canyon
Farwell Canyon Trails
Hoodoos

DURRELL Rd

FARWELL CANYON

Junction
Ross Gulch
Sheep
Iron Pipe Rapids

Toosey IR 3

PORTER Cr FSR

Creek 2028km FSR

Vedan-Chilcotin Trail

SOUTH (2000 Rd)
2033km

2041km

CHILCOTIN
Farwell
Vedan

Cow Lake

GANG (2100 Rd)

Cargile Creek

Chinaman
Chinaman Flat Rapids
Chinaman Flats

Range (4wd)
Junction Sheep Range Trail

Fraser

5-2

Alkali IR 1

Alkali Lake

Alkali Lake
Reidemann Wildlife Sanctuary

2500 Rd

RANCH

Railroad Rapids

Caboose Rapids

Prov
Park

GASPARD

Farwell

WORD
CREEK (2700 Rd)

Rd

McEwen

Alkali Rapids
Old Clemens IR 16

Creek
McEwen Rapids

DOG CREEK

Creek Medkin
Creek

RAPHAEL -MEASON

HANCEVILLE

2600

CREEK (2200 Rd)

5-3

Word

Rd

2214km
2214 Rd

2718km

River

5-3

Wycott's Flat IR 6

Harpers Creek

2221km

Gaspard Camp

(2800 Rd)

Alex Lake

Mt Alex

CREEK

Gaspard

CANOE

Gaspard

Rd

Prentice Gulch

Dog Creek IR 4

DOG CREEK

Dog Creek

pictograph

2231km

GASPARD
Rd
LAKE

Gaspard

William Meadows

3103km 3100 Rd

3100 B

Rd

3100

Gang
Ranch

Churn Creek

3100 Rd

DOG Cr -CANOE Cr Rd

Canoe Creek IR 3

CANOE

(2200 Rd)

Little

CHURN

Stobie Lake

Snake Lake

Blackwater Lake

Churn Creek

Basin Trail

Big

Dry Lake

IRONGATE Rd

put-in

?

3-3

Gaspard (2900 Rd)

FSR

Goose Lakes

Protected

private land

Little Churn

Area

private land

Koster Lake Trail

Koster Cr

Hairy Fish Lk

BC Lake

EMPIRE (2700 Rd)

VALLEY

Gaspard Lake Stobart

GASPARD CREEK

EIGHT Cr

5,740,000m N
5,730,000m N
5,720,000m N
5,710,000m N
5,700,000m N

520,000m E　A
530,000m E　C
540,000m E　E
550,000m E　G

2km 0 2km 4km

2km 0 2km 4km

5-9

Nooseseck River

Flagpole Pt

Windy Bay

Mount Moore

Snooka Creek Valley Route

Noohalk Mountain

52° 20'

N

Laladata Pt
o Port ardy (Van Isl)

Nooseseck Indian Reserve

Loiyentsi Pt

Snootli Peak

5-8

Bentinck Arm

Menzies Pt

Tallheo Pt

Tallheo

M. Gurr Lake & Trail Clayton Pass 1219m

Gray Jay Lake

Mount Fougner

1

52° 15'

Blue Jay Lake Rec Site

Blue Jay Lake

Jay Lakes Snowmobile Area

Howe Lake

Big Snow Mountain

5-8

South

Pacific

2

5-8

CLAYTON FALLS Rd (4wd)

Bensins Island

Tallheo Hot Springs

Bentinck Spire

Giant Cedar Trees

Larso Bay Rec Site

Larso Bay

Bentinck

3

52° 10'

Arm

Ranges

Smitley

See Map 13

4

52° 05'

tna River

FSR

NOEICK

5

52° 05'

NOEICK RIVER

Noeick

Taleomy Indian Reserve

6

Elyak River

Bentinck Narrows

Taleomey

Torrant Creek

52° 00'

5-7

Creek

Tzeo River

7

Kilbella River

Mallon Creek

Asseek River

51° 55'

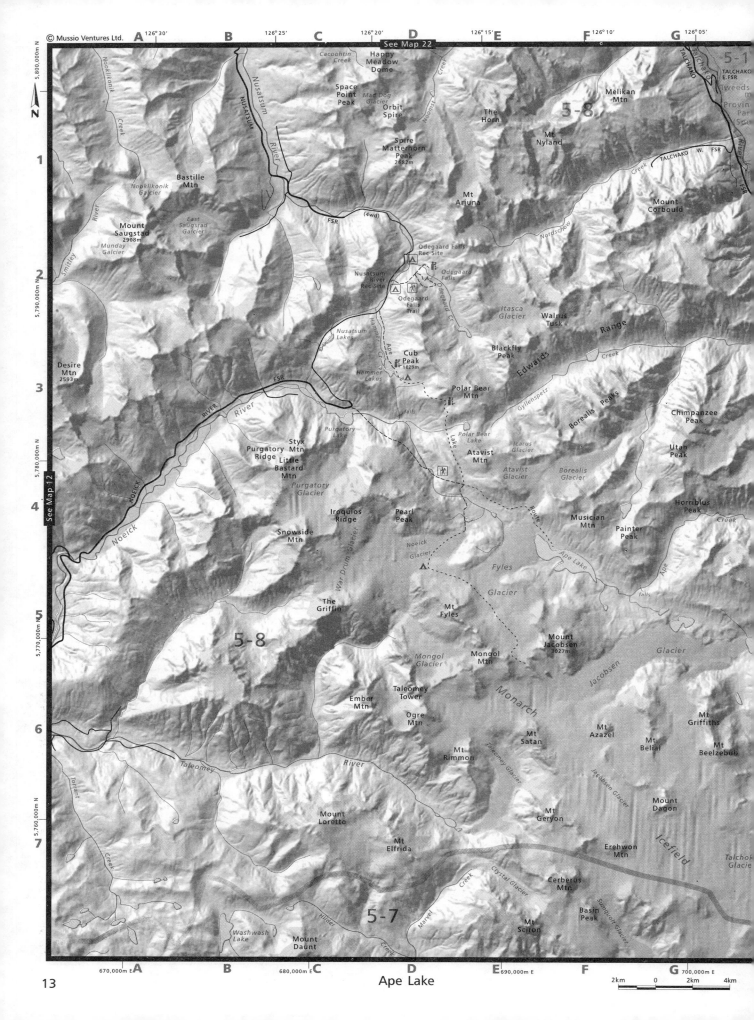

5-1

5-8

TALCHAKO E. FSR

Tweeds
Provin
Par Spur

TALCHAKO W. FSR

Melikan
Mtn

Mount
Corbould

The
Horn

Mt
Nyland

Space
Point
Peak

Happy
Meadow
Dome

Cacoohtin
Creek

Mad Dog
Glacier

Orbit
Spire

Spire
Matterhorn
Peak
2682m

Mt
Arjuna

Odegaard Falls
Rec Site

Odegaard
Falls

Nusatsum River
Rec Site

Odegaard
Falls
Trail

Nusatsum
Lakes

Cub
Peak
1829m

Hammer
Lakes

Itasca
Glacier

Walrus
Tusk

Blackfly
Peak

Polar Bear
Mtn

Edwards

Range

Gyllenspetz

Borealis Peaks

Chimpanzee
Peak

Utan
Peak

Desire
Mtn
2593m

Mount
Saugstad
2908m

Bastille
Mtn

Nooklikonik
Galcier

East
Saugstad
Galcier

Munday
Galcier

Smitley
River

Nooklikonik
Creek

Purgatory
Lake

Styx
Mtn
Ridge

Purgatory
Ridge

Little
Bastard
Mtn

Purgatory
Glacier

Iroquios
Ridge

Snowside
Mtn

Pearl
Peak

Polar Bear
Lake

Atavist
Mtn

Icarus
Glacier

Atavist
Glacier

Borealis
Glacier

Horriblus
Peak

Musician
Mtn

Painter
Peak

Noeick
Glacier

War Drum Glacier

The
Griffin

Mt
Fyles

Fyles

Glacier

Ape Lake

falls

5-8

Mongol
Glacier

Mongol
Mtn

Mount
Jacobsen
3027m

Jacobsen

Glacier

Glacier

Ember
Mtn

Taleomey
Tower

Ogre
Mtn

Mt
Rimmon

Mt
Satan

Monarch

Taleomey Glacier

Mt
Azazel

Mt
Belial

Mt
Griffiths

Mt
Beelzebub

Taleomey

River

Mount
Loretto

Mt
Elfrida

Mt
Geryon

Mount
Dagon

Jacobsen Glacier

Icefield

Erehwon
Mtn

Crystal Glacier

Cerberus
Mtn

Basin
Peak

Sumpoh Glacier

Talchako
Glacier

Mt
Sciron

Washwash
Lake

Mount
Daunt

Hilder

Creek

Markel

Creek

5-7

Toirant
Creek

Creek

NOEICK

RIVER

River

Noeick

River

Noeick
Lake

FSR

FSR

(4wd)

Nusatsum

River

NUSATSUM

Noomst

Creek

Nordschow

Creek

Ape Lake

2km   0   2km   4km

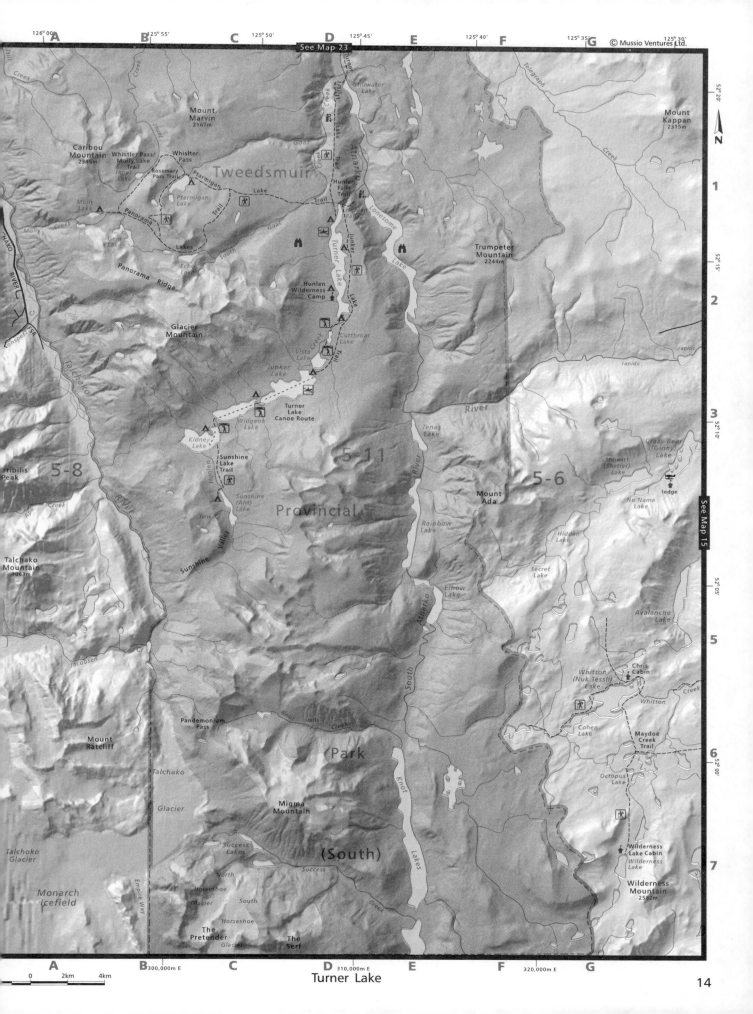

© Mussio Ventures Ltd.

A   126° 00'   B   125° 55'   C   125° 50'   D   125° 45'   E   125° 40'   F   125° 35'   G   125° 30'

52° 20'

N

1

52° 15'

2

52° 10'

3

See Map 15

52° 05'

5

52° 00'

6

7

Mount Kappan 2315m

Mount Marvin 2167m

Caribou Mountain 2345m

Whistler Pass/ Molly Lake Trail
Whistler Pass
Rosemary Pass Trail

Tweedsmuir

Ptarmigan Lake

Ptarmigan Trail

Panorama

Molly Lake

Gem Lake

Molly

Panorama Ridge

Echo Lake

Glacier Mountain

Hunlen Falls Trail

Stillwater Lake

Atnarko

Lonesome

Lake

Goat Creek

Goat Trail

Turner Lake

Junker Lake

Hunlen Wilderness Camp

Cutthroat Lake

Vista Lake

Junker Lake

Trumpeter Mountain 2244m

Hunlen Creek Trail

Turner Lake Canoe Route

Widgeon Lake

Kidney Lake

5-8

rribilis Peak

Talchako Mountain 3063m

Talchako River

Tsilbekuz CFSR

Tenspet FSR

Molly Cr

Ape Creek

Jacobsen Cr

Sunshine Lake Trail

Sunshine (Ant) Lake

Hunlen Falls

Provincial

River

Tenas Lake

Atnarko

Rainbow Lake

Mount Ada

Elbow Lake

South

Knot Falls

Knot Creek

5-11

River

5-6

Telegraph

Crazy Bear (Ginny) Lake

Stewart (Shetler) Lake

lodge

No Name Lake

Hidden Lake

Secret Lake

Avalanche Lake

Whitton (Nuk Tessli) Lake

Chris Cabin

Whitton

Cohen Lake

Maydoe Creek Trail

Octopus Lake

Wilderness Lake Cabin

Wilderness Lake

Wilderness Mountain 2582m

rapids

rapids

Mount Ratcliff

Pandemonium Pass

Park

Talchako Glacier

Migma Mountain

Success Lakes

North Horseshoe Glacier

South Horseshoe Glacier

Success

(South)

Monarch Icefield

Empire Way

Talchako Glacier

The Pretender

The Serf

Knot Lakes

Whitton Creek

A   B   300,000m E   C   D   310,000m E   E   F   320,000m E   G

0   2km   4km

Turner Lake

14

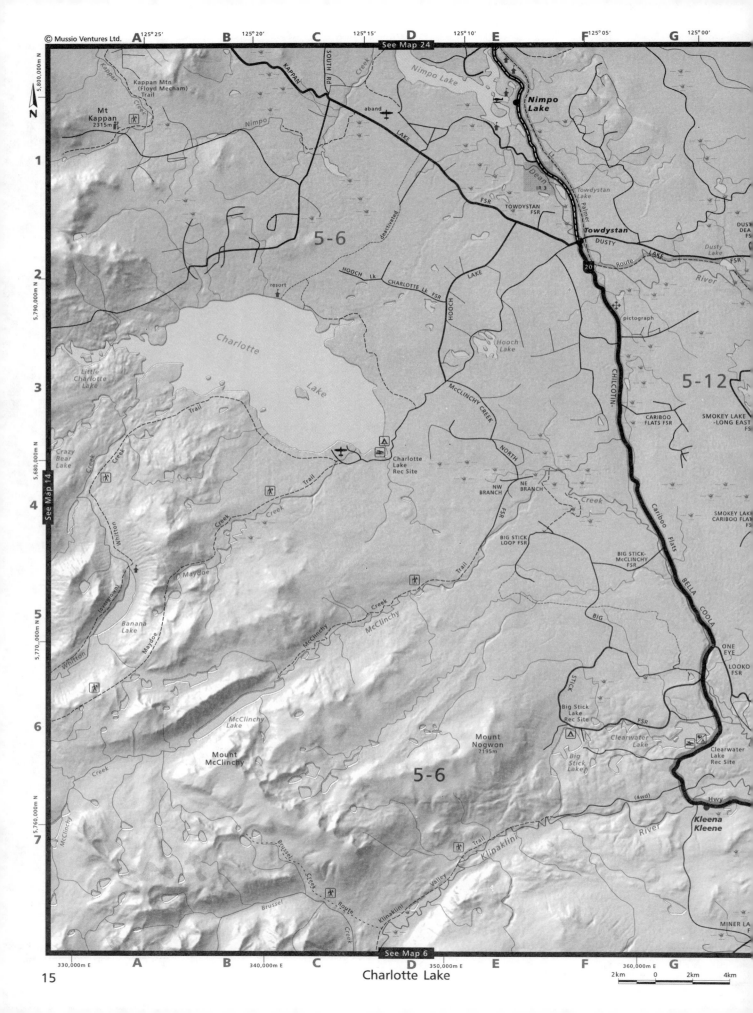

A 125°25' B 125°20' C 125°15' D 125°10' E 125°05' F 125°00' G

Kappan Mtn
(Floyd Mecham)
Trail

Mt
Kappan
2315m

Kappan Creek

Nimpo

5-6

SOUTH Rd

KAPPAN

Creek

aband

LAKE

deactivated

HOOCH Lk

CHARLOTTE Lk FSR

resort

Charlotte

Lake

Little
Charlotte
Lake

Trail

Crazy
Bear
Lake

Creek

Creek

Trail

Charlotte
Lake
Rec Site

Whitton

Maydoe

(overgrown)

Maydoe

Banana
Lake

Creek

Creek

Trail

McClinchy

Creek

McClinchy

Whitton

McClinchy

McClinchy
Lake

Mount
McClinchy

Creek

Nimpo Lake

See Map 24

Nimpo
Lake

IR 3

Towdystan
Lake

Dean

TOWDYSTAN
FSR

Towdystan

DUSTY

20

Route

Palmer

LAKE

HOOCH

LAKE

Hooch
Lake

McCLINCHY CREEK

NORTH

NW
BRANCH

NE
BRANCH

FSR

Creek

BIG STICK
LOOP FSR

Trail

BIG

pictograph

CHILCOTIN-

Cariboo

Flats

BELLA

COOLA

5-12

CARIBOO
FLATS FSR

SMOKEY LAKE
-LONG EAST

DUST
DEA
FSR

Dusty
Lake

FSR

River

SMOKEY LAKE
CARIBOO FLAT
FSR

BIG STICK-
McCLINCHY
FSR

ONE
EYE

LOOKO
FSR

STICK

FSR

Big Stick
Lake
Rec Site

Clearwater
Lake

Big
Stick
Lake

Mount
Nogwon
2195m

5-6

Mount
Nogwon
2195m

Clearwater
Lake
Rec Site

Kleena
Kleene

(4wd)

Hwy

Brussel

Creek

Brussel

Route

Klinaklini

Creek

Trail

Klinaklini

Valley

Klinaklini

River

MINER LA
F

330,000m E A B 340,000m E C D 350,000m E E F 360,000m E G

5,800,000m N

See Map 14

5,680,000m N

5,770,000m N

5,760,000m N

N

Charlotte Lake

2km 0 2km 4km

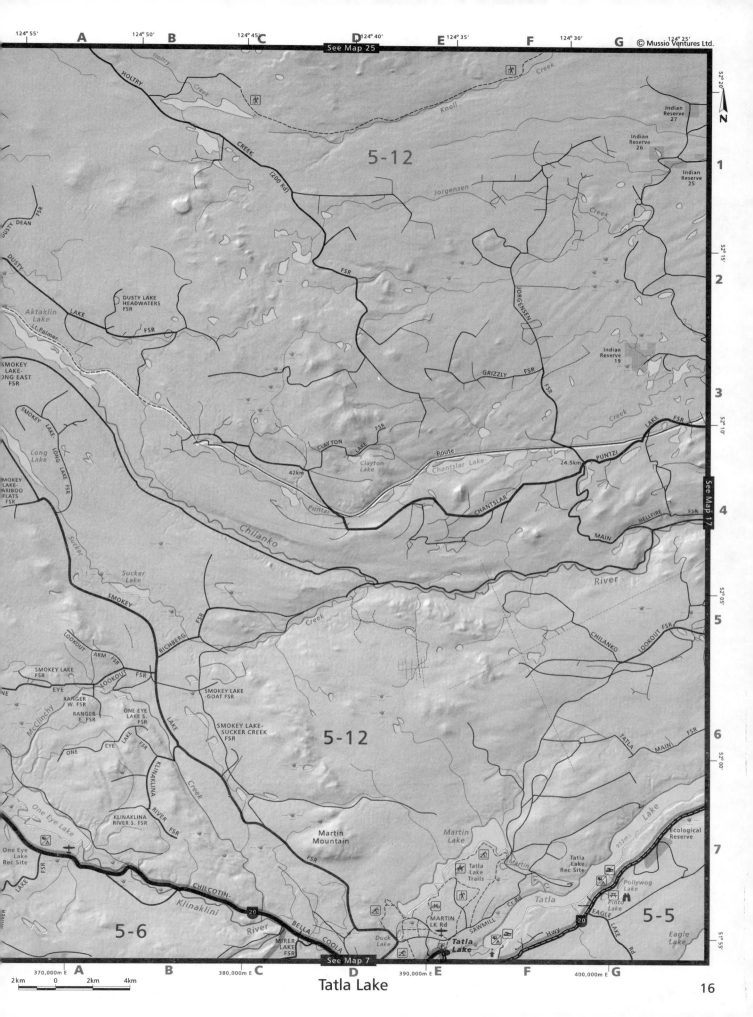

5-12

5-12

5-6

5-5

HOLTRY

Holtry Creek

CREEK (200 Rd)

DUSTY DEAN

DUSTY LAKE

Aktaklin Lake

Lt. Palmer

SMOKEY LAKE-LONG EAST FSR

Long Lake

SMOKEY LAKE LONG LAKE FSR

SMOKEY LAKE-CARIBOO FLATS FSR

Sucker Lake

SMOKEY

SUCKER

RICHBERG

LOOKOUT ARM FSR

SMOKEY LAKE FSR

EYE

LOOKOUT FSR

RANGER W. FSR

RANGER E. FSR

McCLINCHY

ONE EYE LAKE S. FSR

ONE

EYE

LAKE FSR

KLINAKLINA RIVER FSR

KLINAKLINA RIVER S. FSR

SMOKEY LAKE -GOAT FSR

SMOKEY LAKE-SUCKER CREEK FSR

Creek

Chilanko

DUSTY LAKE HEADWATERS FSR

FSR

FSR

FSR

CLAYTON LAKE

42km

Clayton Lake

Puntzi

Route

Chantslar Lake

CHANTSLAR

24.5km

Puntzi Lake

PUNTZI

MAIN

HELLFIRE FSR

LAKE FSR

Jorgensen

Jorgensen Creek

JORGENSEN FSR

GRIZZLY FSR

Creek

Indian Reserve 27

Indian Reserve 26

Indian Reserve 25

Indian Reserve 19

Knoll Creek

River

CHILANKO

LOOKOUT FSR

TATLA MAIN FSR

Martin Mountain

Martin Lake

One Eye Lake

One Eye Lake Rec Site

Klinaklini Creek

CHILCOTIN-

Klinaklini River

MIRER LAKE FSR

BELLA COOLA

Duck Lake

MARTIN LK Rd

Tatla Lake Trails

MARTIN LK Rd

Tatla Lake

SAWMILL

Martin Cr. Rd

Tatla Lake Rec Site

913m

Tatla

Hwy

Pollywog Lake

Pintc Lake

Ecological Reserve

Eagle Lake

EAGLE LAKE Rd

20

20

See Map 7

See Map 17

2km   0   2km   4km   370,000m E   A   B   380,000m E   C   D   390,000m E   E   F   400,000m E   G

52° 20'

52° 15'

52° 10'

52° 05'

52° 00'

51° 55'

1

2

3

4

5

6

7

Tatla Lake

16

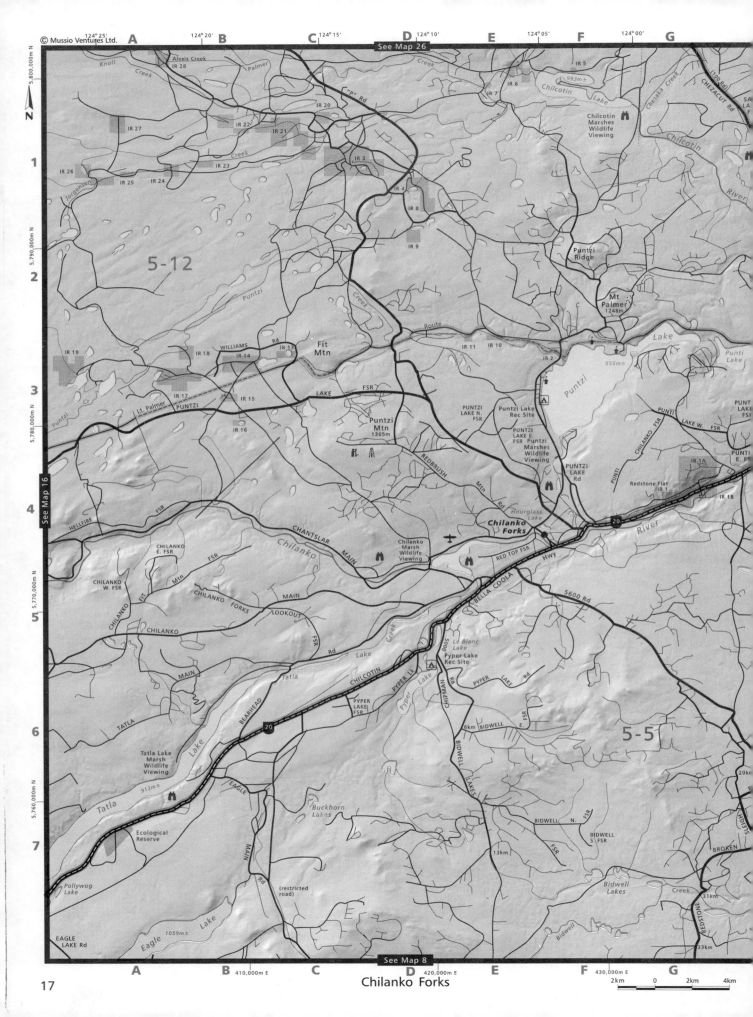

See Map 16

5-12

Knoll Creek
Alexis Creek
IR 28
Palmer
"P" Rd
IR 20
IR 22
IR 27
IR 21
IR 23
IR 26
IR 25
IR 24
Jorgensen
IR 3
IR 4
IR 8
IR 9
Puntzi
Creek
IR 19
WILLIAMS
Rd
IR 18
IR 13
Fit
Mtn
IR 14
Creek
Route
IR 11
IR 10
IR 2
IR 17
IR 15
Lt. Palmer
PUNTZI
LAKE
FSR
Puntzi
Mtn
1365m
IR 16
PUNTZI
Cr

IR 5
IR 6
993m±
IR 7
Chilcotin
Lake
Chilcotin
Marshes
Wildlife
Viewing
Chilcotin
River
Puntzi
Ridge
Mt
Palmer
1248m
Puntzi
Lake
955m±
Punti
Lake
Puntzi Lake N.
FSR
Puntzi Lake
Rec Site
PUNTZI
LAKE E
FSR Puntzi
Marshes
Wildlife
Viewing
PUNTZI
LAKE
Rd
Chilanko
FSR
PUNTI
LAKE W.
FSR
PUNT
LAKE
FSR
PUNTI
E. FSR
Redstone Flat
IR 1
IR 1A
IR 1B
Chesaka Creek
CHEZACUT Rd
(100 Rd)
SA
LA
PUNT

HELLFIRE
FSR
CHILANKO
E. FSR
Chilanko
CHANTSLAR
MAIN
REDBRUSH
Mtn
Rd
Chilanko Marsh
Wildlife
Viewing
Hourglass
Lake
Chilanko
Forks
RED TOP FSR
Hwy
20
River
CHILANKO
W. FSR
Chilanko
PIT
Mtn
FSR
CHILANKO FORKS
MAIN
LOOKOUT
FSR
Lake
BELLA COOLA
5600 Rd
5-5
MAIN
Tatla
CHILCOTIN
Creek
PYPER LK
Pyper Lake
Le Blanc
Lake
Pyper Lake
Rec Site
CHAPMAN
Rd
PYPER
LAKE
Rd
20km

TATLA
BEARHEAD
Eagle
Lake
20
PYPER
LAKE
FSR
Pyper Lake
BIDWELL
6km BIDWELL
BIDWELL
LAKES
BIDWELL
E. FSR
FSR
Tatla Lake
Marsh
Wildlife
Viewing
912m±
Tatla Lake
Ecological
Reserve
Pollywog
Lake
MAIN
Rd
(restricted
road)
Buckhorn
Lakes
13km
BIDWELL N.
FSR
Bidwell
Lakes
BIDWELL
S. FSR
BROKEN
SLEIGH
REDSTONE
31km
Bidwell
Creek
33km
EAGLE
LAKE Rd
1059m±
Eagle
Lake

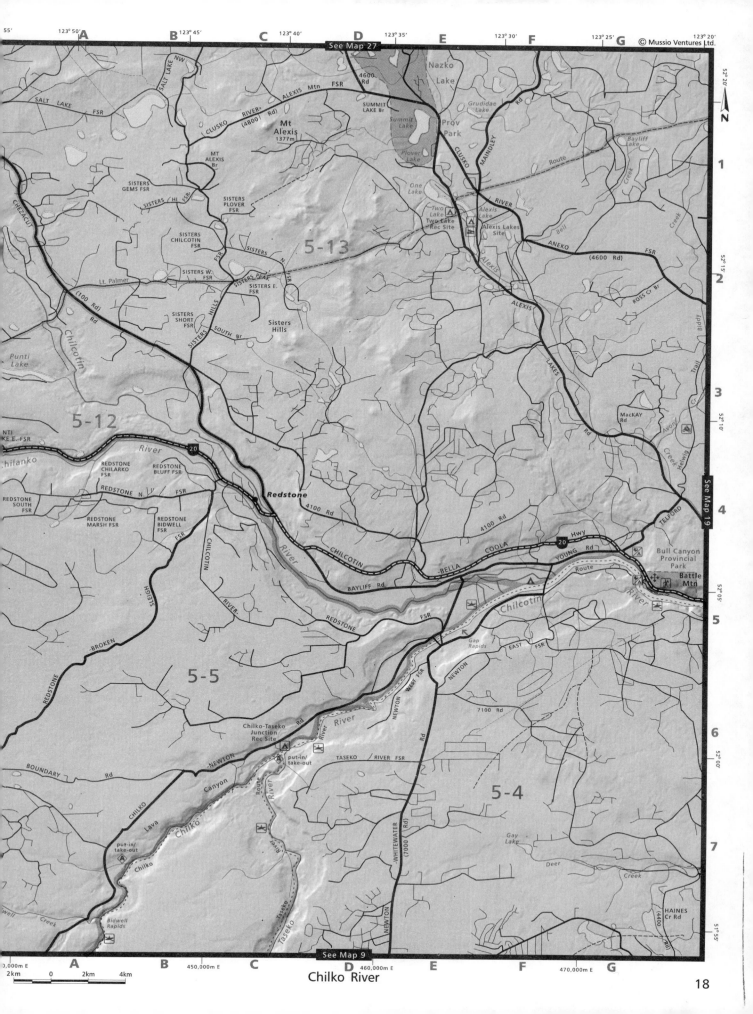

© Mussio Ventures Ltd.

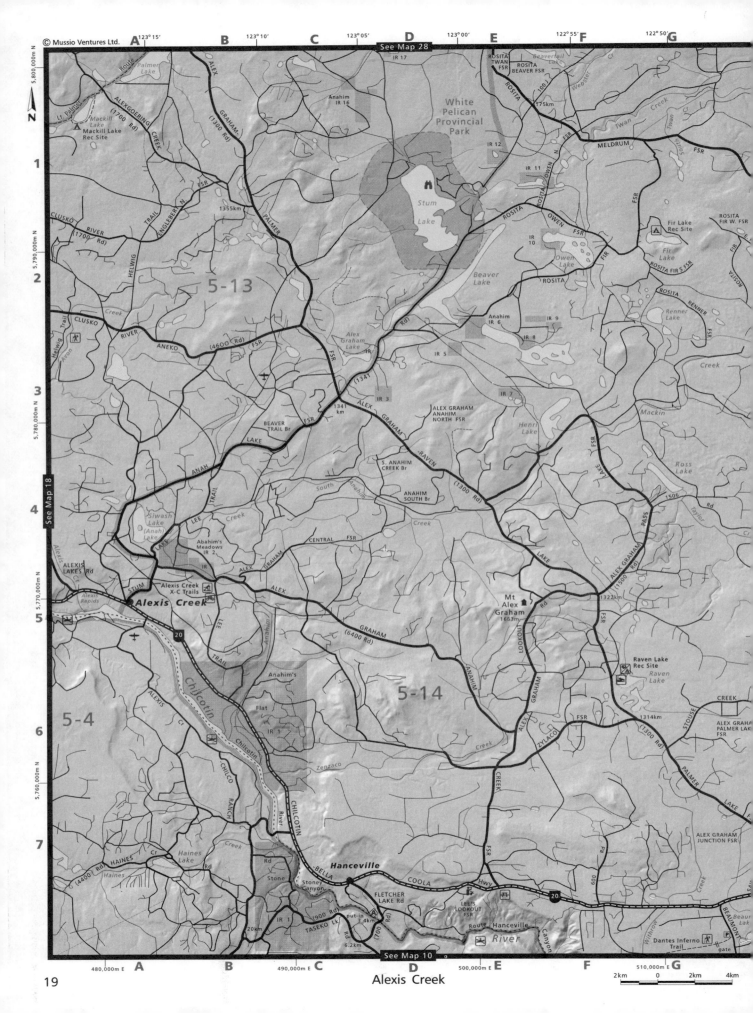

See Map 18

White
Pelican
Provincial
Park

5-13

5-4

5-14

Alexis Creek

Hanceville

Alexis Creek

2km   0   2km   4km

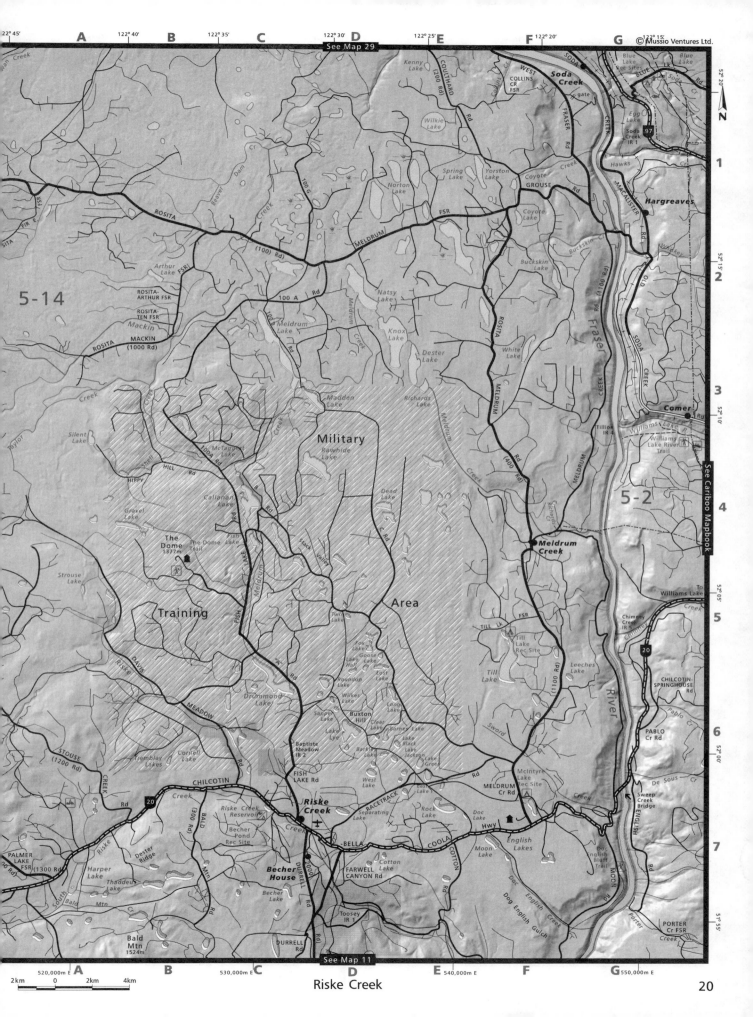

22° 45'

5-14

ROSITA

FIR E FSR

Arthur Lake FSR

ROSITA-ARTHUR FSR

ROSITA-TEN FSR

MACKIN (1000 Rd)

ROSITA

Mackin Creek

(100 Rd)

100 A Rd

100 G

Beaver Dam

100 A Meldrum Lake

Meldrum Creek

MELDRUM FSR

Norton Lake

Spring Lake

Natsy Lake

Knox Lake

Dester Lake

Wilkie Lake

Kenny Lake

COULTHARD (1200 Rd) Rd

COLLINS CR FSR

Collins Cr FSR

WEST SODA CREEK

Soda Creek

gate

Yorston Lake

Coyote GROUSE

Coyote Lake

Buckskin Lake

White Lake

ROSITA MELDRUM (1400 Rd)

Buckskin Creek

FRASER Rd

(1100 Rd) Rd

Hawks

Egg Lake

Soda Creek IR 1

97

Hargreaves

Wrigley Rd

OLD SODA CREEK Rd

MACALISTER

Fraser River

Comer Rd

Williams Lake River Trail

Tillion IR 4

5-2

52° 20'

1

52° 15'

2

52° 10'

3

See Cariboo Mapbook

Silent Lake

Taylor Creek

Shell Creek

HILL Rd

HIPPY

McTaggart Lake

Riske Creek

100A Rd

Callanan Lake

The Dome 1377m

The Dome Trail

Fish Lake

Strouse Lake

Gravel Lake

Madden Lake

Rawhide Lake

Richards Lake

Military

Meldrum Creek

Dead Lake

Richards Creek

MELDRUM (1400 Rd)

Meldrum Creek

Meldrum Creek Rd

52° 05'

4

Training

DAVIS

Riske Creek

FISH LAKE Rd

Meldrum Rd

'A' Rd

Stack Valley

C Rd

Area

Twin Lake

Fox Lake

Goose Lake

Lost Lake

Clam Lake

Till Lk

Till Lake Rec Site

Till Lake

FSR

5-2

52° 05'

5

20

MEADOW

Drummond Lake

Roundup Lake

Wilkes Lake

Sapper Lake

Buxton Hill

Clear Lake

Lake Lye

Barney Lake

Long Lake

Lake Black Lake Jackson

Lake Green

Sword Creek

McIntyre Lake Rec Site

Leeches Lake

CHILCOTIN-SPRINGHOUSE Rd

PABLO Cr Rd

Pablo Cr

52° 00'

6

STOUSE (1200 Rd)

Tremblay Lakes

Cornell Lake

Baptiste Meadow IR 2

FISH LAKE Rd

Riske Creek

Riske Creek Reservoir

CHILCOTIN Rd

20

BALD (300 Rd) Rd

Becher Pond Rec Site

West Lake

Separating Lake

Rock Lake

Doc Lake

MELDRUM Cr Rd

Bella COOLA

Moon Lake

English Lakes

De Sous Cr

Sweep Creek Bridge

ENGLISH MOON Rd

Doc English Bluff Trail

52° 00'

7

PALMER LAKE FSR (1300 Rd)

Harper Lake

Thaddeus Lake

Dester Ridge

Bald Mtn

Bald Mtn 1524m

Riske Creek

DURRELL Rd

Becher House

Toosey IR 1

DURRELL Rd

FARWELL CANYON Rd

Cotton Lake

Separating Lake

Cotton Creek

BELLA COOLA Hwy

Doc English Gulch

Dog Creek

PORTER Cr FSR

English Creek

51° 55'

127° 05'   127° 00'   126° 55'   126° 50'   126° 45'   126° 40'

N

5-9

Sutslem rapids

rapids

Creek

Raphoe Pt

Channel

Engerbrightson Pt

Ironbound Islet

Swallop

Sylvester Pt

Wattie Pt

Dean

5-9

Across

Creek

Mount Saunders

Mount Pootlass 2214m

Nooskulla Peak

Nooskulla Creek

Creek

Kalone Creek

Forward Peak

rapids

rapids

Index Crag

Kalone Peak

Creek

Mount Creswe

Mount

5-8

Christenson Creek

Necteetscannay River

Four Mile Mountain

rapids

Mill Creek Valley Route

Walker Island Regional Park

Snooka Creek Hatchery

Big Cedars

Newmianus Creek

Tallheo

Arm

North Bentinck

Bella Coola

Bella Coola Indian Reserve

Snooka Cr Trails

Snootli Creek Park

Sutlej Pt

Clayton Falls Rec Area

Clayton Falls Creek

dam

CHILCOTIN

Tatsquan Creek

BELLA

20

COOLA

Thorsen Cr

Hwy

Big Bay

River

Nooseseck

River

Niaxash Creek

Humpback Creek

Jump

630,000m E   640,000m E   650,000m E   660,000m E

2km   0   2km   4km

5,850,000m N

5,840,000m N

5,830,000m N

5,820,000m N

5,810,000m N

126° 35' A 126° 30' B 126° 25' C 126° 20' D 126° 15' E 126° 10' F 126° 05' G © Mussio Ventures Ltd.

Tweedsmuir

Dean

rapids

rapids

Dean River Route

Salmon House Falls

5-9

Creek

Crag

Stack Peak

Mount Collins

Compass Mountain

Compass Lakes

Lower Teeztsaytsul Lake

Upper Teeztsaytsul Lake

Tzeetsaytsul Glacier

Tzeetsaytsul Peak 2580m

Thunder Mountain 2681m

Mount Stepp

Mount reswell

Talcheezoone Lakes

Neeteetscannay River

5-8

NOOSE GULCH

CREEK

Tseapseahooiz Creek Route

Salloomt Peak Route

Salloomt Peak 1871m

Salloomt Forest Trail

Salloomt Recreational Trails

SALLOOMT

SALLOOMT

RIVER (WEST)

Lost Lake Trail

SALLOOMT FSR Rd

Bella

Nooshlonik Creek

Hagensborg

NUSATSUM FSR

Nusatsum River

Medby Rock Lookout Trail

Cooks Trail

Nusatsum Mtn Route

Nusatsum Mountain 2574m

Mosquito Pass

CHILCOTIN-

20

"Big Village"

FSR

Firvale

BELLA

COOLA RIVER

CACOONTIN CREEK

CREEK FSR

Defiance Mountain 2669m

Tanya Mountain 1458m

River

Talchako

Kohasganko

(overgrown)

Trail

MacKenzie

Valley

5-10

Provincial

Summit

Mount Leonard

Ulkatcho

Mount MacKenzie 2146m

Rainbow Cabin

Boyd Pass

MacKenzie

Pass

Tweedsmuir Trail

Rainbow Range

Snowmobile Area

Bead Lakes

Capoose

Trail

5-11

King Mountain 2043m

Capoose Range

Park

(South)

Mount Walker 2148m

(overgrown)

Alexander Trail

Horse Camp

Tine Hill 1597m

Long Lake

Summer Trail

Cabin

Bluff Lakes

Silvern Lake

Hump Lake

Alexander MacKenzie Limit

Capoose

Valley View Loop Trail

Alexander MacKenzie Heritage Trailhead (monument)

COOLA

Talchako

McCall Flats Rec Site

20

Steep Roof Launch

Table Mtn 2677m

Stupendous Mountain 2680m

Stupendous Mtn Route

Noomst Creek

NOOMST CREEK FSR

Fisheries Pool Campsite

Stuie

Belarko Launch

Talchako River

lodge

Lester Dorsey's Cabin

Salmon House Falls Campsite

Tanya Lakes

Talatheezi

Creek

52° 45' 1

52° 40' 2

52° 35' 3

See Map 23 4

52° 30' 5

6

52° 25' 7

N

126° 00' A 125° 55' B 125° 50' C 125° 45' D E 125° 40' F 125° 35' G

Tanya Lakes

Alexander
MacKenzie
Heritage
Trail

Tweedsmuir

Rainbow

Tsitsutl
Peak
2029m

5-10

Range

Provincial

North Obsidian Creek

Grizzly Creek

Anahim
Peak
1892m

Obsidian

Creek

5-12

Indian
Reserves
9 & 11

Obsidian Creek
(Anahim Creek)
Trail

Dean

RIVER

UPPER DEAN

Festuea
Creek

rapids

rap

MacKenzie
Valley Heritage
Trail

Boyd
Pass

Rainbow
Cabin

MacKenzie
Valley Heritage
Trail
Connecting
Trail

Crystal
Lake

Crystal
Lake

Rainbow

Valley

Range

Rainbow Trail

Lester's
Camp

Boneshaker
Ridge

Beef

Beef Trail

Trail

Trail

Route

Creek

Beef

Creek

King
Mtn
2043m

Deception
Pass
2043m

Octopus
Lake

Octopus
Trail

Snowmobile

Area

Young Creek

5-11

Park

Range Trail

Trail

Hwy
Heckman

"The
Hill"

Pass

Heckman

X-Country
Ski Trails

Tusulko

TUSULKO
RIVER
S. FSR

Louie

TUSULKO RIVER
ABUNTLET FSR

River

Creek

Natzadalia Creek

5-6

Hotnarko
Mountain
2048m

BELLA COOLA

Mosher Creek

20

(South)

Creek

Camp Creek

precipice

Hotnarko

Lake

The Kadpan
Precipice"

Atnarko

Atnarko

River

Old Rd
(4wd only)

Hotnarko River

The "Great
Slide"

Telegraph Creek

See Map 22

A 300,000m E B C 310,000m E D E 320,000m E F G 330,00

Atnarko

2km 0 2km 4km

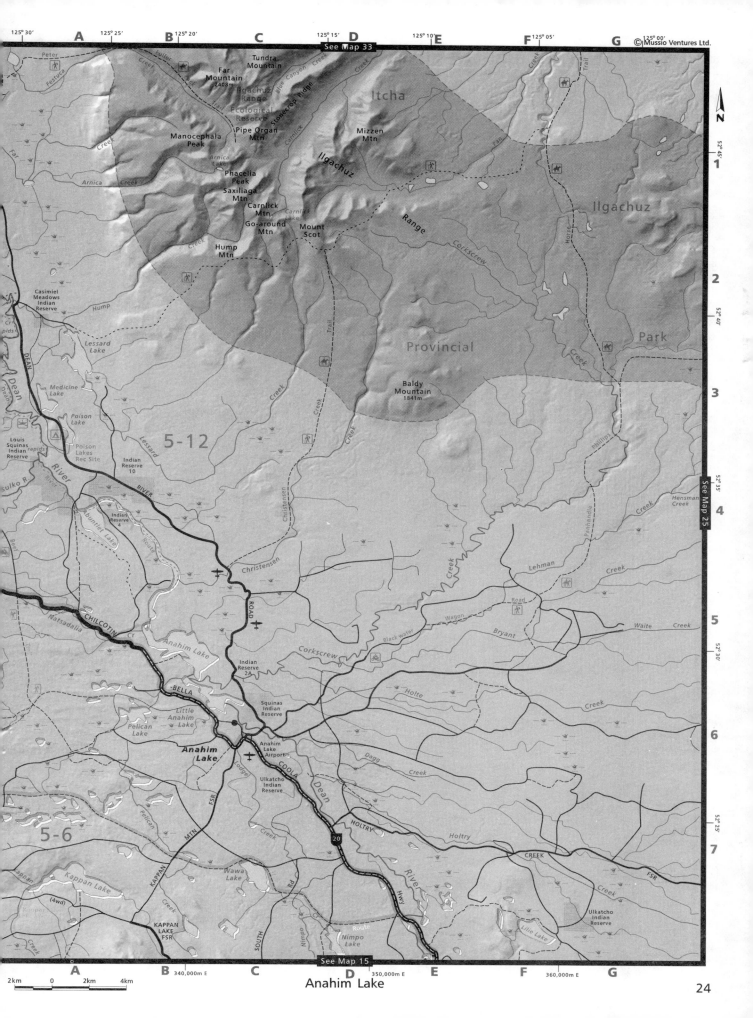

N

Peter
Festuca
Fuller Creek
Tundra Mountain
Far Mountain 2408m
Igachuz Range
Ecological Reserve
Pipe Organ Mtn
Stonecrop Ridge
blue Canyon Creek
Carnlick Creek
Itcha
Mizzen Mtn
Ilgachuz
Manocephala Peak
Arnica Lake
Arnica Creek
Ilgachuz Range
Phacelia Peak
Saxiliaga Mtn
Carnlick Mtn
Carnlick Lake
Ilgachuz
Go-around Mtn
Mount Scot
Range
Park
Hump Mtn
Pan Creek
Horse Creek
Corkscrew Creek
Casimiel Meadows Indian Reserve
Hump Creek
Dean
Lessard Lake
Provincial
Philip Creek
Medicine Lake
Poison Lake
Creek
Baldy Mountain 1841m
Hensman Creek
Louis Squinas Indian Reserve
Poison Lakes Rec Site
rapids
Lessard Creek
5-12
Christensen Creek
Creek
See Map 25
River
Indian Reserve 10
Panhandle
sulko R
RIVER
Labuntlet Lake
Indian Reserve 4
Christensen
Creek
Lehman Creek
Christensen
Route
Dean River
Road
Natsadalia
CHILCOTIN Cr
Anahim Lake
ROAD
Corkscrew
Bryant
Wagon
Waite Creek
Indian Reserve 2A
Black water
Holte
BELLA
Little Anahim Lake
Squinas Indian Reserve
Creek
Pelican Lake
Dagg
Anahim Lake
Anahim Lake Airport
COOLA
Creek
Ulkatcho Indian Reserve
Dean
FSR
Lodgejl
HOLTRY
5-6
MTN
KAPPAN
Pelican Creek
Holtry
Holtry
CREEK
FSR
Kappan
Wawa Lake
South Rd
River
Hwy
Ulkatcho Indian Reserve
Kappan Lake
(4wd)
KAPPAN LAKE FSR
Nimpo
Route
Nimpo Lake
Lille Lake
Creek

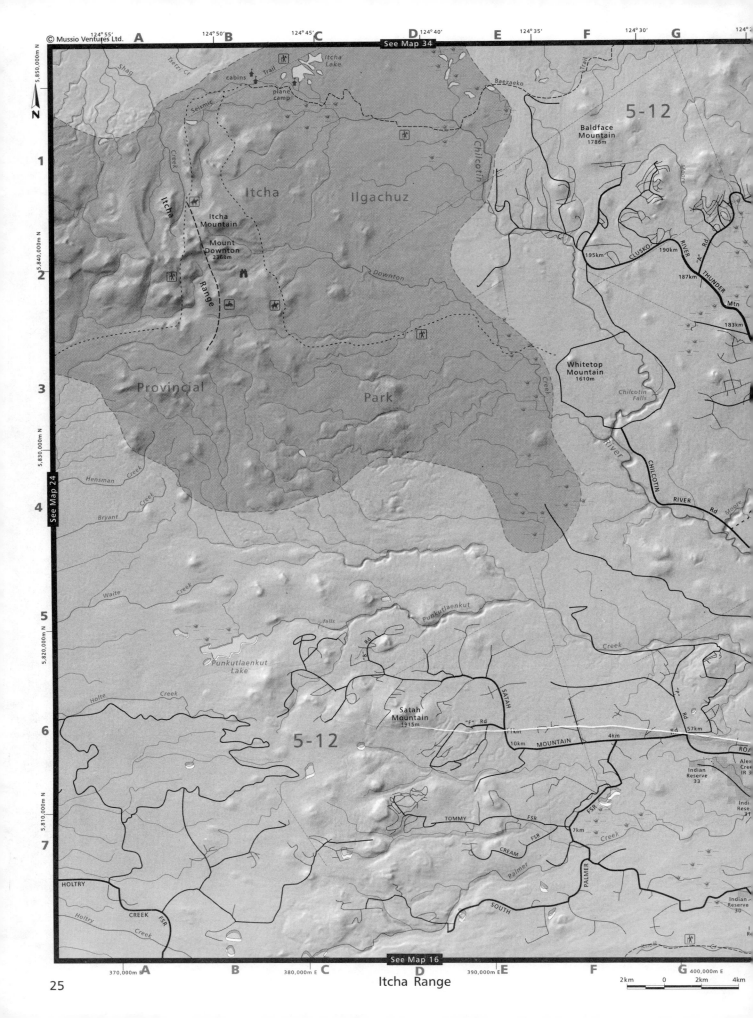

© Mussio Ventures Ltd.

5-12

N

Shag

Tsetzi Cr

cabins

Trail

plane camp

Seismic

Itcha Lake

Baezaeko

Baldface Mountain
1786m

Chilcotin

Moore

195km

CLUSKO

RIVER

190km

187km

THUNDER

Rd

Itcha

Creek

Itcha Mountain

Itcha

Ilgachuz

183km

Mtn

Mount Downton
2368m

Downton

Range

Whitetop Mountain
1610m

Chilcotin Falls

Creek

Provincial

Park

River

CHILCOTIN

RIVER

Rd

Moore

Hensman

Creek

Bryant

Creek

Waite

Creek

falls

Punkutlaenkut

Punkutlaenkut Lake

Creek

Satah Mountain
1915m

SATAH

Rd

Creek

Rd

57km

Holte

Creek

5-12

"F" Rd

11km

10km

MOUNTAIN

4km

Rd

ROA

Alex
Cree
IR 3

Indian Reserve
33

Indi
Rese

TOMMY

FSR

7km

Creek

CREAM

FSR

FSR

Palmer

PALMER

Indian Reserve
30

HOLTRY

Holtry

CREEK

FSR

Creek

SOUTH

Knoll

25

2km   0   2km   4km

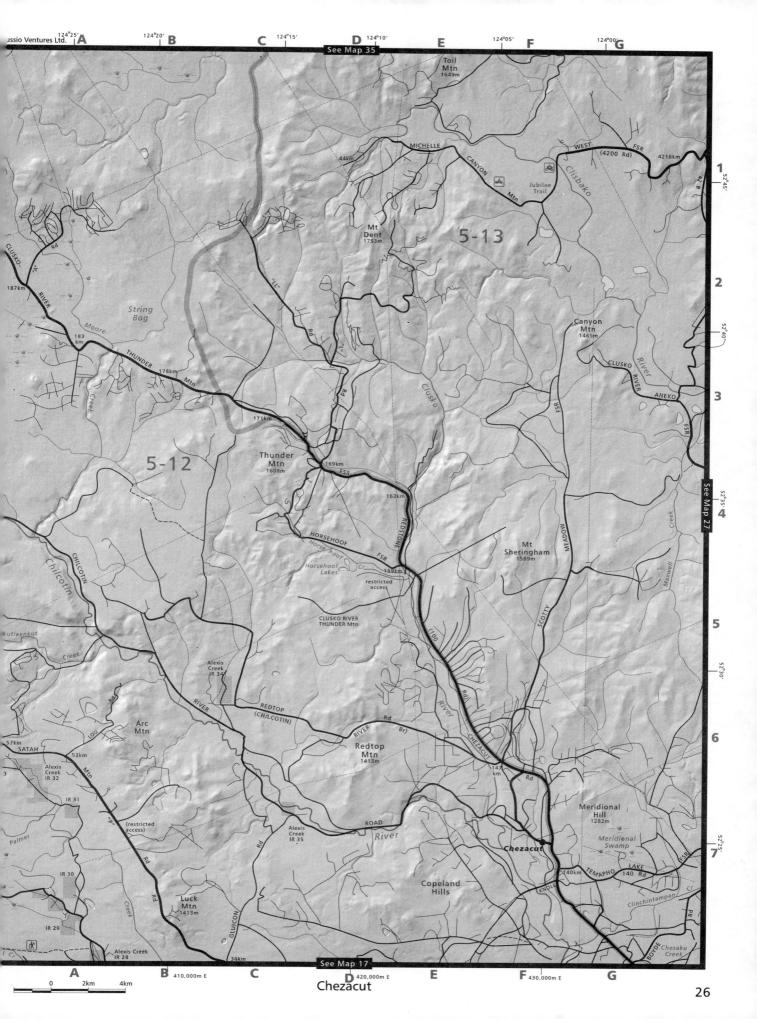

52°45'

52°40'

52°35'

52°30'

52°25'

See Map 27

ussio Ventures Ltd.

124°25' A 124°20' B C 124°15' D 124°10' E 124°05' F 124°00' G

Toil
Mtn
1649m

MICHELLE

WEST (4200 Rd) 4216km

CANYON Clisbako

FSR

42 B

Jubilee
Trail

Mt
Dent
1753m

5-13

CLUSKO
Rd
187km

Moore

Clusko

Canyon
Mtn
1465m

183
km

Creek

THUNDER
178km Mtn

String
Bog

"L"
Rd

CLUSKO RIVER

ANEKO FSR

171km

Clusko

RIVER

Maxwell Creek

Chilcotin

5-12

Thunder
Mtn
1608m

169km FSR

163km

REDSTONE

Mt
Sheringham
1589m

MEADOW

SCOTTY

HORSEHOOF

Horsehoof Cr.

Horsehoof
Lakes

FSR

159km

restricted
access

CLUSKO RIVER
THUNDER Mtn

1100

Chilcotin

kutlaenkut

Creek

Alexis
Creek
IR 34

RIVER

REDTOP
(CHILCOTIN)

RIVER Rd Br

River

Rd

Arc
Mtn

LOU

Redtop
Mtn
1413m

CHEZACUT

147
km Rd

57km
SATAH

53km Mtn

Alexis
Creek
IR 32

IR 31

(restricted
access)

Alexis
Creek
IR 35

ROAD

River

Meridional
Hill
1282m

Meridional
Swamp

Chezacut

Palmer

IR 30

Rd

Copeland
Hills

TEMAPHO LAKE
140km 140 Rd

FSR

KNDLE

IR 29

Luck
Mtn
1413m

GUICON

Clinchintampan

Chesaku
Creek

BOYDE Rd

Creek

Rd

Alexis Creek
IR 28

36km

A 0 2km 4km B 410,000m E C D 420,000m E E F 430,000m E G

Chezacut

26

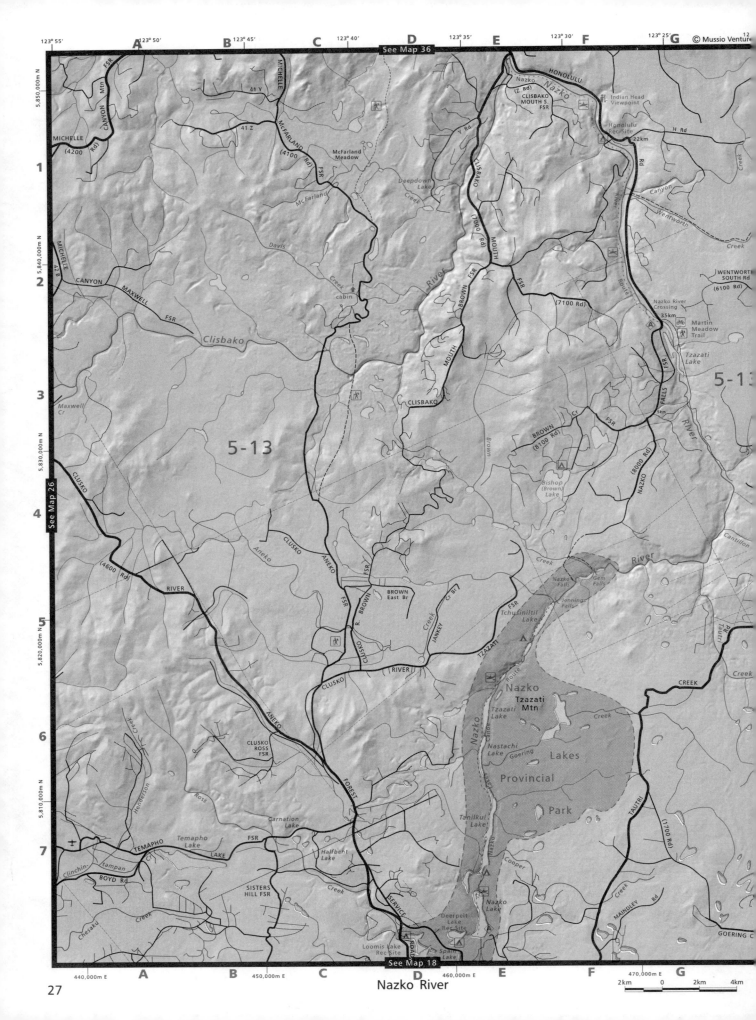

© Mussio Ventures

123° 55'   A   123° 50'   B   123° 45'   C   123° 40'   D   123° 35'   E   123° 30'   F   123° 25'   G   12

5,850,000m N

5,840,000m N

5,830,000m N

5,820,000m N

5,810,000m N

See Map 26

MICHELLE
(4200 Rd)

CANYON Mtn

MICHELLE

42 B

CANYON

MAXWELL

FSR

Clisbako

Maxwell
Cr

5-13

CLUSKO

(4600 Rd)

RIVER

ANEKO

Henderson

Ross Creek

TEMAPHO

Itampan

Clinchin

BOYD Rd

Chesaku   Creek

Temapho
Lake

Carnation
Lake

CLUSKO
ROSS
FSR

LAKE

FSR

Halfbent
Lake

SISTERS
HILL FSR

Creek

41 Y

41 Z

McFARLAND
(4100 Rd)

FSR

McFarland
Meadow

McFarland

Davis

Creek

cabin

Deepdown
Creek
Lake

River

CLISBAKO

5-13

CLUSKO

ANEKO

FSR

CLUSKO R.   BROWN

BROWN
East Br

Cr Br

JANKEY

Creek

CLUSKO   RIVER

ANEKO

FOREST

SERVICE

ROAD

Loomis Lake
Rec Site

Spani
Lake

Nazko   Nazko   HONOLULU

Nazko
(Z Rd)   CLISBAKO
MOUTH S.
FSR

Indian Head
Viewpoint

Honolulu
Rec Site

22km

Y Rd

CLISBAKO

(7000 Rd)

MOUTH

BROWN FSR

FSR

(7100 Rd)

Canyon

Wentworth
Creek

H Rd

WENTWORTH
SOUTH Rd
(6100 Rd)

Route

Nazko River
Crossing

35km

Martin
Meadow
Trail

Tzazati
Lake

5-1

5-1

River

BROWN

Brown

BROWN
(8100 Rd)

Cr

FSR

FALLS

5km

NAZKO

(8000 Rd)

Bishop
(Brown)
Lake

River

Creek

Nazko
Falls

Gem
Falls

Cantillon

Jennings
Falls

FSR

Tchusiniltit
Lake

TZAZATI

Nazko

Tzazati
Mtn

Tzazati
Lake

Route

Nastachi
Lake   Goering

Lakes

Provincial

Park

Creek

Tanilkul
Lake

NAZKO

Cooper

Nazko
Lake

Deerpelt
Lake
Rec Site

River

CREEK

Creek

TAUTRI

(1700 Rd)

Creek

MAINDLEY
Rd

GOERING C

440,000m E   A   B   450,000m E   C   D   460,000m E   E   F   470,000m E   G

27

2km   0   2km   4km

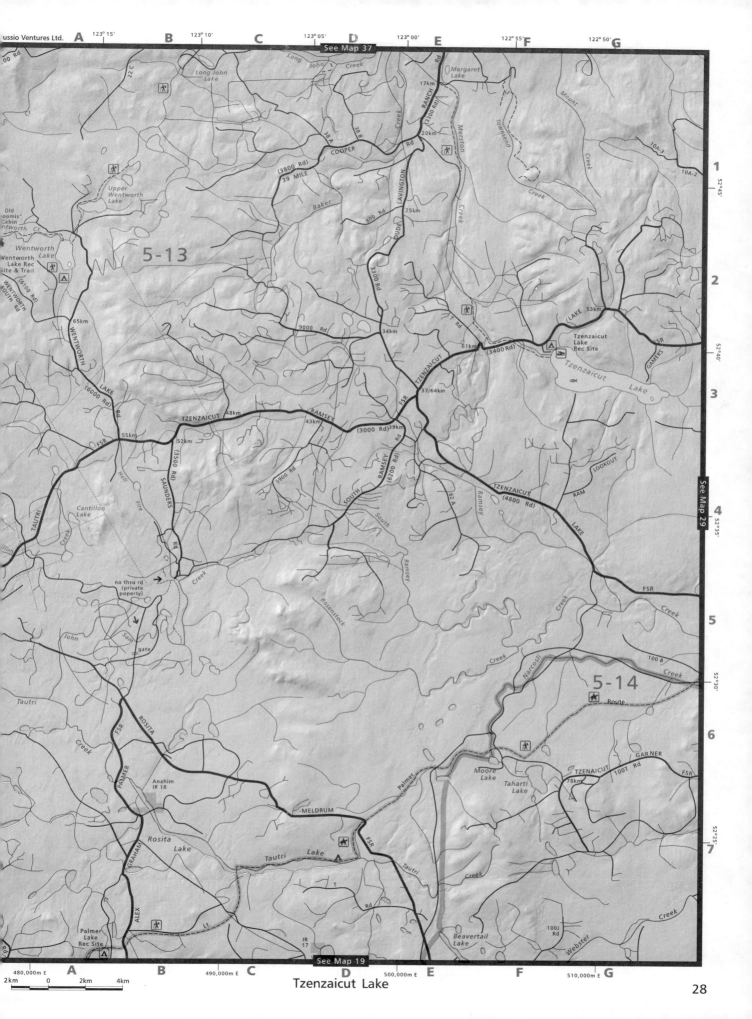

A 123° 15' B 123° 10' C 123° 05' D 123° 00' E 122° 55' F 122° 50' G

52°45'

Long John Lake

Long John Creek

22 C

Upper Wentworth Lake

17km

Margaret Lake

Mount Townsend

10A-3

10A-2

5-13

Cooper

38 A
38 B

RANCH (3300 Rd)

20km

DUDE LAVINGTON Rd

Merston Creek

Old Loomis Cabin Wentworth Cr

Wentworth Lake

Baker

(3800 Rd)
39 MILE

25km

52°40'

Wentworth Lake Rec Site & Trail

WENTWORTH MOUTH Rd

(6100 Rd)

65km

9000 Rd

3300 Rd

800 Rd

34km

T Rd

61km

(3400 Rd)

LAKE 53km

GAMERS FSR

Tzenzaicut Lake Rec Site

Tzenzaicut Lake

WENTWORTH   LAKE   Rd

(6000 Rd)

TAUTRI

FSR

55km

TZENZAICUT 48km

RAMSEY 43km

FSR

TZENZAICUT

37/64km

(3000 Rd) 39km

Ramsey Rd

LOOKOUT

52°35'

52km

(3500 Rd)

5900 Rd

SOUTH RAMSEY (6200 Rd)

62 A

Ramsey

TZENZAICUT (4800 Rd)

RAM

See Map 29

Cantillon Lake

Hell Fire

SAUNDERS Rd

Creek

no thru rd (private property)

Rosenstock

South Ramsey

LAKE

FSR

Creek

John

Sam gate

Narcosli Creek

Creek

100 B Creek

52°30'

5-14

Route

Tautri

ROSITA

FSR

PALMER

Anahim IR 18

Palmer

Moore Lake

Taharti Lake

TZENAICUT

78km

100T Rd

GARNER FSR

52°25'

Creek

GRAHAM

MELDRUM

Rosita Lake

Tautri Lake

FSR

Tautri Creek

52°25'

ALEX

Lt

Rd

IR 17

Beavertail Lake

100J Rd

Webster Creek

Palmer Lake Rec Site

A 480,000m E B 490,000m E C D 500,000m E E F 510,000m E G

2km 0 2km 4km

Tzenzaicut Lake

28

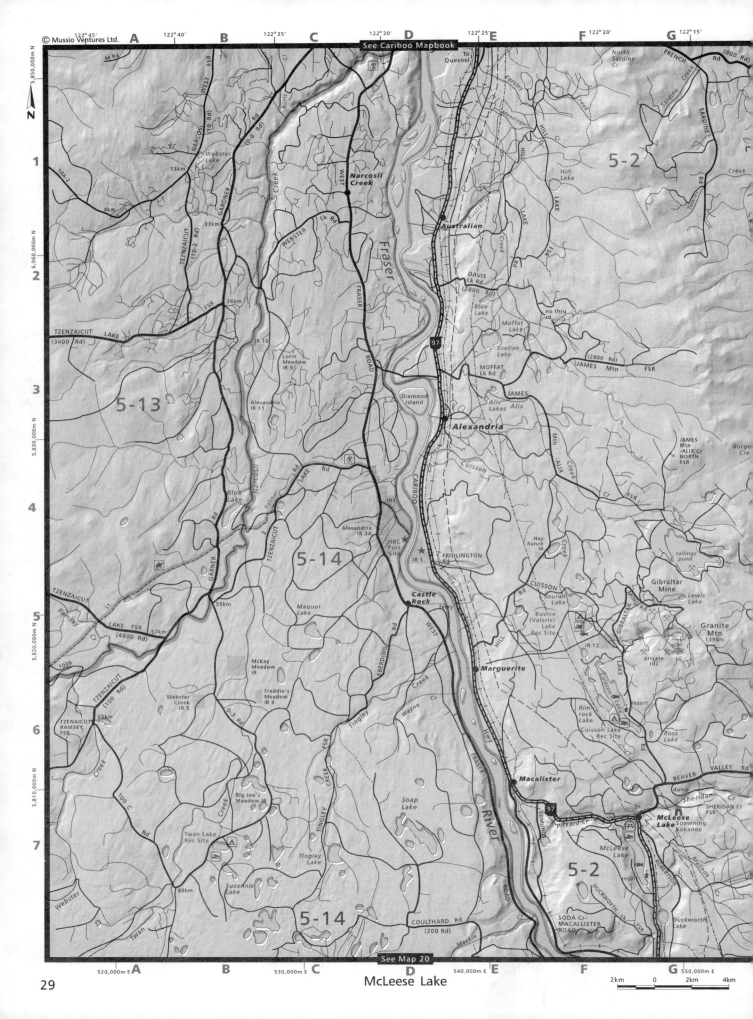

McLeese Lake

29

53° 15'

Cosgrove
Lake

Mount
Cosgrove

Smoky
Creek

Eutsuk

Tweedsmuir

Pondosy
Bay

(Eutsuk
Lake)

Eutsuk
Lake

Mount
Preston
2049m

1

53° 10'

Thumb
Peak

Nature

Salahagen Lake

Farbus
Lake

Pondosy
Lake

6-1

Cam
McEwen
Lake

Wahla Lake

Mount
McVicar

Gable
Mountain
2280m

Conservancy

Creek

Rivers
Peak

Provincial

Pondosy Pass

Tesla   Lake

2

53° 05'

5-9

Trapper
Mountain

Salahagen

Area

Mount
Pondosy
2226m

Narrows
Peak

Stadium
Mountain

Tesla
Mountain

Pattullo

3

George
Peak

Trapper

Creek

Salient
Mountain
2433m

Kimsquit

Park

South

Creek

Butler
Peak

(North)

Range

4

53° 00'

See Map 31

Salient
Creek

Dam
Peak

Creek

Gadsden
Peak

Sakumtha Pass

Tophole
Lake

Tsaydaychez
Peak
2769m

Kimsquit Ridge

King

George

Creek

Sakumtha

River

Sakumtha

Sakumtha
River

Jumble
Mountain
2362m

Iltasyuko R.

5

52° 55'

River

5-9

East

Sakumtha
Crag

Pisgah
Mountain

6

Chatscah
Indian
Reserve

Creek

Skuce

River

Kimsquit
Peak

Creek

Bernhardt

Stick Pass
Mountain

Tweedsmuir
Provincial Park
(South)

7

52° 50'

Hoam

Creek

Kimsquit Narrows

Dean

rapids

River

5-10

rapids

rapids

Kimsquit
Bay

Kimsquit

Kimsquit
Indian
Reserve

rapids

Nooskulla Creek

Nugleigh   Creek

A   B   C   D   E   F   G

See Map 39

N

5,900,000m N

Nechako

Eutsuk   Lake   Reservoir

Connelly
Pt

Connelly
Bay

6-2

Tetachuk
River /
Trail

Redfern
Rapids

Entiako
Protected
Area

6-1

1

Demion
Lake

Mink
Lake

Circuit

Wahla
Lake

Tweedsmuir   Provincial

River

Wahla
Mountain

Ice
Hill

Olaf Lake

Tahuntesko Lake

Detna L

2

Two Bear
Hill

Park

Unchietlat

Creek

Tesla
Lake

(North)

Unchietlat
Lakes

Detna

Chezko

Nadedikus
Mountain
1648m

Tweedsmuir

Nahlouza
Lake

6-1

Holmes

Ridge

Oppy

Creek

3

Oppy   Lake

Nahlouzo

Claire
Lake

Natuza

Creek

Ulkatch
Indian
Reserv

5,880,000m N

Watut
Mountain
1721m

Provincial

5-10

4

Ramsey
Peak
2395m

Creek

Qualcho

She
Lak

Ramsey

5

5,870,000m N

Jumble
Mountain
2362m

Nechako

Sigutlat   Lake

Sigutlat

Creek

Plateau

Pattullo

rapids

Mount
Jones

Creek

Park

6

Stick
Lake

Range

rapids

River

River

Sea
Lion
Peak
2153m

Iltasyuko

Iltasyuko   Lake

(South)

rapids

5,860,000m N

5-10

Iltasyuko

Dean

rapids

River

7

Mount
Bernhardt
2211m

Creek

rapids

rapids

rapids

Bottleneck

5-9

rapids

A   B   C   D   E   F   G

670,000m E   680,000m E   690,000m E   700,00

31   Sigulat Lake

2km   0   2km   4km

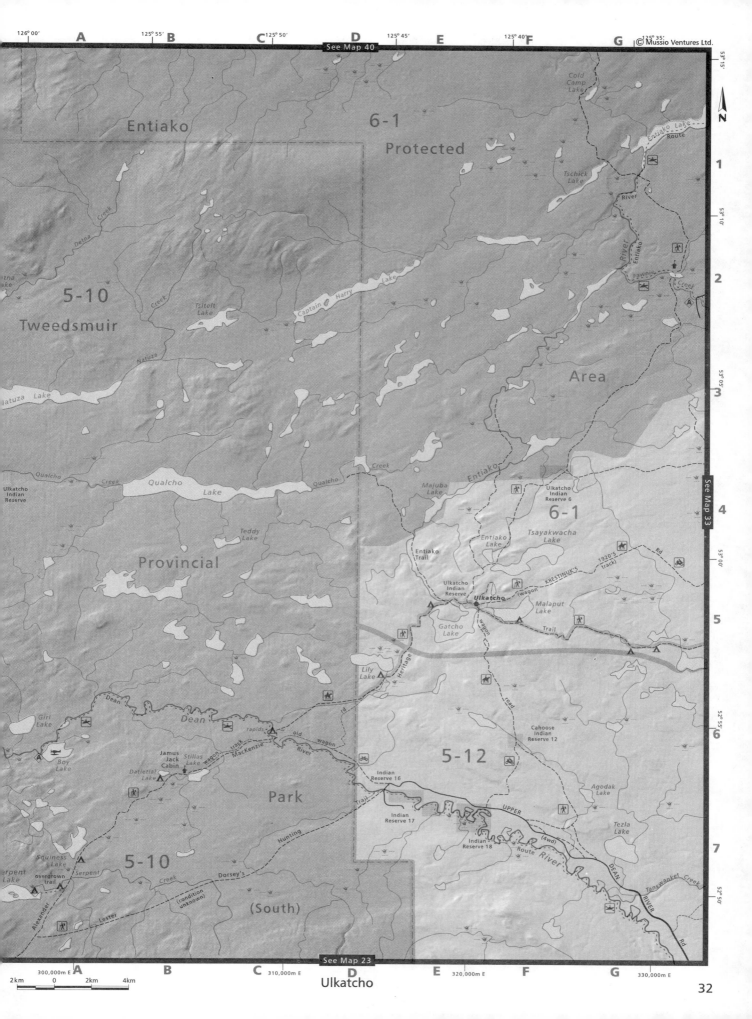

Entiako

6-1

Protected

Cold Camp Lake

Entiako Lake Route

53°10'

Tschick Lake

5-10

Tweedsmuir

Detna Creek

Tsitelt Lake

Captain Harry Lake

Natuza Creek

River

Entiako

Fawnie Creek

Area

53°05'

Natuza Lake

Qualcho Creek

Qualcho Lake

Qualcho Creek

Entiako Creek

Majuba Lake

Ulkatcho Indian Reserve 6

Ulkatcho Indian Reserve

Entiako Lake

Tsayakwacha Lake

1920's track

Rd

53°00'

Teddy Lake

Provincial

Entiako Trail

Ulkatcho Indian Reserve

Ulkatcho

wagon

KRESTINUK'S

Malaput Lake

Gatcho Lake

wagon

Trail

Heritage

Lily Lake

5

Girl Lake

Dean

Dean

rd

52°55'

Boy Lake

Dean River

rapids

old wagon

MacKenzie River

track

Jamus Jack Cabin

Stillas Lake wagon

Datletlal Lake

Cahoose Indian Reserve 12

5-12

Agodak Lake

Indian Reserve 16

Park

Indian Reserve 17

UPPER

Tezla Lake

52°50'

Squiness Lake

Serpent Lake

overgrown trail

Serpent

5-10

Hunting

Indian Reserve 18

Route

River

(4wd)

DEAN

RIVER

Tangswanket Creek

Alexander

Lester

Dorsey's

Creek

(condition unknown)

(South)

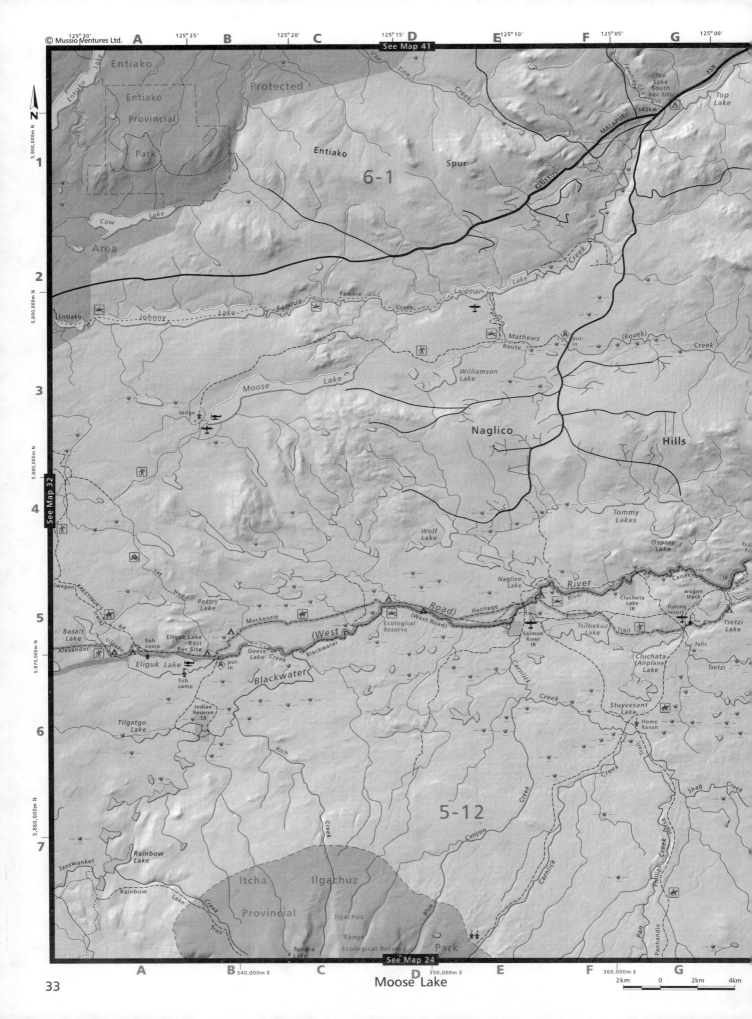

A 125° 30'   125° 25'   B   125° 20'   C   125° 15'   D   E 125° 10'   F 125° 05'   G 125° 00'

See Map 41

Entiako

Entiako

Provincial

Park

Protected

Entiako

Spur

6-1

Area

Cow   Lake

KLUSKUS

MALAPUT

Top Lake South Rec Site

142km

Top Lake

FSR

Fawnier Cr

See Map 32

Entiako

Johnny   Lake

Fawnie

Fawnie   Creek

Laidman   Lake

Creek

Moose   Lake

Mathews Route

put-in

(Rozek)

Creek

lodge

Williamson Lake

Naglico

Hills

Tommy Lakes

Wolf Lake

Osprey Lake

Naglico Lake

River

River

Canoe   rapids

IR

wagon track

KRESTINUK'S TRAIL

(wagon)

cat   trail

Rd

Pettry Lake

Mackenzie

(West   Road)

(West Road)

Heritage

Ecological Reserve

Cluchuta Lake IR

fishing resort

Tsetzi Lake

Basalt Lake

Ulgako

Eliguk Lake East Rec Site

Geese Lake   Creek

Blackwater

Salmon River IR

Tsilbekuz Lake

Trail

falls

Alexander

Eliguk Lake

fish camp

put-in

Blackwater

Camlick   Creek

Cluchata Airplane Lake

Tsetzi

fish camp

Indian Reserve 18

Home Ranch

Stuyvesant Lake

Tilgatgo Lake

Rich

Canyon   Creek

Camlick   Creek

Shag   Creek

5-12

Creek

Tanswanket

Rainbow Lake

Itcha

Ilgachuz

Phillips   Creek

Rose   Creek

Rainbow   Lake   Creek

Trail

Provincial

Ilgachuz

Blue

Park

Pan   Panhandle

Range Ecological Reserve

Tundra Lake

See Map 24

A   B 340,000m E   C   D 350,000m E   E   F 360,000m E   G

Moose Lake

2km 0 2km 4km

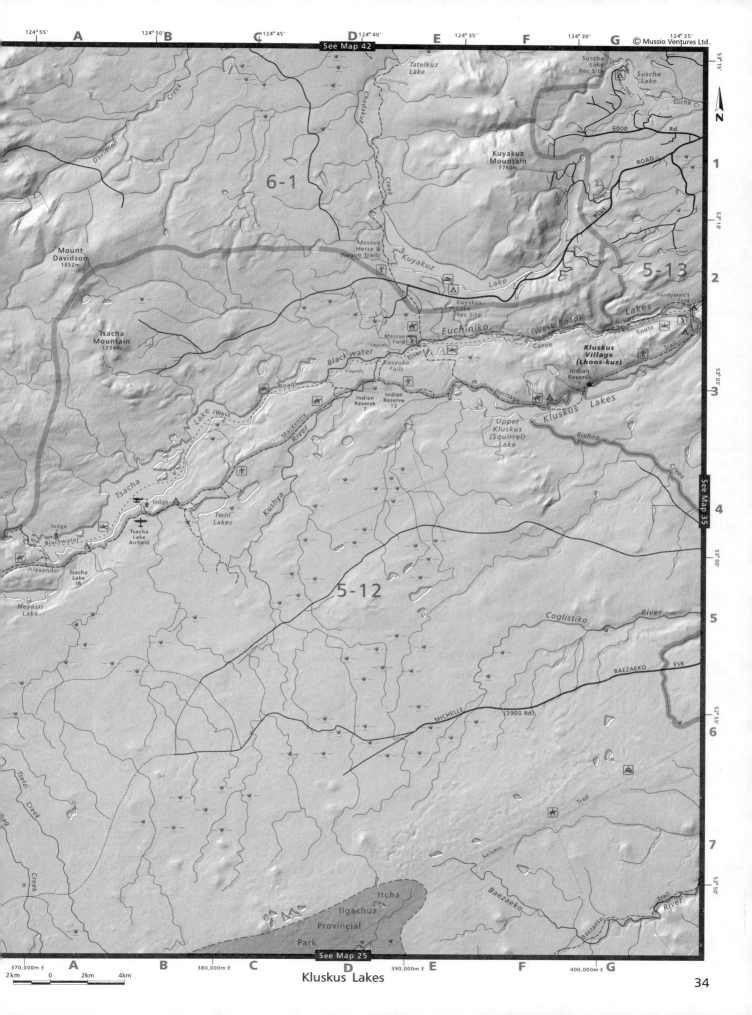

N

Tatelkuz
Lake

Suscha
Lake
Rec Site

Suscha
Lake

Sucha Cr

6-1

6000   Rd

Kuyakuz
Mountain
1780m

ROAD

BLUE

5-13

Mount
Davidson
1852m

Messue
Horse &
Wagon Trails

Kuyakuz   Lake

Sandyman's
Ford

Lakes

Kuyakus
Lake
Rec Site

Euchiniko   (West Road)

River

Tsacha
Mountain
1734m

Route

Canoe   Trail

Blackwater

rapids

Messue
Ford

River

Kluskus
Village
(Lhoos-kuz)

Kusyuko
Falls

rapids

Indian Reserve
1

Road

Indian
Reserve
7

Indian
Reserve
12

IR

Heritage

Kluskus   Lakes

Lake   (West)

Mackenzie

River

Upper
Kluskus
(Squirrel)
Lake

Bishop

Creek

See Map 35

lodge

Kushya

Tsacha

Twin
Lakes

lodge

Tsacha Lake
Airfield

5-12

Coglistiko   River

Blackwater

Alexander

Tsacha Lake
IR

Neyasri
Lake

BAEZAEKO   FSR

MICHELLE   (3900 Rd)

Tsetzi Creek

Coglistiko

Trail

Itcha
Ilgachuz

Seismic

Baezaeko

Provincial

Park

Baezaeko

Creek

Trail   River

See Map 25

A   370,000m E   B   380,000m E   C   390,000m E   D   E   F   400,000m E   G

53° 15'
53° 10'
53° 05'
53° 00'
52° 55'
52° 50'

1   2   3   4   5   6   7

© Mussio Ventures Ltd.

2km   0   2km   4km

Kluskus Lakes

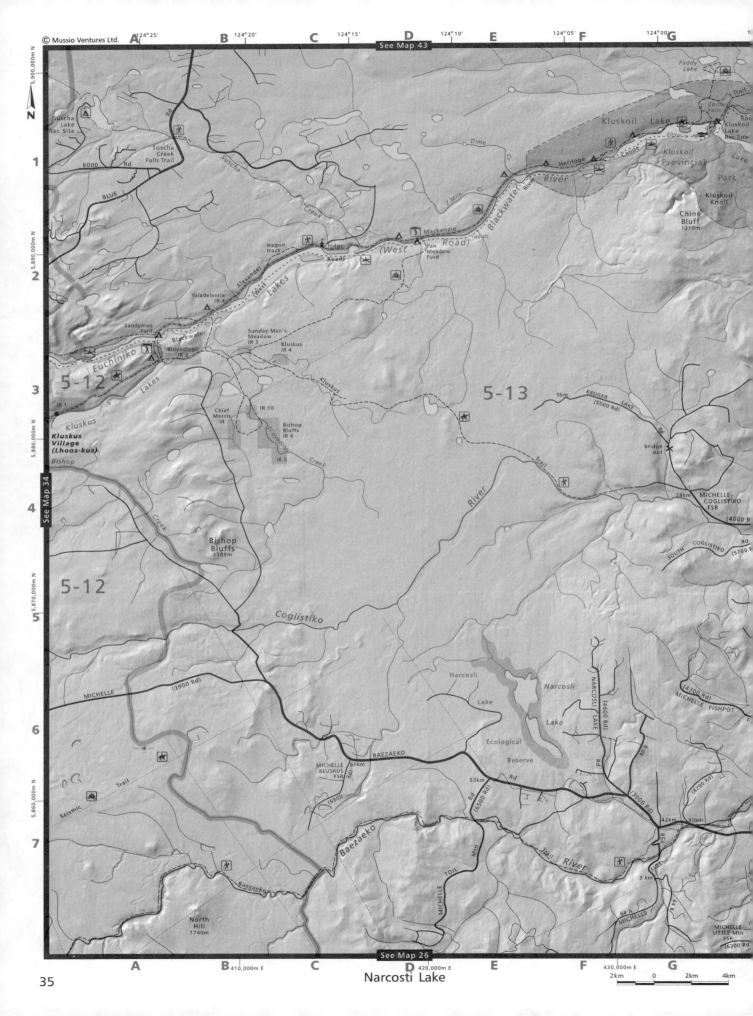

N

124°25' 124°20' 124°15' 124°10' 124°05' 124°00'

A B C D E F G

5,900,000m N

Suscha Lake Rec Site

Suscha Creek Falls Trail

6000 Rd

BLUE

Suscha Creek

Paddy Lake

Chine Falls Rd

Kluskoil Lake

Kluskoil Lake Rec Site

Kluskoil Provincial Park

Kluskoil Knoll

Chine Bluff 1310m

5,890,000m N

Dime Cr

7 Mile Cr

Blackwater River

Mackenzie

rapids

wagon track

Alexander

Lodge

(West Road)

Pan Meadow Ford

West Lakes

Yaladelassia IR 4

Sandyman Ford

Blackwater

Kloyadingli IR 2

Euchiniko Lakes

Sunday Man's Meadow IR 3

Kluskus IR 4

Kluskus

5-13

9km

KRUGER (5500 Rd)

LAKE

5-12

IR 1

Kluskus

Kluskus Village (Lhoos-kuz)

Bishop

Chief Morris IR

IR 10

Tl'oyedinli

IR 5

Bishop Bluffs IR 6

Creek

River

Trail

bridge out

28km

MICHELLE-COGLISTIKO FSR

(4000 R

SOUTH COGLISTIKO Rd (5700 F

5,880,000m N

See Map 34

Bishop Bluffs 1389m

Coglistiko

5-12

MICHELLE

(3900 Rd)

Narcosli Lake

Narcosli Lake

NARCOSLI LAKE

(4600 Rd)

(4300 Rd)

MICHELLE FISHPOT

48 B

Ecological Reserve

5,870,000m N

5,860,000m N

Seismic

Trail

BAEZAEKO

MICHELLE KLUSKUS FSR

61km

(6800)

53km

(6500 Rd)

Rd

(3900 Rd)

42km

39km

(8300 R

Baezaeko

MICHELLE TOIL Mtn

Trail River

3 km

FSR

Baezaeko

North Hill 1740m

64 A

MICHELLE

MICHELLE LITTLE Mtn FSR

(6300 R

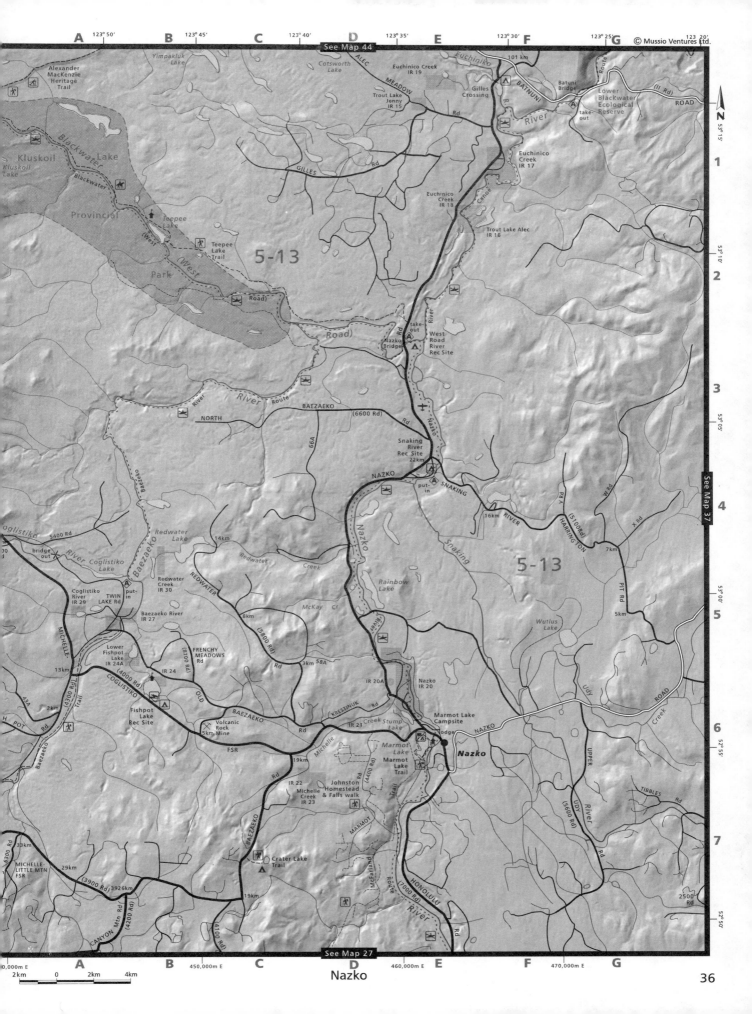

© Mussio Ventures Ltd.

A 123° 50' B 123° 45' C 123° 40' D 123° 35' E 123° 30' F 123° 25' G 123° 20'

Alexander
MacKenzie
Heritage
Trail

Yimpakluk
Lake

Cotsworth
Lake

Euchinico Creek
IR 19

Gilles
Crossing

101 km

Batuni
Bridge

Lower
Blackwater
Ecological
Reserve

take-
out

(II Rd)

ROAD

Trout Lake
Jenny
IR 15

Kluskoil Lake

Kluskoil
Lake

Blackwater

Provincial

Blackwater
Lake

Teepee
Lake

Teepee
Lake
Trail

GILLES

Rd

MEADOW

ALEC

Euchinico
Creek
IR 18

Euchinico
Creek
IR 17

Trout Lake Alec
IR 16

Euchiniko

BATNUNI

River

Route

53° 15'

1

Park

(West

5-13

Road)

Road)

Nazko
(Bridge)

West
Road
River
Rec Site

take-
out

River

Nazko

Canoe

53° 10'

2

River

River
Route

NORTH

BAEZAEKO

(6600 Rd)

Rd

Snaking
River
Rec Site
22km

Nazko

53° 05'

3

66A

NAZKO

put-
in

SNAKING

16km RIVER

Snaking

(5100 Rd)

HARRINGTON

Pit A

W Rd

X Rd

7km

53° 05'

See Map 37

4

Coglistiko

5400 Rd

Baezaeko

Redwater
Lake

14km

Redwater

Creek

McKay Cr.

Rainbow
Lake

5-13

Wutlus
Lake

PIT Rd

5km

53° 00'

5

bridge
out

River Coglistiko
Lake

Coglistiko
River
IR 29

TWIN
LAKE Rd

put-
in

Redwater
Creek
IR 30

Baezaeko River
IR 27

13km

MICHELLE

(4300 Rd)

Lower
Fishpot
Lake
IR 24A

IR 24

FRENCHY
MEADOWS
Rd

(8700 Rd)

(4000 Rd)

IS800 Rd)

Rd

3km 58A

IR 20A

Nazko
IR 20

Udy

Creek

ROAD

UPPER

52° 55'

6

45A

2km

COGLISTIKO

Fishpot
Lake
Rec Site

OLD
BAEZAEKO

Volcanic
Rock
5km Mine

FSR

KRESTINUK

Rd

Creek Stump
Lake

IR 23

Marmot Lake
Campsite

Lodge

Marmot
Lake

Marmot Lake
Trail

Nazko

NAZKO

UDY
River

TIBBLES
Rd

52° 55'

H POT
Rd

Baezaeko

19km

Michelle

Rd

IR 22
Michelle
Creek
IR 23

Johnston
Homestead
& Falls walk

(4400 Rd)

Trail

(5600 Rd)

(2500
Rd)

7

6300 Rd 30km

MICHELLE-
LITTLE MTN
FSR

29km

(3900 Rd) 3926km

CANYON Mtn Rd

(4200 Rd)

BAEZAEKO

Rd

19km

(4100 Rd)

Crater Lake
Trail

MARMOT

McClelland

Route

HONOLULU

(7000 Rd)

Rd

River

52° 50'

7

A 450,000m E B C 450,000m E C D E 460,000m E E F 470,000m E G

0,000m E

2km 0 2km 4km

Nazko

36

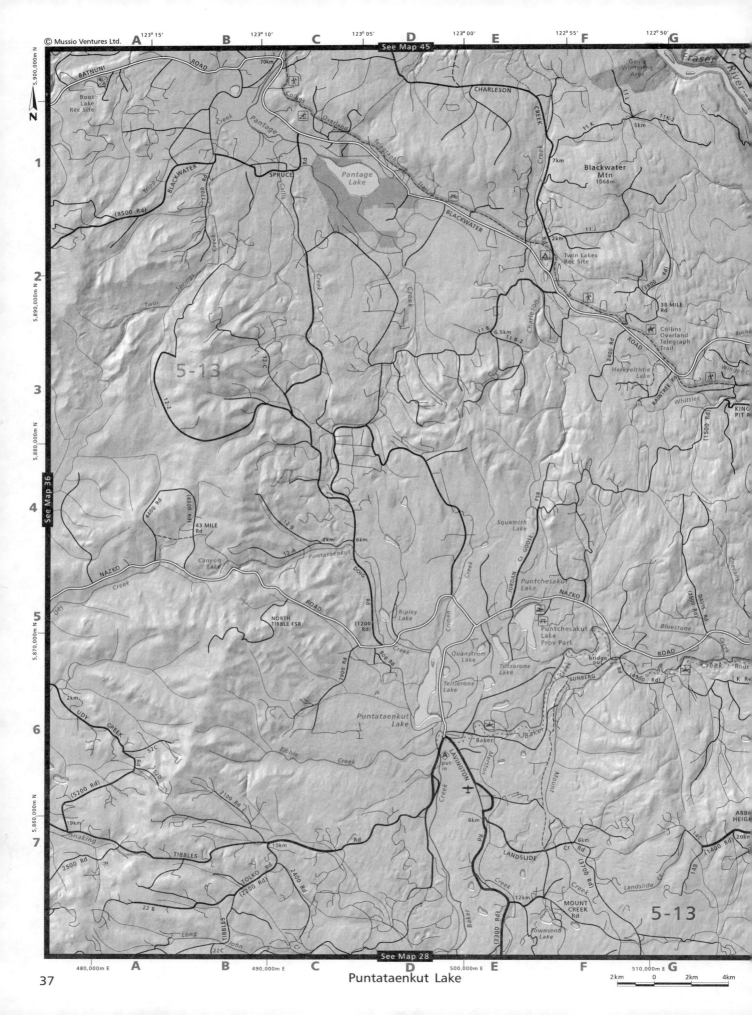

A   123° 15'   B   123° 10'   C   123° 05'   D   123° 00'   E   122° 55'   F   122° 50'   G

See Map 36

BATNUNI

Boot
Lake
Rec Site

ROAD

70km

Collins

Overland

Pantage

SPRUCE

Pantage
Lake

Calls

Rd

Telegraph

Trail

BLACKWATER

CHARLESON

CREEK

Gang
Wintering
Area

Fraser River

Blackwater
Mtn
1068m

11 K

5km

11K-2

7km

7km

11 J

2km

Twin Lakes
Rec Site

ROAD

3800 Rd

38 MILE
Rd

Collins
Overland
Telegraph
Trail

BLACKWATER

Rd

7700 Rd

(8500 Rd)

Twin

Springs

Creek

Rd

Creek

Creek

Creek

11 B

6.5km

11 B-2

Charleson

Creek

3400 Rd

RANTREE Rd

Herkyelthtie I
Lake

Whittier

Wing Cr

(1500 Rd)

KING
PIT R

5-13

12-C

12-1

4400 Rd

4300 Rd

43 MILE
Rd

12-B

Canyon
Lake

12-A

Puntataenkut

2km

6km

DOIG

Rd

Squamish
Lake

Gr GOOSE

FSR

JORDAN

Puntchesakut
Lake

NAZKO

Creek

2500 Rd

Chevan

NAZKO

Creek

Udy

Creek

NORTH
TIBBLE FSR

1300 Rd

(1200
Rd)

900 Rd

Creek

Ripley
Lake

Crooked

Creek

Quanstrom
Lake

Tiltzarone
Lake

Teiterone
Lake

Puntchesakut
Lake
Prov Park

SUNBERG

bridge
out

(4900
Rd)

ROAD

Bluestone

Creek

Rout

K Re

2km

UDY

CREEK

52C

52D

Rd

Tibble

Creek

Puntataenkut
Lake

put
in

LAVINGTON

Baker

Baker

Mureton

Mount

(5200 Rd)

19km

Snaking

2500 Rd

R

TIBBLES

2100 Rd

John

10km

TOLKO Rd

(2200 Rd)

2400 Rd

Rd

22 B

22 C

TIBBLES

Long

Baker

6km

Creek

Rd

Pit

3300 Rd

LANDSLIDE

12km

6km

Cr

Rd

3700 Rd

MOUNT
CREEK
Rd

Townsend
Lake

Landslide

14 E

14 B

1400 Rd

20km

ABBO
HEIGH

5-13

A   480,000m E   B   490,000m E   C   D   500,000m E   E   F   510,000m E   G

2km   0   2km   4km

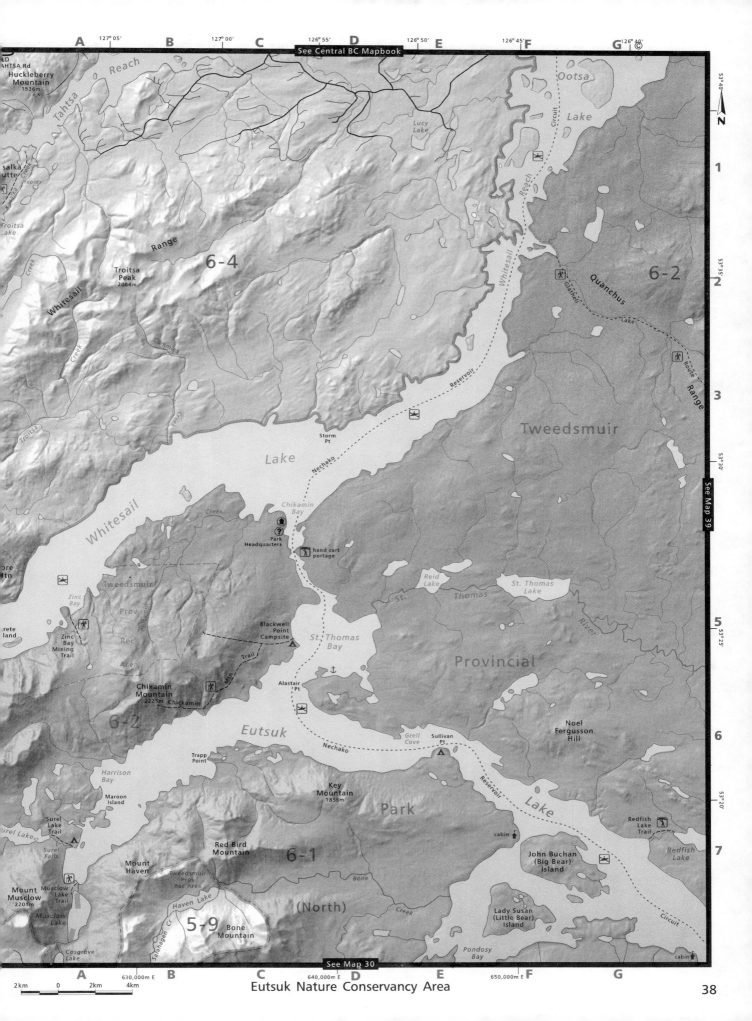

A   127° 05'   B   127° 00'   C   126° 55'   D   126° 50'   E   126° 45'   F   G   126° 40'   ©

53° 40'   1

53° 35'   2

Huckleberry
Mountain
1536m

Tahtsa   Reach

Ootsa   Lake

Lucy
Lake

6-4

Troitsa
Peak
2084m

Range

Whitesail   Reach

Quanchus

6-2

Clemiss   Creek

Tweedsmuir

Folta   Range

53° 30'   3

Reservoir

Nechako

Storm
Pt

Lake

Whitesail

St. Thomas
Lake

Reid
Lake

Chikamin
Bay

Park
Headquarters

hand cart
portage

St.   Thomas

River

Zinc Bay

Tweedsmuir

Blackwell
Point
Campsite

St. Thomas
Bay

Provincial

5   53° 25'

Zinc Bay
Mining Trail

Prov

Rec

Area

Alastair
Pt

Chikamin
Mountain
2225m   Chikamin

Mtn   Trail

Noel
Fergusson
Hill

6-2

Eutsuk

Grell
Cove

Sullivan
Pt

6   53° 20'

Nechako

Trapp
Point

Harrison
Bay

Key
Mountain
1856m

Reservoir

Lake

Maroon
Island

Park

Redfish Lake
Trail

Surel
Lake
Trail

Surel Lake

Red Bird
Mountain

6-1

cabin

John Buchan
(Big Bear)
Island

Redfish
Lake

7

Surel
Falls

Mount
Haven

Mount
Musclow
2201m

Musclow
Lake
Trail

Tweedsmuir
Prov
Rec Area

(North)

Bone   Creek

Lady Susan
(Little Bear)
Island

Musclow
Lake

Haven Lake

5-9

Bone
Mountain

Cosgrove
Lake

Salahagen Cr

Pondosy
Bay

cabin

See Map 39

See Map 30

2km   0   2km   4km

A   630,000m E   B   C   640,000m E   D   E   650,000m E   F   G

Eutsuk Nature Conservancy Area

38

126° 35'   A   126° 30'   B   126° 25'   C   126° 20'   D   126° 15'   E   126° 10'   F   126° 05'   G

See Central BC Mapbook

N

Tweedsmuir

5,950,000m N

Tweedsmuir
Peak
2182m

Blanchet

1

Glatheli   Lake

Lake

Chelaslie

Michel
Lake

Ghitezli Lake

Sabina
Lake

Route

2

5,940,000m N

Michel
Peak
2254m

6-2

Route

River

Thietelban
Lake

Lake

Wutak
Lake

Route

3

5,930,000m N

Glatheli

Quanchus

rapids

Goodrich
Lake

shelter

Fenton   Lake

Morgan
Lake

Nutli
Lake

Lake

Blanchet

River

rapids

4

Provincial

Chef

Wells Gray
Peak
2198m

Blanchet

Justa
Lake

Etalie
Lake

Michel

Creek

rapids

River

Ridge

5

5,920,000m N

River

Range

Blanchet
Lake

Tlutlias
Lake

Lena
Lake

Thomas

Grizzly
Hill

Tlutlias

6

Junction
Hill

Park

Tlutlias
Cone

6-2

St.

Goosefoot
Lake

Eutsuk
Peak
1914m

5,91 0,000m N

Redfish
Lake

7

(North)

Tetachuk
Lake

Sandy
Cabin
Bay

Eutsuk   Lake

cabin

Tetachuk
River Trail

6-

660,000m E   A   B   670,000m E   C   D   680,000m E   E   F   690,000m E   G

See Map 31

2km   0   2km   4km

See Map 38

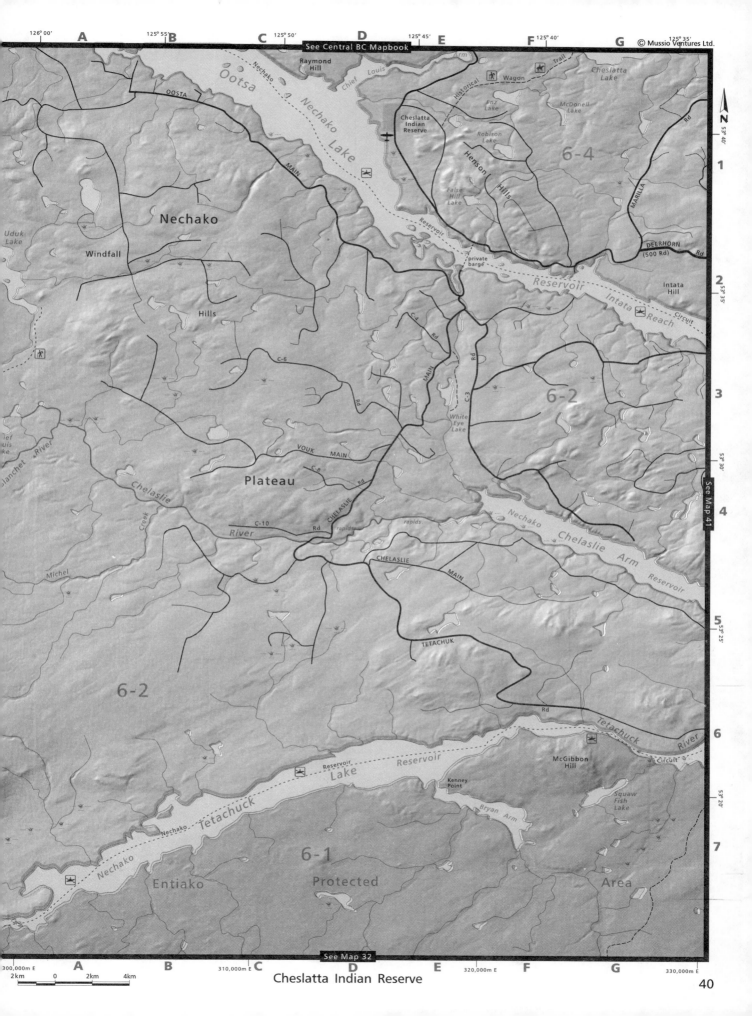

© Mussio Ventures Ltd.

Ootsa

Nechako Lake

Nechako

Hills

Plateau

Chelaslie

River

Creek

Michel

Windfall

Uduk
Lake

Chief
Louis
Lake

Blanchet River

6-2

Raymond
Hill

Chief Louis Arm

Nechako

Cheslatta
Indian
Reserve

Reservoir

private barge

Historical

Wagon

Trail

Enz
Lake

Robison
Lake

Henson Hills

False
Hill
Lake

McDonell
Lake

Cheslatta
Lake

6-4

MARILLA

Rd

DEERHORN
(500 Rd)

Intata
Hill

Reservoir

Intata Reach

Circuit

6-2

White
Eye
Lake

MAIN

C-4
Rd

C-3

Rd

VOUK MAIN

C-8

Rd

CHELASLIE

C-10   Rd   rapids

rapids

Nechako

Chelaslie Arm

Reservoir

CHELASLIE

MAIN

TETACHUK

Rd

Tetachuck

River

Circuit

McGibbon
Hill

Squaw
Fish
Lake

6-2

6-1   Protected   Area

Reservoir Lake

Reservoir

Kenney
Point

Bryan Arm

Nechako Tetachuck

Nechako

Entiako

C-6

Rd

Cheslatta Indian Reserve

See Map 41

OOSTA

MAIN

2km   0   2km   4km

300,000m E

310,000m E

320,000m E

330,000m E

126° 00'   125° 55'   125° 50'   125° 45'   125° 40'   125° 35'

53° 40'

53° 35'

53° 30'

53° 25'

53° 20'

A   B   C   D   E   F   G

1

2

3

4

5

6

7

40

N

© Mussio Ventures Ltd.

N

125° 30'   125° 25'   125° 20'   125° 15'   125° 10'   125° 05'   125° 00'

A   B   C   D   E   F   G

5,950,000m N

MARILLA   Rd

MARILLA
NEW
BIRD
Rd

Chaoborus
Lake

BIRD

MARILLA   LAKE

Murray

1

Davidson
Lake

MacKenzie
Lake

Indian
Reserve
4

Bird
Lake

Lake

Rum Cache
(Cicuta)
Lake

Rum Cache
Lake
Rec Site

M 25   RD

Smith
Lake

6-4

Sam
Hardy
Lake

M-12

M32

Rd

DEERHORN

Nechako

Deerhorn
Hill
1415m

The Devil's
Thumb
1287m

Lucas

2

5,940,000m N

Thumb
Lake

Lucas   Lake

DEERHORN   ROAD

536km

Knewstubb
Lake

Saunders
Hill

Creek

Intata

Nechako

Table
Hill
1277m

562km

Emmett
Lake

Plateau

3

5,930,000m N

ROAD

Hoult
Lake

6-2

Reach

Reservoir

Woodpecker
Hill

(500 Rd)

Leon
IR

Knewstubb Lake

4

WOODPECKER

Rd

Circuit

Yellow
Moose
Lake

Jim
Smith
Point

Chelaslie   Arm

Echu   Reach

Nechako   Reservoir

Route

5

5,920,000m N

Cheda
Arm

Entiako

River

River

6

Aslin

River

Creek

Mount
Swannell
1821m

5,910,000m N

Capoose

Capoose
Lake

6-1

Tutiai
Mountain

Little
Capoose
Lake

7

Entiako

Entiako

Protected

Creek

Entiako
Provincial
Park

Fawnie

Saddle
Hump

Faw
Do
17

Entiako
Lake

Area

Fawnie
Nose
1926m

Fawnie
Cr

Fawnie
Creek
Falls

Van   Tine   Creek

See Map 40

See Map 33

A   B   340,000m E   C   D   350,000m E   E   F   360,000m E   G

Lucas Lake

2km   0   2km   4km

41

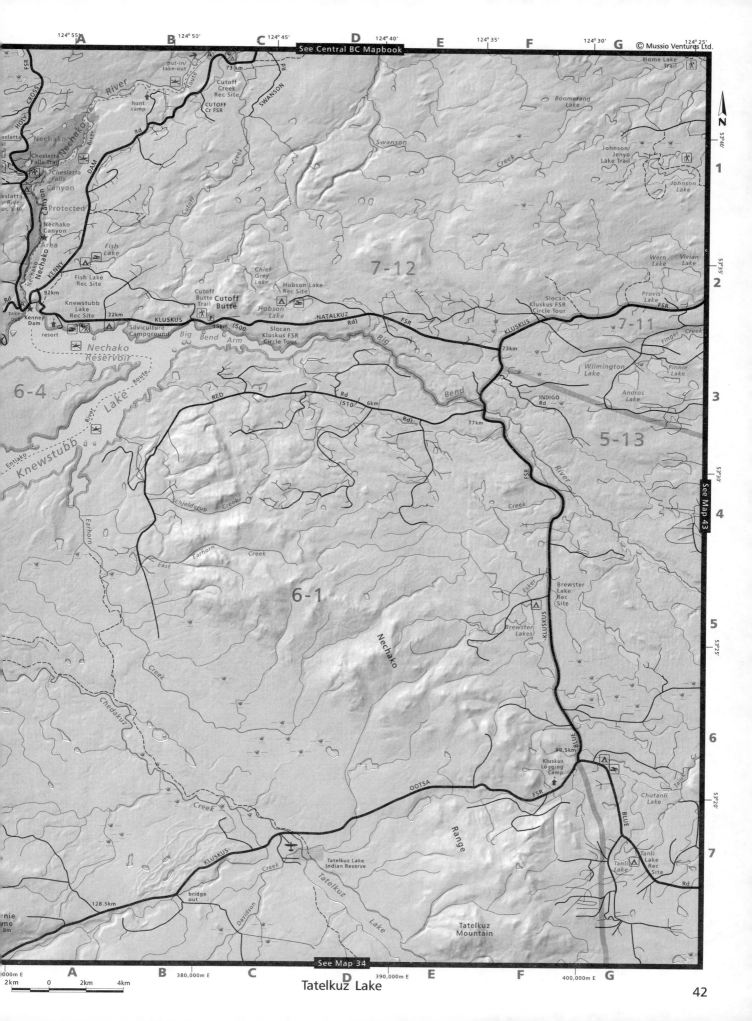

© Mussio Ventures Ltd.

A   124° 55'   B   124° 50'   C   124° 45'   D   124° 40'   E   124° 35'   F   124° 30'   G   124° 25'

N

53°40'   1
53°35'   2
53°30'   3
53°25'   4
5
53°25'
6
53°20'
7

7-12

7-11

6-4

5-13

6-1

Boomerang Lake

Home Lake Trail

Johnson/ Jenyo Lake Trail

Johnson Lake

Wern Lake   Vivian Lake

Provis Lake

Slocan Kluskus FSR Circle Tour

Finger Creek

Wilmington Lake

Finnie Lake

Andros Lake

INDIGO Rd

KLUSKUS FSR

73 km

Swanson Creek

Swanson Rd

Cutoff Creek Rec Site
CUTOFF Cr FSR
Cutoff Cr FSR

put-in/ take-out
73 km

hunt camp

Cutoff Creek

HOLY CROSS FSR

Nechako River
River Rd

Cheslatta Trail
Cheslatta Falls Trail
Cheslatta Falls

Nechako Canyon
Canyon Protected Area

Nechako Canyon

Cheslatta River Rec Site

take-out
Rd

DAM

KENNY

Kenney Dam

92km

resort

Fish Lake

Fish Lake Rec Site

Knewstubb Lake Rec Site   22km

Silviculture Campground

KLUSKUS

Nechako Reservoir

Big Bend Arm

Cutoff Butte Trail
Cutoff Butte

Chief Grey Lake

Hobson Lake Rec Site
Hobson Lake

15km (500   Slocan Kluskus FSR Circle Tour

NATALKUZ   Rd)   FSR

Big   Bend

73 km

KLUSKUS

Knewstubb Lake

River Route

Entiako

6km

Rd (510)

RED

Rd)

77km

FSR

River

Nechako

Creek

Schielderup Creek

East   Earhorn Creek

Earhorn

Chedakuz

Creek

Brewster Lakes

Brewster Lake Rec Site

Esker

KLUSKUS

99.5km

Kluskus Logging Camp

BLUE

OOTSA FSR

Creek

Range

Chutanli Lake

BLUE

Tapli

Tanli Lake
Tanli Lake Rec Site
Rd

KLUSKUS

bridge out

128.5km

Davidson Creek

Tatelkuz Lake Indian Reserve

Tatelkuz   Creek

Tatelkuz   Lake

Tatelkuz Mountain

ernie me 8in

See Map 43

See Map 34

2km   0   2km   4km

000m E   A   2km   B   380,000m E   C   D   390,000m E   E   F   400,000m E   G

Tatelkuz Lake

A   124° 25'   B   124° 20'   C   124° 15'   D   124° 10'   E   124° 05'   F   124° 00'   G

See Central BC Mapbook

Paddle
Lake

Home
Lake

Home
Lake
Rec Site

Boomerang
Lake

Nulki
Hills

Frank Lake
Rec Site

Frank
Lake

427km   400   Rd

42.5km

7-12

Johnson
Lake

Johnson   Jenyo
Lake   Trail

Meridian
Road
Ecological
Reserve

(600 Rd)

TATUK Rd 600

1100   Rd

Gluten
Lake

Gluten
Lake
Trail

611km

BOBTAIL

Wren
Lake

Vivian
Lake

Secord
Lake

Duten
Lake

7-11

Koshe
Falls

155km

Provis
Lake

bridge
out

Finger

Iron
Knoll

KLUSKUS

59km

Finger
Lake

Arthur
Lake

Finnie   Finge   Arthur Lake
Lake   Rec Site

Hawley   Kaiser
Lake   Lake

Jardine
Lake

Willington
Lake

Stefiuk
Lake

Tatuk
Lake
IR

Fire
Lake

Falls

Creek

Chilako
River
Ecological
Reserve

Andros
Lake

Ray
Lake

Otter
Lake

resort

Tatuk   **Lake**

Tatuk Lake
Campsite

Upper
Chilako River
Campsite

137km

(100 Rd)

Thomas
Lake

Kobes
Lake

Smolock
Lake

Tatuk Lake
West Campsite

Tatuk

Tatuk Lake
Campsite

Chilako

Expansion
Lake

River

PELICAN   CHILKO

Tatuk
Hill
1321m

Slims
Lake

Johny
Lake

Tatuk

Hills

Inez
Lake

Mountain
Lake

Provincial

no
through

Lavoie
Lake

Turff
Lake

Vance
Lake

Park

Hay
Lake

Bodley
Lake

Harp
Lake

Cory
Lake

Euchiniko

Klunchatistli
Lake

Batnuni
Cone

Bourgeois

River

Batnuni
Lake W
Rec Site

BATNUNI

LAKE

FSR

Comstock
Lake

Batnuni

Creek

Chutanli
Lake

Tatuk

Lake

Batnuni
Lake E
Rec Site

132km

Snag
Lake

BLUE

Tanli
Lake

Chuniar
Lake

Tanli Lake
Rec Site

5-13

Jerryboy

Hills

Swede

Creek

KLUSKUS   FSR

11 H

CREEK

SWEDE

FSR

Pilot
Knoll

Marc
Hills
1291m

A   410,000m E   B   C   D   420,000m E   E   F   430,000m E   G

Tatuk Lake

2km   0   2km   4km

5,950,000m N
5,940,000m N
5,930,000m N
5,920,000m N
5,910,000m N

N

1
2
3
4
5
6
7

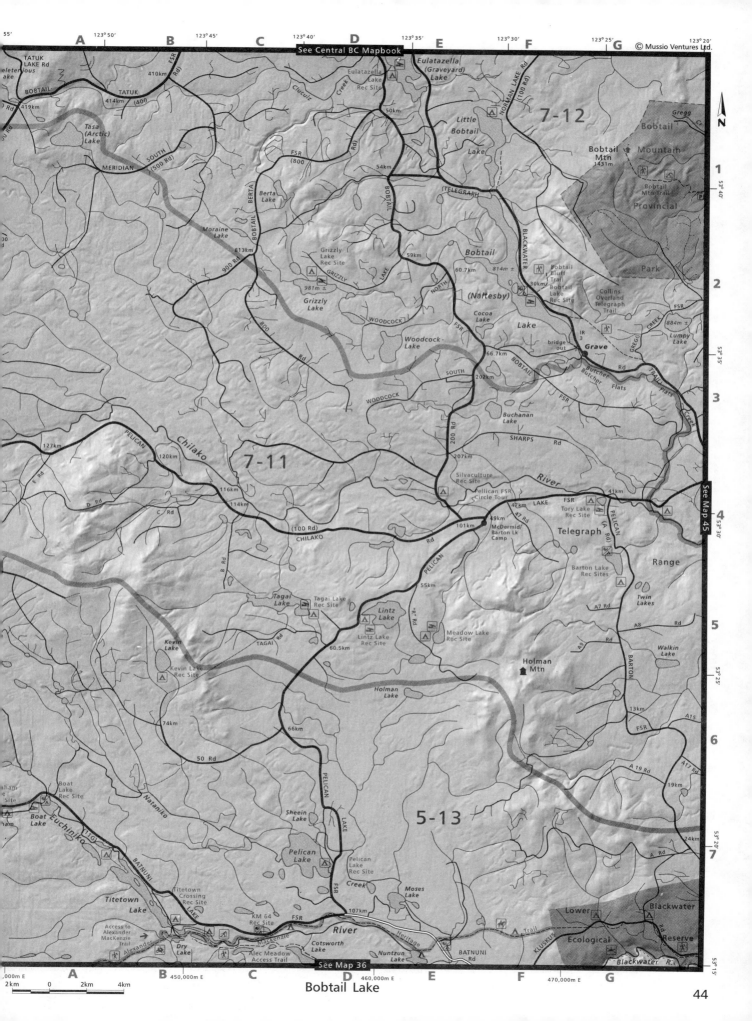

© Mussio Ventures Ltd.

See Central BC Mapbook

TATUK LAKE Rd

BOBTAIL

Tasa (Arctic) Lake

TATUK

410km

414km (400

419km

MERIDIAN

SOUTH (500 Rd)

Moraine Lake

Clucuiz Creek

Eulatazella Lake Rec Site

Eulatazella (Graveyard) Lake

50km

Little Bobtail Lake

NORMAN LAKE Rd (100 Rd)

7-12

Bobtail Mtn 1431m

Bobtail Mtn Trail

Bobtail

Provincial

Gregg Cr

Park

1

53°40'

BERTA

Berta Lake

BOBTAIL

FSR (800

54km

(TELEGRAPH

BLACKWATER

Bobtail

Collins Overland Telegraph Trail

884m ±

Lumpy Lake

FSR

2

53°35'

813km

900 Rd

Grizzly Lake Rec Site

981m ±

Grizzly Lake

GRIZZLY

LAKE

NORTH

WOODCOCK

59km

60.7km

814m ±

(Naltesby)

Cocoa Lake

30km

Bobtail Bluff Trail

Bobtail Lake Rec Site

Lake

IR 3

bridge out

Grave

Butcher

Butcher Flats

GREGG CREEK

TRAIL Flats

800 Rd

Woodcock Lake

FSR

66.7km

BOBTAIL

3

53°35'

PELICAN

127km

Chilako

120km

116km

114km

7-11

SOUTH

WOODCOCK

200 Rd

202km

SHARPS Rd

Buchanan Lake

207km

River

Silvaculture Rec Site

Pellican FSR Circle Tour

41km

FSR

LAKE

47 Rd

47km

Tory Lake Rec Site

A

PELICAN Rd

See Map 45

4

53°30'

E Rd

D Rd

C Rd

B Rd

(100 Rd)

CHILAKO

101km

Rd

49km

McDermid/ Barton Lk Camp

Telegraph

Barton Lake Rec Sites

A7 Rd

Range

A8 Rd

Twin Lakes

Tagai Lake

Tagai Lake Rec Site

Lintz Lake

PELICAN

55km

Meadow Lake Rec Site

BARTON

Walkin Lake

5

53°25'

Kevin Lake

Kevin Lake Rec Site

TAGAI Rd

Lintz Lake Rec Site

60.5km

"R" Rd

Holman Mtn

13km

FSR

A15

74km

50 Rd

66km

Holman Lake

A 19 Rd

A17 Rd

19km

6

Natankio

PELICAN

LAKE

5-13

24km

53°20'

Boat Lake Rec Site

ham Site

Boat Lake

Euchinko

(11G)

BATNUNI

Sheein Lake

PELICAN CREEK

FSR

Moses Lake

Lower

Blackwater

A Rd

7

Titetown Crossing Rec Site

Titetown Lake

LAKE

KM 64 Rec Site

FSR

107km

Pelican Lake

Pelican Lake Rec Site

Heritage

Trail

KLUSKUS Rd

Ecological

Lower Blackwater

Reserve

Blackwater R.

Access to Alexander MacKenzie Trail

Dry Lake

Alexander

MacKenzie

Alec Meadow Access Trail

Cotsworth Lake

River

Nuntzun Lake

BATNUNI Rd

53°15'

N

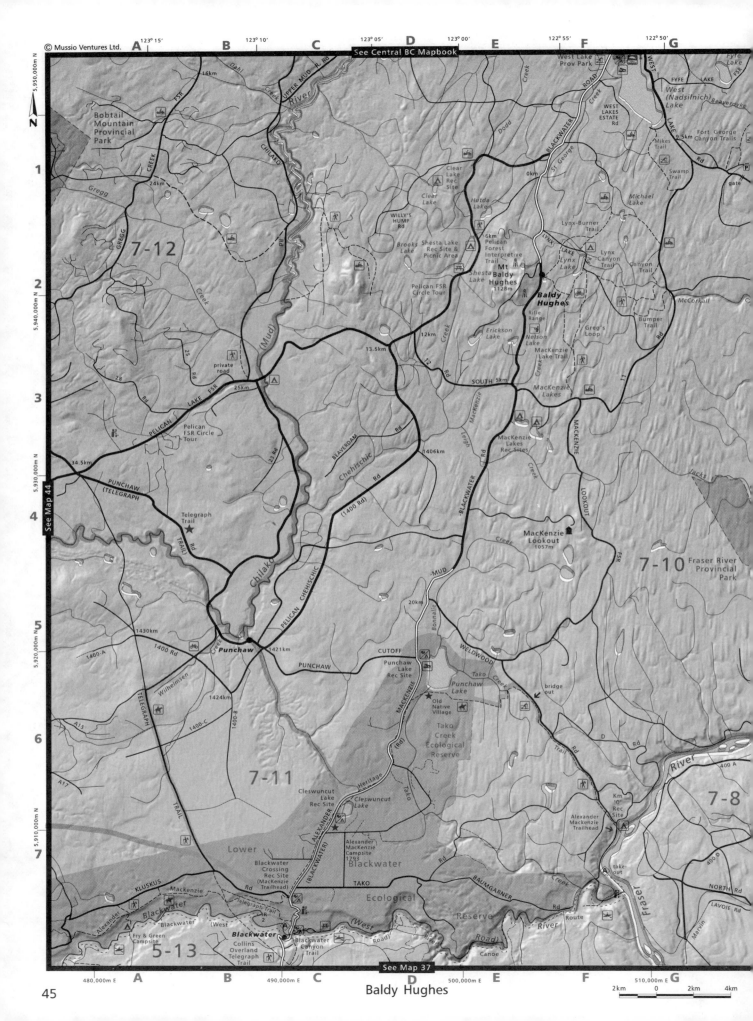

© Mussio Ventures Ltd.

N

Bobtail
Mountain
Provincial
Park

West Lake
Prov Park

FYFE
LAKE

Fyfe
Lake

West
(Nadsilnich)
Lake

WEST LAKES
ESTATE Rd

Fort George
Canyon Trails

Mikes
Trail

9.5km

gate

Michael
Lake

Swamp
Trail

Gregg

Gregg

24km

7-12

Dehi

UPPER MUD R. Rd

River

CHILAKO

Creek

Dodd

Creek

BLACKWATER

St. George

0km

LYNX

Lynx-Burner
Trail

McCorkall

Clear
Lake
Rec
Site

Clear
Lake

WILLY'S
HUMP
Rd

Brooks
Lake

Hutda
Lake

Shesta Lake
Rec Site &
Picnic Area

6km
Pelican Forest
Interpretive
Trail

Mt
Baldy
Hughes
1128m

Lynx
Lake

Lynx
Canyon
Trail

Canyon
Trail

Baldy
Hughes

private
road

Rd

(Mud)

Creek

25km

Pelican FSR
Circle Tour

Shesta
Lake

13.5km

12km

12
Rd

Creek

Rifle
Range

Erickson
Lake

Nelson
Lake

MacKenzie
Lake Trail

Greg's
Loop

Bumper
Trail

25

28

Rd

PELICAN

LAKE
FSR

25km

Pelican
FSR Circle
Tour

23 Rd

BEAVERDAM

Chehischic

Rd

1406km

SOUTH

5km

MacKenzie

Mackenzie

Leigh

Rd

MacKenzie
Lakes

MacKenzie
Lakes
Rec Sites

34.5km

PUNCHAW
(TELEGRAPH

Telegraph
Trail

Chilako

PELICAN

CHEHISCHIC

(1400 Rd)

BLACKWATER

Creek

MacKenzie
Lookout
1057m

LOOKOUT

FSR

7-10 Fraser River
Provincial
Park

Jacks

TRAIL)

Rd

1430km

1400-A

1400 Rd

Punchaw

1421km

PUNCHAW

Creek

CUTOFF

MUD

Bonnallie

20km

Punchaw Lake
Rec Site

WELDWOOD

Tako
Creek

bridge
out

Telegraph

Wilhelmsen

1424km

1400-B

1400-C

MACKENZIE

(Rd)

Punchaw
Lake

Old
Native
Village

Tako
Creek
Ecological
Reserve

Tako

Creek

D

Rd

A15

7-11

Heritage

Creek

Trail

Rd

7-8

A17

TRAIL

Cleswuncut Lake
Rec Site

Cleswuncut
Lake

ALEXANDER

(BLACKWATER)

Rd

Alexander
Mackenzie
Campsite
1793

Rd

Baumgarner

Alexander
Mackenzie
Trailhead

Km
10'
Rec
Site

400 A

River

Lower

Blackwater
Crossing
Rec Site
(MacKenzie
Trailhead)

Blackwater

TAKO

Ecological

Rd

400 D

take-out

KLUSKUS

Mackenzie

Telegraph Trail

IR
2

(West

Road)

Reserve

BAUMGARNER

Rd

Route

Fraser

NORTH Rd

LAVOIE Rd

Alexander

Blackwater

(West

River

Marvin

Fry & Green
Campsite

Blackwater

5-13

Collins
Overland
Telegraph Trail

Blackwater

Blackwater
Canyon Trail

Road)

Canoe

45

Baldy Hughes

2km 0 2km 4km

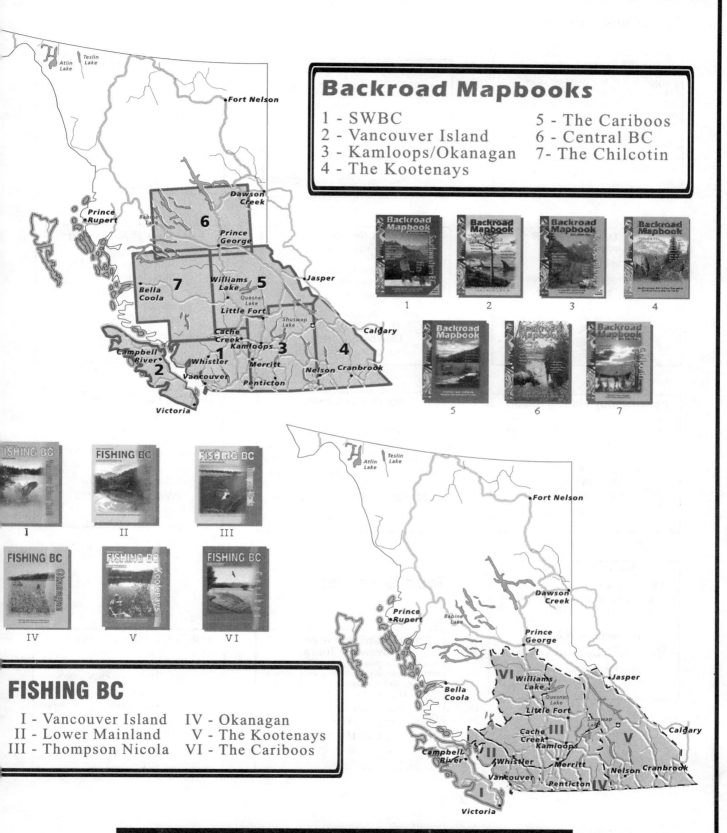

Mussio Ventures Presents...
The **Backroad Mapbooks** and **FISHING BC** series

Backroad Mapbooks

1 - SWBC
2 - Vancouver Island
3 - Kamloops/Okanagan
4 - The Kootenays
5 - The Cariboos
6 - Central BC
7 - The Chilcotin

FISHING BC

I - Vancouver Island   IV - Okanagan
II - Lower Mainland   V - The Kootenays
III - Thompson Nicola   VI - The Cariboos

Service Providers

Accommodations

Chilcotin Lodge

Historic country Inn (Est. 1940) located in beautiful Chilcotin grasslands. Uniquely restored bedrooms, fireplace, licenced dining room, home-style cooking, RV hookups - camp-sites - hot showers. Only 40 minutes west of Williams Lake on Highway 20!

P.O. Box 2, Riske Creek, BC V0L 1T0

Ph/Fax: 250-659-5646

Toll free: 888-659-5688

www.chilcotinlodge.com

Chilko River Lodge

Fishing, River Boat Tours, Horseback Riding, Full Accommodations, Restaurant and Saloon, 16" telescope, reasonable prices.

P.O. Box 43,
Tatla Lake, BC
V0L 1V0

250-394-4105

www.bcadventure.com/chilkoriverlodge

Cochin Lake Resort

18km south of Tatla Lake on Tatlayoko Road. Deluxe modern log chalet; private dry sites in natural treed setting; boat launch; boat rental; nature trails; bird & wildlife watching, cross country skiing.

Box 49

Tatla Lake, BC V0L 1V0

T: 250-476-1132

F: 250-476-1251

Dew Duck Inn B & B

Nearest Accomodation to

Rainbow Range Trailhead

Quality meals - Great rates - Sauna

Boat Rentals

Box 3351 Anahim Lake, BC
V0L 1C0 **1-888-277-6733**
dewduckinnbb@midbc.com
www.bctravel.com/dewduckinn

Eagle's Nest Resort

We offer you great fishing, dining, guided hiking tours,
birdwatching, hot tubbing under the stars, library. Enjoy true nature unspoiled.

PO Box 3403, Highway 20

Anahim Lake, BC V0L 1C0

Ph 250-742-3707

Fax 250-742-3489

www.eaglesnest-resort.com

Heritage River Rafting

Drift in the quiet
beauty of the historic
Bella Coola river with
our licensed guides

Contact: Ron or Willow Sturrock

PH 250-982-2972

Canoe crossing 35km east of Bella Coola

Kokanee Bay Fishing Resort

Fishing (Rainbow trout's /Kokanee 2lb & more) Hiking, mountain biking, icefishing, x-country

Comfi cabins & camping
3904 Puntzi Lake Road
Chilanko Forks, B.C., V0L 1H0

1-250-481-1130
kokanee@bcadventure.com

www.bcadventure.com/kokanee

Rip Rap Campsite

Hwy 20 - Hagensborg
Bella Coola Valley
20 Riverfront Sites - Camping Cabin
Your Hosts: Jim & Amber Knudsen

250-982-2752 www.bellacoola.ca

"Come and Relax!"

The Log Cabin B&B

3 comfortable, self-contained log cabins with private baths. Full breakfast served at main loghouse.

Hiking trails, fishing, aircharters and giftshop.

Highway 20
Kleena Kleene, B.C.

Ph/Fax: 250-476-1155
e-mail: logcabin@coyote.chilcotin.bc.ca
www.pixsell.bc.ca/bb/5247.htm

Tweedsmuir Lodge

A Beautiful Lodge Within Tweedsmuir Park

Fishing, Eco Walks and Viewing, winter Heli-skiing - 12 minutes west from Base of "The Hill" Hwy 20. Cabins - Chalets - Dining

Tel/Fax (250) 982-2402

Email: visit@tweedsmuirlodge.com
www.tweedsmuirlodge.com

Tours & Guides

Cariboo Chilcotin Backroad Adventure Tours

Customized sightseeing tours of the cariboo-chilcotin. Camping, ranch stays, atv & snowmo-bile tours, 4x4 tours based out of Clinton BC. Day trips to week long tours.

Box 423

Clinton, BC V0K 1K0

1-866-459-2172
www.backroadadventures.ca
backroadadventures@telus.net

Nuk Tessli Alpine Experience

(Map page 14/G5-6)

For Hikers, Naturalists, Photographers.
Your host:
Best-selling author CHRIS CZAJKOWSKI

Nimpo Lake, BC V0L 1R0

www.chilcotin.bc.ca/nuktessli

Index

IMPORTANT NUMBERS

General
BC Ferries 1-888-223-3779
Enquiry BC 1-800-663-7867
Highways Report 1-800-550-4997
To Report Forest Fires 1-800-663-5555
....*5555 (cellular phones)
Tourism BC 1-800-435-5622
....www.hellobc.com
Updates ....http://www.backroadmapbooks.com
Weather Conditionshttp://www.weatheroffice.ec.gc.ca/canada_e.html

BC Forest Service (Road & Trail Conditions)
Ministry of Forests ....http://www.gov.bc.ca/for/
Cascade(Lillooet)Forest District.................(250)378-8400
Central Coast Forest District........................(250)956-5000
Chilcotin Forest District............................(250)394-4700
Williams Lake Forest District.......................(250)305-2001

Fish & Wildlife
Fish and Wildlife Conservation 1-800-663-9453
Observe, Record and Report
Sport Fishing Information.............. http://www.sportfishing.bc.ca

Parks
BC Parks .... http://wlapwww.gov.bc.ca/bcparks/index.htm
Williams Lake District.............................(250)398-4530
Park Reservations........(604)689-9025 or 1-800-689-9025
....www.discovercamping.ca

Local Clubs & Organizations
Bella Coola Valley Trail and Nature Club (250)799-5508or(250)982-2526
New Caledonia Canoe Club .... (250) 567-4112
Northwest Brigade Paddling Club .... (250) 962-2217
....www.mag-net.com/~paddle/
Red Shreds (Local Cycling Info) .... (250) 398-7873

Math

Activity Book

3

K12 Summit
CURRICULUM

Book Staff and Contributors

Lisa White   *Lead Content Specialist*
Megan Simmons   *Content Specialist*
Lauralyn Vaughn   *Manager, Instructional Design*
Maureen Steddin   *Text Editor*
Tricia Battipede   *Senior Creative Manager*
Jayoung Cho   *Senior Visual Designer*
Caitlin Gildrien   *Visual Designer*
Sheila Smith   *Cover Designer*
Deborah Benton, Dana Crisafulli, Alisa Steel   *Writers*
Amy Eward   *Senior Manager, Writing and Editing*
Abhilasha Parakh   *Senior Project Manager*

Doug McCollum   *Senior Vice President, Product Development*
Kristin Morrison   *Vice President, Design, Creative, and UX*
Kelly Engel   *Senior Director, Curriculum*
Christopher Frescholtz   *Senior Director, Program Management*
Erica Castle   *Director, Creative Services*
Lisa Dimaio Iekel   *Senior Production Manager*

Illustrations Credits

All illustrations © K12 unless otherwise noted.
Characters: Tommy DiGiovanni, Matt Fedor, Ben Gamache, Shannon Palmer
Cover: Fox. © cavemanboon/Getty Images; Fox pup. © DenisProduction.com/Shutterstock; Pastel wallpaper patterns. © mxtama/iStock.
Interior Pattern: Pastel wallpaper patterns. © mxtama/iStock.

About K12 Inc.
K12 Inc. (NYSE: LRN) drives innovation and advances the quality of education by delivering state-of-the-art digital learning platforms and technology to students and school districts around the world. K12 is a company of educators offering its online and blended curriculum to charter schools, public school districts, private schools, and directly to families. More information can be found at K12.com.

ISBN: 978-1-60153-601-3

Printed by Walsworth, Saint Joseph, MI, USA, September 2020

Table of Contents

Fractions

Measurement: Liquid Volume and Mass

Data Displays

Practice Writing Number Names and Numbers in Standard Form

Follow the steps to answer the question.

1. What is the number name of 649?

   a. Write 649 in the place-value chart.

Ones		
hundreds	tens	ones

   b. Write the number name of each digit.

   _____   _____   _____

   c. Write the number name of 649.

   _____

Write the number name.

2. 513

   _____

3. 603

   _____

4. 26

_____

5. 880

_____

Follow the steps to answer the question.

6. What is seven hundred ninety-two in standard form?

   a. Write seven hundred ninety-two in the
      place-value chart.

Ones		
hundreds	tens	ones

   b. Write the number in standard form. _____

Write the number in standard form.

7. four hundred one

   _____

8. three hundred sixty-five

   _____

9. seven hundred fourteen

   _____

10. eighty-one

    _____

Practice Writing Numbers in Standard Form and Expanded Form

Follow the steps to answer the question.

1. What is 388 in expanded form?

    a. Write 388 in the place-value chart.

Ones		
hundreds	tens	ones

    b. Write the value of each digit in standard form.

    _____   _____   _____

    c. Write the expanded form of 388. _____

Write the number in expanded form.

2. 903

3. 678

    _____   _____

4. 24

_____

5. 414

_____

Follow the steps to answer the question.

6. $400 + 90 + 4$

   a. Write $400 + 90 + 4$ in the place-value chart.

Ones		
hundreds	tens	ones

   b. Write the standard form of $400 + 90 + 4$. _____

Write the number in standard form.

7. $600 + 1$

_____

8. $500 + 90$

_____

9. $300 + 20 + 8$

_____

10. $300 + 40 + 9$

_____

Practice Solving Problems with Numbers in Different Forms

Three friends play a beanbag game. Each beanbag scores 1, 10, or 100 points depending on where it lands.

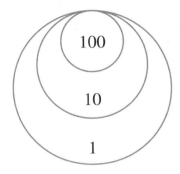

Follow the steps to answer the questions.

1. James lands 3 beanbags in the 100-point area, 4 beanbags in the 10-point area, and 1 beanbag in the 1-point area.

   How many points does James score in all?

   a. Write James's score in expanded form. _____

   b. Write James's score in standard form. _____

   c. James tells his friends his score.

      Write the number name that James says.

      _____

2. Jessica lands 5 beanbags in the 100-point area,
1 beanbag in the 10-point area, and 2 beanbags
in the 1-point area.

How many points does Jessica score in all?

   a. Write Jessica's score in expanded form. _____

   b. Write Jessica's score in standard form. _____

   c. Jessica tells her friends her score.

   Write the number name that Jessica says.

   _____

3. Juan lands 3 beanbags in the 100-point area,
0 beanbags in the 10-point area, and 5 beanbags
in the 1-point area.

How many points does Juan score in all?

   a. Write Juan's score in expanded form. _____

   b. Write Juan's score in standard form. _____

   c. Juan tells his friends his score.

   Write the number name that Juan says.

   _____

Compare and Order Numbers (A)

Practice Comparing Numbers

Follow the steps to compare the numbers.

1. 82 and 79

   a. Plot 82 and 79 on the number line.

   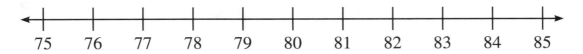

   b. Fill in the blanks to make the sentence true.

   82 is to the _____ of 79, so 82 is _____ than 79.

   c. Write <, >, or = in each box.

   82 ☐ 79   79 ☐ 82

2. 43 and 46

   a. Plot 43 and 46 on the number line.

   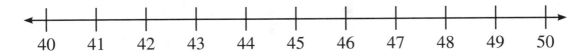

   b. Write <, >, or = in each box.

   43 ☐ 46   46 ☐ 43

3. 851 and 874

a. Write both numbers in the place-value chart.

Ones		
hundreds	tens	ones

b. Write <, >, or = in each box.

8 hundreds ☐ 8 hundreds   5 tens ☐ 7 tens

c. Write <, >, or = in each box.

851 ☐ 874   874 ☐ 851

Compare the numbers. Write <, >, or = in the box.

4. 315 ☐ 92   **5.** 508 ☐ 512

6. 963 ☐ 963   **7.** 794 ☐ 791

8. 400 ☐ 379   **9.** 672 ☐ 627

10. 456 ☐ 456   **11.** 334 ☐ 332

Compare and Order Numbers (B)

Practice Ordering Numbers

Follow the steps to answer the question.

1. Order 57, 53, and 58 from least to greatest.

   a. Plot the numbers on the number line.

   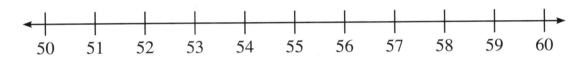

   b. Write the numbers in order from least to greatest.

   _____ < _____ < _____

Order the numbers from least to greatest.

2. 706, 783, 684, 759   _____ < _____ < _____ < _____

3. 543, 534, 43, 540   _____ < _____ < _____ < _____

What does each 2 mean in this number?

220

Follow the steps to answer the question.

4. Order 511, 92, and 510 from greatest to least.

   a. Write each number in the place-value chart.

Ones		
hundreds	tens	ones

   b. Fill in the blanks to complete each statement.

   _____ has no hundreds and is the least value.

   _____ and _____ have the same numbers of hundred and tens.

   _____ has more ones than _____, so it is the greater value.

   c. Write the numbers in order from greatest to least.

   _____ > _____ > _____

Order the numbers from greatest to least.

5. 98, 171, 176, 92   _____ > _____ > _____ > _____

6. 27, 20, 270, 220   _____ > _____ > _____ > _____

Compare and Order Numbers (C)

Practice Comparing and Ordering Numbers in Real-World Problems

A fruit stand has these items.

Item	Amount
apricots	167
bananas	281
apples	285
peaches	164
watermelons	61

Use the table and follow the steps to answer the questions.

1. Does the fruit stand have more apricots or peaches?

   a. Plot the number of apricots and the number of peaches on the number line.

   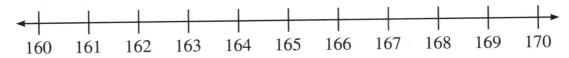

   160   161   162   163   164   165   166   167   168   169   170

   b. Compare the numbers. Write <, >, or = in the box.

   167 ☐ 164

   c. Fill in the blank.

   The fruit stand has more _____ .

2. Order the amounts of fruit from least to greatest.

   a. Write each amount of fruit in the place-value charts.

Ones		
hundreds	tens	ones

Ones		
hundreds	tens	ones

Ones		
hundreds	tens	ones

   b. Fill in the blanks to compare the hundreds.

   _____ has no hundreds and is the least value.

   _____ and _____ both have _____ hundred.

   _____ and _____ both have _____ hundreds.

   c. Fill in the blanks to compare the tens.

   _____ and _____ both have _____ tens.

   _____ and _____ both have _____ tens.

   d. Fill in the blanks to compare the ones.

   _____ has more ones than _____, so it is the greater value.

   _____ has more ones than _____, so it is the greater value.

   e. Order the numbers from least to greatest.

   _____ < _____ < _____ < _____ < _____

Rounding Numbers (A)

Practice Rounding a 2-Digit Number to Nearest 10

Follow the steps to answer the questions.

1. What is 57 rounded to the nearest ten?

    a. Plot 57 on the number line.

    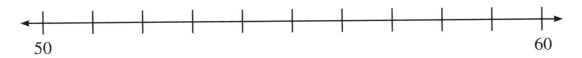

    50   60

    b. Fill in the blanks.

    57 is between _____ and _____.

    57 is closer to _____, so 57 rounds to _____.

2. What is 64 rounded to the nearest ten?

    a. Write 64 in the place-value chart.

Ones		
hundreds	tens	ones

I love to round!

b. Fill in the blanks.

64 is between _____ and _____ .

Use the _____ place to round to the nearest ten.

The digit _____ rounds _____ .

64 rounds to _____ .

Round to the nearest ten.

3. 26 _____

4. 43 _____

5. 12 _____

6. 95 _____

7. 25 _____

8. 13 _____

9. 59 _____

10. 74 _____

Rounding Numbers (B)

Practice Rounding a 3-Digit Number to Nearest 100

Follow the steps to answer the questions.

1. What is 143 rounded to the nearest hundred?

   a. Plot 143 on the number line.

   100   200

   b. Fill in the blanks.

   143 is between _____ and _____ .

   143 is closer to _____ , so 143 rounds to _____ .

2. What is 850 rounded to the nearest hundred?

   a. Write 850 in the place-value chart.

Ones		
hundreds	tens	ones

b. Fill in the blanks.

850 is between _____ and _____.

Use the _____ place to round to the nearest hundred.

The digit _____ rounds _____.

850 rounds to _____.

Round to the nearest hundred.

3. 652 _____

4. 719 _____

5. 949 _____

6. 150 _____

7. 406 _____

8. 245 _____

9. 350 _____

10. 117 _____

Practice Rounding a 3-Digit Number to Nearest 10

Follow the steps to answer the questions.

1. What is 853 rounded to the nearest ten?

   a. Plot 853 on the number line.

   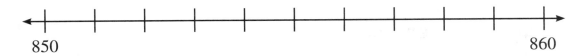

   850   860

   b. Fill in the blanks.

   853 is between _____ and _____ .

   853 is closer to _____ , so 853 rounds to _____ .

2. What is 217 rounded to the nearest ten?

   a. Write 217 in the place-value chart.

Ones		
hundreds	tens	ones

b. Fill in the blanks.

217 is between _____ and _____.

Use the _____ place to round to the nearest ten.

The digit _____ rounds _____.

217 rounds to _____.

Round to the nearest ten.

3. 785 _____

4. 997 _____

5. 354 _____

6. 192 _____

7. 335 _____

8. 709 _____

9. 105 _____

10. 604 _____

Rounding Numbers (D)

Practice Rounding in Real-World Problems

Aisha writes down how long she spends on activities one weekend. Her times are in this table.

Activity	Time (minutes)
reading	204
hiking	293
playing sports	75
sleeping	962

Use the table and follow the steps to answer the question.

1. About how long does Aisha spend playing sports?
   Round to the nearest ten minutes.

   a. Plot 75 on the number line.

   70   80

There is a rounding rule for 5!

b. Describe how you know whether to round 75 up or down.

_____

_____

_____

c. Fill in the blank.

Aisha spends about  minutes playing sports.

Use the table to answer the questions.

2. About how long does Aisha spend sleeping?
Round to the nearest hundred minutes.

about _____ minutes

3. About how long does Aisha spend reading?
Round to the nearest ten minutes.

about _____ minutes

4. About how long does Aisha spend hiking?
Round to the nearest hundred minutes.

about _____ minutes

Practice Estimating Sums

Answer the questions.

1. What is a compatible number?

    _____

    _____

2. What two numbers do compatible numbers usually end in?

    _____

Fill in the blanks.

3. Estimate the sum $48 + 19$ by rounding to the nearest ten.

    a. 48 rounds to _____ and 19 rounds to _____ .

    b. The estimated sum is _____ .

4. Estimate the sum $517 + 268$ by rounding to the
    nearest hundred.

    a. 517 rounds to _____ and 268 rounds to _____ .

    b. The estimated sum is _____ .

5. Estimate the sum $385 + 196$ by rounding to the nearest hundred.

   a. 385 rounds to _____ and 196 rounds to _____.

   b. The estimated sum is _____.

6. Estimate the sum $52 + 23$ using compatible numbers.

   a. 52 is compatible to _____ and 23 is compatible to _____.

   b. The estimated sum is _____.

7. Estimate the sum $219 + 548$ using compatible numbers.

   a. 219 is compatible to _____ and 548 is compatible

   to _____.

   b. The estimated sum is _____.

8. Estimate the sum $187 + 301$ using compatible numbers.

   a. 187 is compatible to _____ and 301 is compatible

   to _____.

   b. The estimated sum is _____.

Practice Estimating Differences

Fill in the blanks.

1. Estimate the difference 63 − 41 by rounding to the nearest ten.

   a. 63 rounds to _____ and 41 rounds to _____ .

   b. The estimated difference is _____ .

2. Estimate the difference 56 − 18 by rounding to the nearest ten.

   a. 56 rounds to _____ and 18 rounds to _____ .

   b. The estimated difference is _____ .

3. Estimate the difference 935 − 294 by rounding to the nearest hundred.

   a. 935 rounds to _____ and 294 rounds to

   _____ .

   b. The estimated difference is _____ .

4. Estimate the difference 413 − 268 by rounding to the nearest hundred.

    a. 413 rounds to _____ and 268 rounds to _____ .

    b. The estimated difference is _____ .

5. Estimate the difference 98 − 27 using compatible numbers.

    a. 98 is compatible to _____ and 27 is compatible to _____ .

    b. The estimated difference is _____ .

6. Estimate the difference 848 − 621 using compatible numbers.

    a. 848 is compatible to _____ and 621 is compatible

    to _____ .

    b. The estimated difference is _____ .

7. Estimate the difference 579 − 214 using compatible numbers.

    a. 579 is compatible to _____ and 214 is compatible

    to _____ .

    b. The estimated difference is _____ .

Strategies for Exact Sums and Differences (A)

Practice Using Strategies to Add or Subtract

Fill in the boxes and blanks.

1. Use the number line to find $354 + 123$.

   a. Model the sum on the number line.

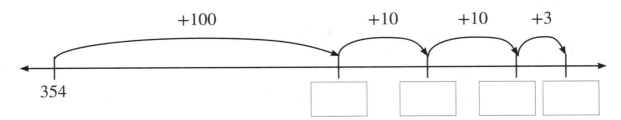

   b. $354 + 123 =$ _____

2. Use the number line to find $903 - 86$.

   a. Model the difference on the number line.

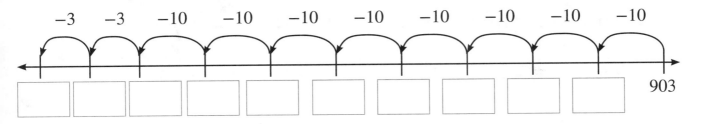

   b. $903 - 86 =$ _____

3. Use compatible numbers to find $435 + 357$.

    a. A good compatible number for 357 is _____.

    b. Move _____ from 435 to 357 to make the numbers compatible.

    c. The compatible numbers are _____ and _____.

    d. The sum is _____.

4. Use compatible numbers to find $698 - 282$.

    a. A good compatible number for 698 is _____.

    b. Add _____ to both numbers to make them compatible.

    c. The compatible numbers are _____ and _____.

    d. The difference is _____.

Find the sum or difference. Show your work.

5. $193 + 236 =$ _____

6. $968 - 613 =$ _____

7. $704 - 156 =$ _____

8. $615 + 148 =$ _____

Practice Using Properties to Add

Fill in the blanks.

1. You can add 0 to any number using the _____ property of addition.

2. You can change the order of addends without changing the sum

   because of the _____ property of addition.

3. You can group addends differently without changing the sum

   because of the _____ property of addition.

Follow the steps to find the sum.

4. $175 + 0$

   a. Remember that the sum of any number and 0

      is _____ .

   b. Apply the property to add. _____

You can use properties to add and subtract.

5. $53 + 89 + 47$

    a. Change the order of the numbers.

        _____ + _____ + 89

    b. Use mental math to find the sum. _____

6. $460 + 245 + 140$

    a. Change the order of the numbers.

        _____ + _____ + _____

    b. Use mental math to find the sum. _____

7. $35 + 85 + 72$

    a. Place parentheses around the two numbers that should be added first.

        $35 + 85 + 72$

    b. Use mental math to find the sum. _____

8. $163 + 172 + 128$

    a. Place parentheses around the two numbers that should be added first.

        $163 + 172 + 128$

    b. Use mental math to find the sum. _____

Strategies for Exact Sums and Differences (C)

Practice Using the Break Apart Strategy

Follow the steps to find the sum.

1. $174 + 552$

    a. Break apart each number into expanded form.

    $174 = $ _____ $+$ _____ $+$ _____

    $552 = $ _____ $+$ _____ $+$ _____

    b. Add each place value. Sum $=$ _____ $+$ _____ $+$ _____

    c. Write the sum in standard form. Sum $=$ _____

2. $286 + 317$

    a. Break apart each number into expanded form.

    $286 = $ _____ $+$ _____ $+$ _____

    $317 = $ _____ $+$ _____ $+$ _____

    b. Add each place value. Sum $=$ _____ $+$ _____ $+$ _____

    c. Write the sum in standard form. Sum $=$ _____

Follow the steps to find the difference.

3. 976 – 145

    a. Break apart each number into expanded form.

        976 = _____ + _____ + _____

        145 = _____ + _____ + _____

    b. Subtract each place value.

        Difference = _____ + _____ + _____

    c. Write the difference in standard form.

        Difference = _____

4. 799 – 604

    a. Break apart each number into expanded form.

        799 = _____ + _____ + _____

        604 = _____ + _____ + _____

    b. Subtract each place value.

        Difference = _____ + _____ + _____

    c. Write the difference in standard form.

        Difference = _____

TRY IT

Using a Standard Addition Algorithm (A)

Practice Adding Vertically to 100

Follow the steps to find the sum.

1. Use the place-value chart to find $36 + 53$.

Ones		
hundreds	tens	ones
+		

a. Write the digits of each number in the place-value chart.

b. Add each place value.

2. Use the place-value chart to find $29 + 27$.

Ones		
hundreds	tens	ones
+		

a. Write the digits of each number in the place-value chart.

b. Add the ones and regroup:

$9 + 7 =$ ______

$=$ ______ ten and ______ ones

c. Add the tens.

Add.

3. $54 + 31 = $ _____

4. $28 + 48 = $ _____

5. $39 + 61 = $ _____

6. $23 + 45 = $ _____

7. $33 + 64 = $ _____

Sometimes you must regroup when you add!

8. $15 + 39 = $ _____

Using a Standard Addition Algorithm (B)

Practice Adding Vertically to $1,000$

Follow the steps to find the sum.

1. Use the place-value chart to find $263 + 125$.

	Ones		
	hundreds	tens	ones
+			

   a. Write the digits of each number in the place-value chart.

   b. Add each place value.

2. Use the place-value chart to find $458 + 267$.

	Ones		
	hundreds	tens	ones
+			

   a. Write the digits of each number in the place-value chart.

   b. Add the ones and regroup:

   $8 + 7 =$ _____

   $=$ _____ ten and _____ ones

   c. Add the tens and regroup:

   $1 + 5 + 6 =$ _____ tens $=$ _____ hundred and _____ tens

   d. Add the hundreds.

Add.

3. $175 + 394 =$ _____

4. $217 + 640 =$ _____

5. $803 + 165 =$ _____

6. $439 + 561 =$ _____

7. $537 + 445 =$ _____

8. $629 + 182 =$ _____

Using a Standard Addition Algorithm (C)

Practice Solving Problems with Addition

Answer the questions. Show your work in the place-value chart.

1. A party supply store has 309 blue balloons. The store has 73 more green balloons than blue balloons.

   a. How many green balloons does the store have?

Ones		
hundreds	tens	ones

   b. How many green and blue balloons combined does the store have?

Ones		
hundreds	tens	ones

c. The party supply store also has 256 red balloons and 587 orange balloons.

How many red and orange balloons combined does the store have?

	Ones	
hundreds	tens	ones
+		

Add.

2. Kiki has 192 pumpkin seeds and 399 watermelon seeds.

   How many seeds does Kiki have altogether?

   _____ seeds

3. A farmer has 245 pounds of green beans and 103 pounds of peas.

   How many pounds of green beans and peas does the farmer have altogether?

   _____ pounds

4. A fish store has 123 fish. The store receives 219 more fish.

   How many fish does the store have altogether?

   _____ fish

5. Jake's club collects 273 cans and 160 bottles to be recycled.

   How many items does Jake's club collect altogether?

   _____ items

Using a Standard Subtraction Algorithm (A)

Practice Subtracting Vertically without Regrouping

Follow the steps to find the difference.

1. Use the place-value chart to find 68 − 41.

    a. Write the digits of each number in the place-value chart.

    b. Subtract each place value.

Ones		
hundreds	tens	ones

2. Use the place-value chart to find 884 − 71.

    a. Write the digits of each number in the place-value chart.

    b. Subtract each place value.

Ones		
hundreds	tens	ones

I always subtract from right to left!

3. Use the place-value chart to find 537 − 123.

	Ones	
hundreds	tens	ones

   a. Write the digits of each number in the place-value chart.

   b. Subtract each place value.

Subtract.

4. 87 − 25 = _____

5. 708 − 403 = _____

6. 592 − 71 = _____

7. 999 − 894 = _____

Using a Standard Subtraction Algorithm (B)

Practice Subtracting Vertically to 100 with Regrouping

Follow the steps to find the difference.

1. Use the place-value chart to find
   74 − 25.

   a. Write the digits of each number
      in the place-value chart.

   b. Regroup one ten.

   c. Subtract each place value.

Ones		
hundreds	tens	ones

2. Use the place-value chart to find
   86 − 28.

   a. Write the digits of each number
      in the place-value chart.

   b. Regroup one ten.

   c. Subtract each place value.

Ones		
hundreds	tens	ones

3. Use the place-value chart to find 60 – 14.

   a. Write the digits of each number in the place-value chart.

   b. Regroup one ten.

   c. Subtract each place value.

Ones		
hundreds	tens	ones

Subtract.

4. 51 – 37 = _____

5. 82 – 47 = _____

6. 96 – 28 = _____

7. 75 – 29 = _____

Using a Standard Subtraction Algorithm (C)

Practice Subtracting Vertically to 1,000 with Regrouping

Follow the steps to find the difference.

1. Use the place-value chart to find 826 − 149.

   a. Write the digits of each number in the place-value chart.

   b. Regroup one ten. Then subtract the ones.

   c. Regroup one hundred. Then subtract the tens.

   d. Subtract the hundreds.

	Ones	
hundreds	tens	ones

2. Use the place-value chart to find 509 − 234.

   a. Write the digits of each number in the place-value chart.

   b. Subtract the ones.

   c. Regroup one hundred. Then subtract the tens.

   d. Subtract the hundreds.

	Ones	
hundreds	tens	ones

3. Use the place-value chart to find
   783 − 316.

Ones		
hundreds	tens	ones

   a. Write the digits of each number
      in the place-value chart.

   b. Regroup one ten. Then subtract
      the ones.

   c. Subtract the tens.

   d. Subtract the hundreds.

Subtract.

4. 732 − 198 = _____

5. 407 − 382 = _____

6. 814 − 75 = _____

7. 681 − 483 = _____

Practice Solving Problems with Addition and Subtraction

This table shows the number of tickets that were sold for each movie at a theater on a Saturday. Use the table to answer the questions.

Movie	Number of Tickets Sold
A	349
B	731
C	258
D	88

1. How many more tickets were sold to Movie C than to Movie D?

   a. I must _____ to find the difference in tickets.

   b. Show your work to find the answer.

   _____ tickets

2. How many tickets were sold to Movie B and Movie C in all?

   a. I must _____ to find the total.

   b. Show your work to find the answer.

      _____ tickets

3. How many more tickets were sold to Movie B than to all other movies combined?

   a. I must _____ then _____ to find the answer.

   b. Show your work to find the answer.

      _____ tickets

Solve.

4. A shop sells 280 sandwiches in one week.
The shop sells 545 sandwiches the next week.

How many more sandwiches did the shop
sell the second week?   _____ sandwiches

5. An art gallery has 458 paintings in its collection.
The gallery purchases 257 more paintings.

How many paintings does the art gallery
have after their purchase?   _____ paintings

Practice Finding the Perimeter of Shapes

Follow the steps to find the perimeter.

1. Find the perimeter of this rectangle.

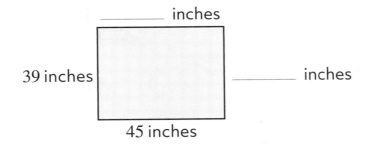

_____ inches

39 inches

_____ inches

45 inches

   a. Write in the missing side lengths.

   b. Finish the equation that can be used to find the perimeter.

$$P = \rule{8cm}{0.4pt}$$

   c. What is the perimeter? _____ inches

2. Find the perimeter of this shape.

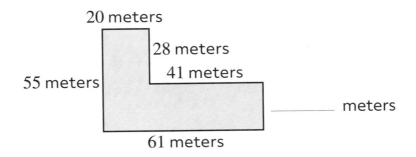

20 meters

28 meters

41 meters

55 meters

_____ meters

61 meters

   a. Write in the missing side length.

b. Finish the equation that can be used to find the perimeter.

$P =$ _____

c. What is the perimeter? _____ meters

Find the perimeter.

3.

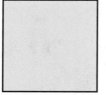

4 centimeters

$P =$ _____ centimeters

4.

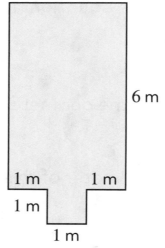

8 cm   1 cm

Note: *cm* stands for "centimeter."

$P =$ _____ centimeters

5.

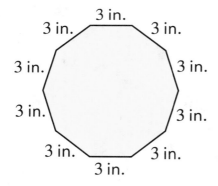

3 in. 3 in. 3 in.
3 in. 3 in.
3 in. 3 in.
3 in. 3 in.
3 in.

Note: *in.* stands for "inch."

$P =$ _____ inches

6.

6 m

1 m   1 m

1 m

1 m

Note: *m* stands for "meter."

$P =$ _____ meters

Practice Finding Missing Side Lengths

Follow the steps to find the missing side length.

1. The perimeter of this triangle is 128 centimeters.

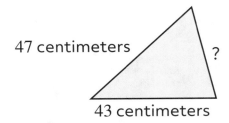

47 centimeters

?

43 centimeters

   a. Subtract one side length from the perimeter:

   128 – _____ = _____

   b. Now subtract the other side length from the difference: _____

   c. What is the missing side length? _____ centimeters

2. The perimeter of this pentagon is 138 feet.

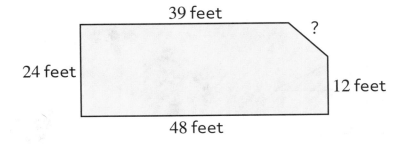

39 feet

?

24 feet

12 feet

48 feet

   a. Find the sum of the four known side lengths: _____

b. Subtract the sum of the known side lengths from

the perimeter: _____

c. What is the missing side length? _____ feet

Use the figure to find the missing side length.

3. $P = 23$ feet

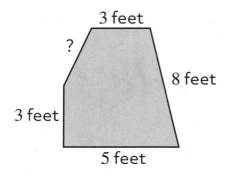

3 feet

?

8 feet

3 feet

5 feet

What is the missing side

length? _____ feet

4. $P = 60$ centimeters

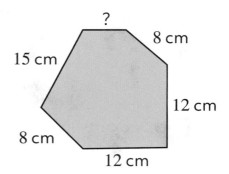

?

8 cm

15 cm

12 cm

8 cm

12 cm

Note: *cm* stands for "centimeter."

What is the missing side

length? _____ centimeters

5. $P = 12$ inches

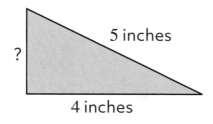

5 inches

?

4 inches

What is the missing side

length? _____ inches

Perimeter is the distance around a figure!

Perimeter (C)

Practice Finding Perimeter in Real-World Problems

Follow the steps to solve the problem.

1. A pillow is in the shape of a triangle. The trim around the edge of the pillow is 87 centimeters long.

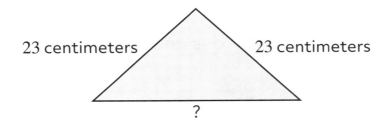

23 centimeters   23 centimeters

?

Find the length of the third side of the pillow.

a. Subtract one side length from the perimeter:

87 − _____ = _____

b. Subtract the other side length from the difference: _____

c. What is the missing side length? _____ centimeters

2. A designer sews trim around the edges of 2 pillows. Each pillow is in the shape of this rectangle.

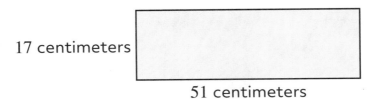

17 centimeters

51 centimeters

Find the amount of trim the designer uses.

a. Finish the equation that can be used to find the perimeter of one pillow.

$P =$ _____

b. Find the perimeter of one pillow. _____ centimeters

c. Write and solve an equation to find the amount of trim

used for two pillows. _____

d. How much trim does the designer use? _____ centimeters

Solve.

3. There are 64 squares on this game board. Each small square is 1 inch long.

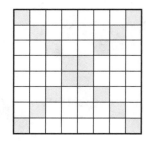

What is the perimeter of the game board?

_____ inches

4. The perimeter of this street sign is 122 inches.

25 inches   25 inches

18 inches   18 inches

?

What is the missing side length?

_____ inches

Skip Counting Patterns (A)

Practice Skip Counting by 5s and 10s

Fill in the boxes.

1. Use the number line to skip count by 5.

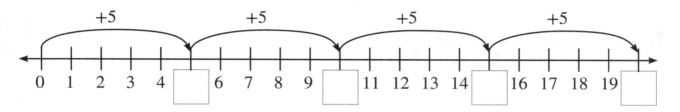

2. Use the number line to skip count by 10.

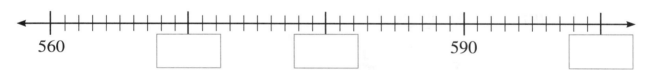

Fill in the blank to complete the pattern.

3. 420, 430, _____, 450, 460

4. 585, _____, 595, 600, 605

5. 735, 740, 745, _____, 755

6. 20, 30, 40, 50, _____, 70, 80

Answer the questions.

7. Start at 450 and skip count by 10.

    How many times must you skip count by 10 to get 500? _____

8. Start at 900 and skip count by 5.

    How many times must you skip count by 5 to get 915? _____

9. Start at 520. Skip count by 10 eight times.

    What number do you get? _____

10. Start at 150. Skip count by 5 seven times.

    What number do you get? _____

Figure out whether to add 5 or 10!

Skip Counting Patterns (B)

Practice Skip Counting by 2s and 3s

Fill in the boxes.

1. Use the number line to skip count by 3.

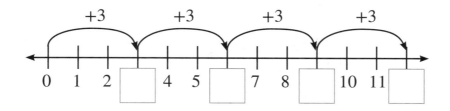

2. Use the number line to skip count by 2.

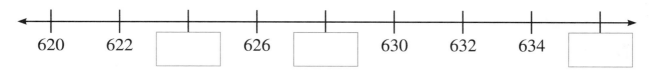

Fill in the blank to complete the pattern.

3. 447, 450, 453, —————, 459

4. 963, 966, —————, 972, 975

5. 36, 38, —————, 42, 44, 46, 48

6. 192, —————, 196, 198, 200

Answer the questions.

7. Start at 762 and skip count by 2.

   How many times must you skip count by 2 to get 778? _____

8. Start at 33 and skip count by 3.

   How many times must you skip count by 3 to get 51? _____

9. Start at 146. Skip count by 2 four times.

   What number do you get? _____

10. Start at 270. Skip count by 3 five times.

    What number do you get? _____

You can use patterns to skip count!

Practice Skip Counting Patterns

Answer the questions.

1. Jordan counts, "630, 636, 642, 648, 654, 660."

   What number does Jordan use to skip count? _____

2. Divya counts, "768, 776, 784, 792, 800, 808."

   What number does Divya use to skip count? _____

3. You can skip count to 20 using two different numbers.

   a. Start at 0 and skip count by 4 to 20 on the
      number line.

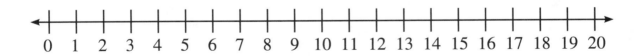

   b. How many times do you skip count by 4 to get 20? _____

c. Start at 0 and skip count by 5 to 20 on the number line.

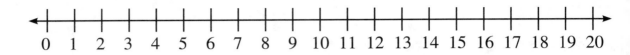

d. How many times do you skip count by 5 to get 20? _____

Fill in the boxes.

4. +7 +7 +7 +7

0, ☐ , ☐ , ☐ , ☐

5. +9 +9 +9 +9

63, ☐ , ☐ , ☐ , ☐

Fill in the blank to complete the pattern.

6. 777, 784, 791, _____ , 805

7. 150, _____ , 162, 168, 174

8. 441, 450, _____ , 468, 477

9. _____ , 380, 384, 388, 392

10. 80, 88, _____ , 104, 112

Practice Modeling and Representing Multiplication

Follow the instructions.

1. There are different ways to think about the
    multiplication expression 4 × 3.

    a. Fill in the blanks: 4 × 3 means _____ groups of _____.

    b. Draw a dot model of 4 × 3.

    c. Skip count on the number line to model 4 × 3.

    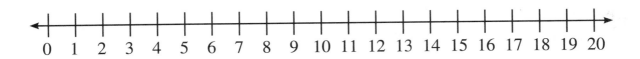

    d. What is 4 × 3? _____

2. There are different ways to think about the
    multiplication expression 8 × 5.

    a. Fill in the blanks: 8 × 5 means _____ groups of _____.

    b. Draw a dot model to represent the multiplication expression.

    c. What is 8 × 5? _____

Write a multiplication equation to represent the model.

3.

4.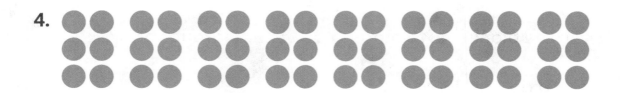

Multiply.

5. 2×8 _____

6. 5×9 _____

7. 7×3 _____

8. 4×10 _____

Practice Using Arrays and Working with Commutative Property

Follow the instructions.

1. Natalie plants 40 roses in her garden. She plants the roses in 5 rows with 8 roses in each row.

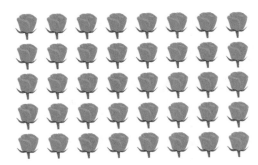

   a. Fill in the blanks to represent the array of roses.

   _____ × _____ = 40

   b. Natalie also plants 40 tulips. This time she plants 8 rows with the same number of tulips in each row.

   How many tulips are in each row? _____

   c. Draw an array to model Natalie's tulips.

   d. Fill in the blanks to represent the array of tulips.

   _____ × _____ = 40

Draw an array to model the multiplication expression.

2. 2×3

3. 4×6

Write a multiplication equation to represent the array.

4.

_____

5. ● ● ● ● ● ● ● ● ● ●
● ● ● ● ● ● ● ● ● ●

_____

6. ▲ ▲ ▲ ▲ ▲ ▲
▲ ▲ ▲ ▲ ▲ ▲
▲ ▲ ▲ ▲ ▲ ▲
▲ ▲ ▲ ▲ ▲ ▲
▲ ▲ ▲ ▲ ▲ ▲
▲ ▲ ▲ ▲ ▲ ▲

_____

7. ★ ★ ★ ★ ★ ★ ★
★ ★ ★ ★ ★ ★ ★
★ ★ ★ ★ ★ ★ ★
★ ★ ★ ★ ★ ★ ★
★ ★ ★ ★ ★ ★ ★

_____

Fill in the blanks.

8. $6 \times 7 = 42$, so $7 \times 6 =$ _____ .

9. $5 \times 10 = 50$, so _____ $\times$ _____ $= 50$.

Practice Multiplying by 0 and 1

Fill in the blanks.

1. The identity property of multiplication says that any

   number times _____ is itself.

2. The zero property of multiplication says that any

   number times 0 equals _____ .

Write the missing factor in the box.

3. $4 \times \boxed{} = 4$

4. $\boxed{} \times 6 = 0$

5. $\boxed{} \times 10 = 10$

6. $8 \times \boxed{} = 0$

7. $\boxed{} \times 9 = 9$

8. $3 \times \boxed{} = 3$

Multiply.

9. 5×1 _____

10. 1×6 _____

11. 9×0 _____

12. 0×1 _____

13. 1×1 _____

14. 10×0 _____

15. 0×5 _____

16. 2×1 _____

17. 0×0 _____

18. 1×5 _____

Practice Multiplying by 10

Fill in the blanks.

1. The product of 10 and a number always ends in _____.

2. To multiply by 10, you can skip count by _____.

3. Jordan has 3 boxes of markers. Each box has 10 markers.

   How many markers does Jordan have?

   $3 \times 10 =$ _____   Jordan has _____ markers.

4. Eloise has 10 baskets of apples. Each basket has 6 apples.

   How many apples does Eloise have?

   $10 \times 6 =$ _____   Eloise has _____ apples.

5. A group of children run relay races. There are 5 teams with 10 children on each team.

   How many children run in the relay races?

   $5 \times 10 =$ _____   _____ children run in the races.

Multiply.

6. 7×10 _____

7. 4×10 _____

8. 10×2 _____

9. 10×9 _____

10. 3×10 _____

11. 10×10 _____

12. 1×10 _____

13. 10×0 _____

14. 2×10 _____

15. 10×6 _____

16. 10×5 _____

17. 9×10 _____

18. 10×7 _____

19. 8×10 _____

Practice Multiplying by 5

Fill in the blanks.

1. The product of 5 and a number always ends in _____ or _____.

2. To multiply by 5, you can skip count by _____.

3. Eloise has 5 bags. Each bag has 6 crackers.

    How many crackers does Eloise have in all?

    $5 \times 6 =$ _____   Eloise has _____ crackers.

4. Aisha reads her book for 3 days. She reads 5 pages each day.

    How many pages does Aisha read in all?

    $3 \times 5 =$ _____   Aisha reads _____ pages.

5. Cans of paint are placed on 5 shelves. Each shelf has
    8 cans of paint.

    How many cans of paint are on the shelves in all?

    $5 \times 8 =$ _____   The shelves have _____ cans.

Multiply.

6. 4×5 _____

7. 8×5 _____

8. 5×2 _____

9. 5×9 _____

10. 6×5 _____

11. 5×3 _____

12. 1×5 _____

13. 5×0 _____

14. 7×5 _____

15. 5×6 _____

16. 5×5 _____

17. 9×5 _____

18. 5×8 _____

19. 5×4 _____

Practice Multiplying by 2 and 4

Follow the instructions.

1. This model has counters in equal groups.

    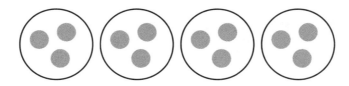

    a. Fill in the blanks: The model has _____ equal groups with

        _____ counters in each group. The model has a total of

        _____ counters.

    b. Write an equation for this model. _____

2. Draw a model to find 2×6.

    $2 \times 6 =$ _____

3. Skip count on the number line to find 5×2.

    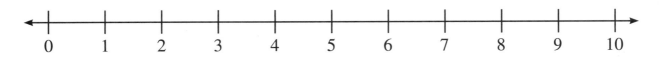

    $5 \times 2 =$ ☐

4. Skip count on the number line to find 6×4.

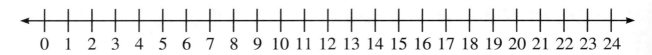

$6 \times 4 = $ ⬚

5. Describe how to use doubles to find 4×7.

_____

_____

Multiply.

6. 3×2 _____

7. 2×5 _____

8. 4×4 _____

9. 4×9 _____

10. 2×2 _____

11. 8×4 _____

12. 4×5 _____

13. 2×8 _____

Multiplication Patterns (B)

Practice Multiplying by 3 and 6

Follow the instructions.

1. This table shows some multiplication facts for 6. The products follow a pattern.

Multiplication Expression	Product
2×6	12
3×6	18
4×6	24
5×6	30
6×6	36

a. State a pattern that you notice.

_____

b. Explain the pattern.

_____

_____

2. Draw a model to find 3×4.

$3 \times 4 = \boxed{}$

3. Skip count on the number line to find 3×6.

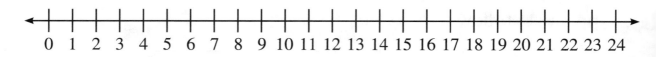

$3 \times 6 = \boxed{}$

4. Describe how to use doubles to find 6×6.

_____

_____

Multiply.

5. 3×8 _____

6. 9×6 _____

7. 5×6 _____

8. 6×1 _____

9. 2×6 _____

10. 6×4 _____

11. 7×6 _____

12. 3×7 _____

Multiplication Patterns (C)

Practice Understanding the Distributive Property

Follow the instructions.

1. Fill in the boxes to find 3×6.

$$3 \times 6 = \left(3 \times \boxed{}\right) + \left(\boxed{} \times 1\right)$$

$$3 \times 6 = \boxed{} + \boxed{}$$

$$3 \times 6 = \boxed{}$$

2. Draw a line to break apart this array to show the equation $4 \times 4 = (4 \times 2) + (4 \times 2)$.

3. Jeremy finds 4×6. He finds the sums $4 + 5$ and $4 + 1$. Then Jeremy multiplies the sums. Is Jeremy correct? Explain.

_____

_____

Draw a line to break apart the array. Then write the product.

4.

$4 \times 9 =$ _____

5.

$4 \times 8 =$ _____

6.

$6 \times 9 =$ _____

Practice Multiplying by 7

Follow the instructions.

1. This array represents 7×4.

    a. Draw a line to break the array into two equal groups.

    b. Fill in the boxes to find 7×4.

    $$7 \times 4 = \left(7 \times \boxed{}\right) + \left(7 \times \boxed{}\right)$$

    $$7 \times 4 = \boxed{} + \boxed{}$$

    $$7 \times 4 = \boxed{}$$

2. Skip count on the number line to find 7×3.

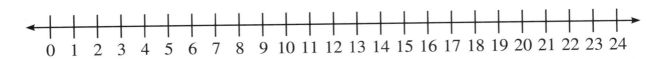

$7 \times 3 = \boxed{}$

3. Describe how to use doubles to find 7×6.

_____

_____

Answer the question.

4. Jane walks her dog 7 miles each week.

   How many miles does she walk her dog in 10 weeks? _____

Multiply.

5. 7×6 _____

6. 3×7 _____

7. 0×7 _____

8. 7×5 _____

9. 7×1 _____

10. 7×7 _____

11. 8×7 _____

12. 7×9 _____

Strategies for Multiplying (A)

Practice Understanding the Associative Property

Follow the steps to find the product.

1. $9 \times 2 \times 5$

   a. Write parentheses in each expression to group the factors two different ways.

      $9 \times 2 \times 5$ $9 \times 2 \times 5$

   b. Choose which expression you will use to find the product. Explain your choice.

   _____

   _____

   c. Find the product. _____

Rewrite the expression to regroup the factors. Then find the product.

2. $2 \times (3 \times 7)$ 3. $6 \times (7 \times 2)$ 4. $(6 \times 2) \times 2$ 5. $5 \times (2 \times 4)$

   _____   _____   _____   _____

   _____   _____   _____   _____

Use the associative property to find the product.

6. $7 \times 2 \times 2$

_____

7. $2 \times 3 \times 9$

_____

8. $7 \times 9 \times 1$

_____

9. $4 \times 2 \times 5$

_____

10. $2 \times 2 \times 4$

_____

11. $8 \times 7 \times 1$

_____

12. $3 \times 0 \times 9$

_____

13. $6 \times 2 \times 3$

_____

Answer the questions.

14. A roller coaster has 4 cars. Each car has 3 rows of seats. Each row has 2 seats.

How many seats does the roller coaster have? _____

15. Stella feeds her cat twice a day. She gives her cat 4 ounces of food at each feeding.

How many ounces of food does Stella feed her cat

in 6 days? _____

16. Bela drinks 5 ounces of milk twice each day.

How much milk does he drink in 7 days? _____

Strategies for Multiplying (B)

Practice Multiplying by 8 and 9

Follow the steps to find the product.

1. 8×3

   a. Double 3 to get _____.

   b. Double again to get _____.

   c. Double one last time to get _____.

Follow the instructions.

2. This table shows some multiplication facts for 9. The products follow a pattern.

   a. State a pattern that you notice.

   _____

   _____

   _____

Multiplication Expression	Product
2×9	18
3×9	27
4×9	36
5×9	45
6×9	54

   b. Explain the pattern.

   _____

   _____

Multiply.

3. 9×7 _____

4. 8×6 _____

5. 9×3 _____

6. 4×9 _____

7. 9×2 _____

8. 6×9 _____

Answer the questions.

9. Rita saved $5. Paco saved 9 times as much money as Rita.

   How much did Paco save? _____

10. How are doubles used to find 8×9?

    _____

    _____

11. Dante says he can use doubles to find 9×7. Is Dante correct? Explain.

    _____

    _____

Can I always use doubles to multiply?

Strategies for Multiplying (C)

Practice Finding an Unknown Factor

Follow the steps to find the unknown factor n.

1. $n \times 8 = 32$

   a. Add rows to the array to show 32 counters with 8 counters in each row.

   b. Fill in the blanks: The array has _____ rows of counters.

   So the unknown factor n is _____ .

Finding an unknown factor is like a puzzle!

Use the multiplication table to find the unknown factor.

Multiplication Table

×	1	2	3	4	5	6	7	8	9	10
1	1	2	3	4	5	6	7	8	9	10
2	2	4	6	8	10	12	14	16	18	20
3	3	6	9	12	15	18	21	24	27	30
4	4	8	12	16	20	24	28	32	36	40
5	5	10	15	20	25	30	35	40	45	50
6	6	12	18	24	30	36	42	48	54	60
7	7	14	21	28	35	42	49	56	63	70
8	8	16	24	32	40	48	56	64	72	80
9	9	18	27	36	45	54	63	72	81	90
10	10	20	30	40	50	60	70	80	90	100

2. $n \times 2 = 8$

3. $7 \times ? = 42$

4. $? \times 9 = 81$

5. $5 \times n = 40$

6. $? \times 6 = 36$

7. $n \times 4 = 12$

8. $4 \times a = 28$

9. $3 \times ? = 24$

10. $6 \times n = 30$

11. $9 \times b = 45$

12. $8 \times ? = 72$

13. $3 \times n = 6$

14. $9 \times ? = 54$

15. $n \times 7 = 49$

Strategies for Multiplying (D)

Practice Multiplying by Multiples of 10

Follow the steps to find the product.

1. Use the associative property to find 2×40.

   a. Think of 40 as _____ $\times 10$.

   $2 \times 40 = 2 \times \left(\boxed{} \times 10 \right)$

   b. Draw parentheses to regroup the factors.

   $2 \times 40 = 2 \times \boxed{} \times 10$

   c. Multiply.

   $2 \times 40 = \boxed{} \times 10$

   $2 \times 40 = \boxed{}$

2. Use the associative property to find 5×20.

   $5 \times 20 = 5 \times \left(\boxed{} \times 10 \right)$

   $5 \times 20 = \left(5 \times \boxed{} \right) \times 10$

   $5 \times 20 = \boxed{} \times 10$

   $5 \times 20 = \boxed{}$

3. Use place value to find 6×50.

$$6 \times 50 = 6 \times \boxed{} \text{ tens}$$

$$= \boxed{} \text{ tens}$$

$$= \boxed{}$$

Multiply.

4. 6×20

5. 9×50

6. 70×3

7. 6×40

_____

_____

_____

_____

8. 20×8

9. 5×90

10. 8×80

11. 6×70

_____

_____

_____

_____

Answer the question.

12. Kelly buys 3 packs of string cheese. Each pack has 20 pieces of cheese.

How many pieces of cheese does Kelly buy in all? _____

Problem Solving with Multiplication (A)

Practice Finding Unknown Products in Real-World Problems

Follow the steps to solve the problem.

1. Simone makes 4 posters. She puts 9 stickers on each poster.
   How many stickers does Simone use in all?

   a. Use base-10 blocks to make 4 groups of 9. Draw
      your model.

   b. Regroup the ones cubes into tens rods. Draw
      your model.

   c. Skip count by tens and then count on by ones to

      find the number of blocks in your model. _____

   d. Write an equation you can use to solve the problem. _____

   e. Answer the question. _____

2. Rami has 4 boxes of model cars. There are 7 cars in each box.

   How many model cars does Rami have in all?

   a. Draw an array to model the problem.

   b. Write an equation you can use to solve the problem.

      Use *m* for the unknown. _____

   c. How many model cars does Rami have? _____

Answer the questions.

3. Theo has 5 bags of peaches. There are 6 peaches in each bag.

   How many peaches does Theo have in all? _____

4. Daniel puts muffins in a box. He makes 5 rows of muffins.
   He puts 2 muffins in each row.

   How many muffins does Daniel put in the box? _____

5. Rachel has 5 boxes of buttons. Each box has 7 buttons.

   How many buttons does Rachel have? _____

6. Darnell buys some stamps. He buys 4 rows of stamps.
   Each row has 5 stamps.

   How many stamps does Darnell buy? _____

Problem Solving with Multiplication (B)

Practice Finding Group Sizes and Numbers of Groups in Problems

Follow the steps to solve the problem.

1. A group of 24 people attend a picnic. Each picnic table seats 6 people.

   How many picnic tables does the group need?

   a. Draw a model that shows 24 counters split into equal groups of 6.

   b. How many equal groups are in your model? _____

   c. Write an equation you can use to solve the problem.

   _____

   d. Answer the question. _____

2. Cecilia has a quilt with 35 square patches. Each row of the quilt has 5 squares.

   How many rows of squares are in the quilt?

   a. Write an equation to represent the problem. Use ?

   for the unknown. _____

b. Draw an array to model the problem.

c. Answer the question. _____

Answer the questions.

3. Danny buys 6 boxes of granola bars. Each box has the same number of granola bars. Danny buys 36 granola bars in all.

   How many granola bars are in each box? _____

4. Adeem buys 24 crayons. There are 8 crayons in each box.

   How many boxes of crayons does Adeem buy? _____

5. Sally plants 18 pepper plants in 3 rows. The same number of pepper plants are in each row.

   How many pepper plants are in each row? _____

6. Sela has a sheet of 20 stickers. There are 4 stickers in each row.

   How many rows of stickers are there? _____

Problem Solving with Multiplication (C)

Practice Solving Two-Step Problems with Multiplication

Follow the instructions.

1. Katie goes to the beach for 5 days. She collects
   9 seashells each day. She gives 8 seashells to her sister.

   How many seashells does Katie have at the end of her trip?

   a. List steps you can take to solve this problem.

   _____

   _____

   b. Write an equation that represents the problem. _____

   c. Which operation should you perform first? Why?

   _____

   _____

   d. Answer the question.

   _____

   e. Is your answer reasonable? Explain.

   _____

   _____

2. Write a story problem that can be solved using this equation.

$$22 + 3 \times 5 = ?$$

_____

_____

Use the order of operations to find the unknown number.

3. $2 \times 4 + 3 = n$

$n =$ _____

4. $19 - 2 \times 5 = ?$

$? =$ _____

5. $7 + 6 \times 4 = n$

$n =$ _____

Solve.

6. Yasmine buys 5 cartons of eggs. Each carton has 2 rows of eggs with 3 eggs in each row.

How many eggs does Yasmine buy? _____

7. Six friends go to a fair. Each friend rides the roller coaster 2 times. A ride costs $2.

How much money in all do the friends spend riding

the roller coaster? _____

Division Concepts (A)

Practice Dividing to Find the Size of Equal Groups

Follow the instructions.

1. Draw a model of $30 \div 5$.

2. Write a story problem that models $21 \div 7$.

   _____

   _____

3. Label the dividend, divisor, and quotient in this division problem.

   $$36 \qquad \div \qquad 9 \qquad = \qquad 4$$

   _____ _____ _____

Follow the steps to answer the question.

4. 18 bees are split into 2 equal groups.

   How many bees are in each group?

   a. Circle 2 equal groups of bees.

   b. Count the number of bees in each group. _____

5. 24 butterflies are split into 4 equal groups.

How many butterflies are in each group?

    a. Circle 4 equal groups of butterflies.

    b. Count the number of butterflies in each group. _____

Answer the questions.

6. 35 tennis balls are split into 7 equal groups.

How many tennis balls are in each group?

_____

7. 32 ladybugs are split into 8 equal groups.

How many ladybugs are in each group?

_____

Practice Dividing to Find the Number of Equal Groups

Follow the instructions.

1. Draw a model of $20 \div 4$.

2. Write a story problem that models $32 \div 8$.

   _____

   _____

Follow the steps to answer the question.

3. 21 apples are split into groups of 3 apples each.

   How many groups are there?

   a. Circle as many groups of 3 apples as possible.

   b. Count the number of groups. _____

4. 45 flowers are split into groups of 9 flowers each.

How many groups are there?

    a. Circle as many groups of 9 flowers as possible.

    b. Count the number of groups. _____

Answer the questions.

5. 18 basketballs are split into groups of 6 basketballs.

How many groups are there?

_____

6. 40 fireflies are split into groups of 10 fireflies.

How many groups are there?

_____

Practice Dividing Using Arrays and Repeated Subtraction

Follow the instructions.

1. $6 \div 2$ can be modeled in different ways.

   a. Draw 6 squares in 2 equal groups.

   b. Draw 6 squares with 2 squares in each group.

   c. Draw an array with 6 squares.

   d. Fill in the boxes to subtract 2 from 6 until you get to 0.

   $\boxed{} - 2 = \boxed{}$

   $\boxed{} - 2 = \boxed{}$

   $\boxed{} - 2 = \boxed{}$

   e. What is $6 \div 2$? _____

2. Draw a model of 36 ÷ 9. Use an array.

3. Fill in the boxes to model 28 ÷ 7 with repeated subtraction.

$$\boxed{} - 7 = \boxed{}$$

$$\boxed{} - 7 = \boxed{}$$

$$\boxed{} - 7 = \boxed{}$$

$$\boxed{} - 7 = \boxed{}$$

4. Write a story problem that models 21 ÷ 3 with an array.

_____

_____

5. What are the parts of 54 ÷ 9 = 6? Fill in the blanks.

The dividend is _____. The divisor is _____.

The quotient is _____.

Practice Solving Division Problems

Answer the questions.

1. Which operations are inverse operations?

    _____

    _____

2. What is the multiplication fact family for the factors
    4 and 7?

    _____   _____

    _____   _____

3. How do you use a multiplication table to divide?
    Fill in the blanks.

    Step 1. Start at the _____ in the first column.

    Step 2. Move _____ until you get to the _____ .

    Step 3. Move _____ to the top of the column to find

    the _____ .

Fill in the blanks.

4. $16 \div 2 =$ _____ because _____ $\times 2 = 16$.

5. $36 \div$ _____ $= 4$ because _____ $\times 4 = 36$.

6. _____ $\times 6 = 18$ because $18 \div 6 =$ _____.

7. _____ $\div 10 = 6$ because $10 \times 6 =$ _____.

8. $7 \times 5 =$ _____ because _____ $\div 7 = 5$.

Use the multiplication table to divide.

9. $63 \div 9$ _____

10. $56 \div 7$ _____

11. $20 \div 4$ _____

12. $6 \div 2$ _____

×	1	2	3	4	5	6	7	8	9	10
1	1	2	3	4	5	6	7	8	9	10
2	2	4	6	8	10	12	14	16	18	20
3	3	6	9	12	15	18	21	24	27	30
4	4	8	12	16	20	24	28	32	36	40
5	5	10	15	20	25	30	35	40	45	50
6	6	12	18	24	30	36	42	48	54	60
7	7	14	21	28	35	42	49	56	63	70
8	8	16	24	32	40	48	56	64	72	80
9	9	18	27	36	45	54	63	72	81	90
10	10	20	30	40	50	60	70	80	90	100

Division Patterns (A)

Practice Dividing by 1 and Dividing 0 by Any Number

Fill in the blanks.

1. The identity property of division says that any number

   divided by _____ equals _____ .

2. Use the identity property of division when the _____ is _____ .

3. Write a division fact that uses the identity property

   of division. _____

4. The zero property of division says that _____ divided

   by any number equals _____ .

5. Use the zero property of division when the _____ is _____ .

6. Write a division fact that uses the zero property

   of division. _____

Divide.

7. $6 \div 1$ _____

8. $18 \div 1$ _____

9. $0 \div 10$ _____

10. $0 \div 8$ _____

11. $7 \div 1$ _____

12. $0 \div 1$ _____

13. $27 \div 1$ _____

14. $33 \div 1$ _____

15. $0 \div 4$ _____

16. $28 \div 1$ _____

17. $0 \div 5$ _____

18. $46 \div 1$ _____

19. $0 \div 7$ _____

20. $10 \div 1$ _____

Practice Dividing by 5

Follow the steps to answer the question.

1. What is $20 \div 5$?

   a. Subtract 5 from 20 until you get to to 0.

   _____

   _____

   b. Count the number of times you subtracted 5. _____

   c. $20 \div 5 =$ _____

2. What is $40 \div 5$?

   a. Write a related multiplication fact.

   _____

   b. Fill in the blanks.

   The factor _____ is the _____ of
   the division problem.

   c. $40 \div 5 =$ _____

Divide.

3. $30 \div 5$ _____

4. $10 \div 5$ _____

5. $5 \div 5$ _____

6. $45 \div 5$ _____

7. $35 \div 5$ _____

8. $25 \div 5$ _____

9. $50 \div 5$ _____

10. $15 \div 5$ _____

Dividing is the opposite of multiplying.

Practice Dividing by 10

Follow the steps to answer the question.

1. What is $80 \div 10$?

   a. Subtract 10 from 80 until you get to 0.

   b. Count the number of times you subtracted 10. _____

   c. $80 \div 10 =$ _____

2. What is $40 \div 10$?

   a. Write a related multiplication fact. _____

   b. Fill in the blanks.

      The factor _____ is the _____
      of the division problem.

   c. $40 \div 10 =$ _____

3. What is $70 \div 10$?

    a. Fill in the blanks.

        The pattern for dividing by 10 is to drop the digit _____

        from the end of the _____.

    b. $70 \div 10 =$ _____

Divide.

4. $20 \div 10$ _____   **5.** $90 \div 10$ _____

6. $10 \div 10$ _____   **7.** $100 \div 10$ _____

8. $50 \div 10$ _____   **9.** $30 \div 10$ _____

10. $60 \div 10$ _____

Practice Dividing by 2 and 4

Follow the steps to answer the question.

1. What is $14 \div 2$?

    a. Draw 14 counters split into these two equal groups.

    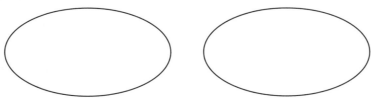

    b. Fill in the blanks: The model has _____ counters split

    into _____ equal groups of _____ counters.

    c. Write an equation for this model. _____

2. What is $12 \div 4$?

    a. Draw a model of $12 \div 4$.

    b. Fill in the blank.

    $12 \div 4 =$ _____

Fill in the blanks.

3. $12 \div 2 = $ _____ because _____ $\times\, 2 = 12.$

4. $40 \div 4 = $ _____ because _____ $\times\, 4 = 40.$

Divide.

5. $2\overline{)\,10}$ with $\square$ on top

6. $4\overline{)\,32}$ with $\square$ on top

7. $4\overline{)\,28}$ with $\square$ on top

8. $2\overline{)\,6}$ with $\square$ on top

9. $36 \div 4$ _____

10. $20 \div 2$ _____

11. $8 \div 2$ _____

12. $24 \div 4$ _____

13. $4 \div 2$ _____

14. $8 \div 4$ _____

Practice Dividing by 3 and 6

Follow the steps to answer the question.

1. What is $18 \div 3$?

   a. Draw an array to model $18 \div 3$.

   b. Fill in the blank.

   $18 \div 3 =$ _____

   c. Write another division equation that this array

   represents. _____

Fill in the blanks.

2. $24 \div 6 =$ _____ because _____ $\times 6 = 24$.

3. $30 \div 3 =$ _____ because _____ $\times 3 = 30$.

4. $27 \div 3 =$ _____ because _____ $\times 3 = 27$.

5. $12 \div 6 =$ _____ because _____ $\times 6 = 12$.

Divide.

6. $3\overline{)\,9}$ □

7. $3\overline{)\,15}$ □

8. $6\overline{)\,30}$ □

9. $6\overline{)\,36}$ □

10. $54 \div 6$ _____

11. $60 \div 6$ _____

12. $3 \div 3$ _____

13. $27 \div 3$ _____

14. $21 \div 3$ _____

15. $42 \div 6$ _____

Practice Dividing by 7, 8, and 9

Follow the steps to answer the question. Use the multiplication table.

1. What is $49 \div 7$?

   a. The divisor is 7. Point to 7 in the left column.

   b. The dividend is 49. Move right to 49.

   c. Move up to the first row. The number where you end up is the quotient.

   d. Fill in the blank.

   $49 \div 7 =$ _____

×	1	2	3	4	5	6	7	8	9	10
1	1	2	3	4	5	6	7	8	9	10
2	2	4	6	8	10	12	14	16	18	20
3	3	6	9	12	15	18	21	24	27	30
4	4	8	12	16	20	24	28	32	36	40
5	5	10	15	20	25	30	35	40	45	50
6	6	12	18	24	30	36	42	48	54	60
7	7	14	21	28	35	42	49	56	63	70
8	8	16	24	32	40	48	56	64	72	80
9	9	18	27	36	45	54	63	72	81	90
10	10	20	30	40	50	60	70	80	90	100

2. What is $81 \div 9$?

   a. The divisor is 9. Point to 9 in the left column.

   b. The dividend is 81. Move right to 81.

   c. Move up to the first row. The number where you end up is the quotient.

   d. Fill in the blank. $81 \div 9 =$ _____

3. What is $32 \div 8$?

   a. The divisor is 8. Point to 8 in the left column.

   b. The dividend is 32. Move right to 32.

   c. Move up to the first row. The number where you end up is the quotient.

   d. Fill in the blank.

     $32 \div 8 = $ _____

×	1	2	3	4	5	6	7	8	9	10
1	1	2	3	4	5	6	7	8	9	10
2	2	4	6	8	10	12	14	16	18	20
3	3	6	9	12	15	18	21	24	27	30
4	4	8	12	16	20	24	28	32	36	40
5	5	10	15	20	25	30	35	40	45	50
6	6	12	18	24	30	36	42	48	54	60
7	7	14	21	28	35	42	49	56	63	70
8	8	16	24	32	40	48	56	64	72	80
9	9	18	27	36	45	54	63	72	81	90
10	10	20	30	40	50	60	70	80	90	100

Divide.

4. $7\overline{)\ 21}$

5. $9\overline{)\ 36}$

6. $7\overline{)\ 70}$

7. $8\overline{)\ 48}$

8. $18 \div 9$ _____

9. $42 \div 7$ _____

10. $24 \div 8$ _____

11. $90 \div 9$ _____

12. $42 \div 7$ _____

13. $56 \div 8$ _____

Practice Finding an Unknown Number in a Division Equation

Fill in the blanks.

1. Use the words *dividend*, *divisor*, and *quotient* in each part.

   a. _____ ÷ _____ = _____

   b. The product of the _____ and the

      _____ is the _____ .

Answer the questions to find the missing number.

2. $35 \div ? = 5$

   a. Which number is missing from this equation? Circle your answer.

      dividend   divisor   quotient

   b. How can you find the missing number?

      _____

      _____

   c. What is the missing number? _____

3. $? \div 6 = 9$

    a. Which number is missing? Circle your answer.

        dividend   divisor   quotient

    b. How can you find the missing number?

    _____

    _____

    c. What is the missing number? _____

Fill in the boxes.

4. $\boxed{} \div 3 = 8$ because $8 \times 3 = \boxed{}$.

5. $28 \div \boxed{} = 7$ because $7 \times \boxed{} = 28$.

6. $27 \div 9 = \boxed{}$ because $\boxed{} \times 9 = 27$.

Fill in the box with the missing number.

7. $16 \div \boxed{} = 8$ **8.** $45 \div 9 = \boxed{}$ **9.** $\boxed{} \div 3 = 3$

10. $20 \div \boxed{} = 5$ **11.** $\boxed{} \div 6 = 7$ **12.** $\boxed{} \div 6 = 3$

Problem Solving with Division (A)

Practice Solving Division Group Problems

Follow the steps to answer the question.

1. Caitlyn has 56 pins. She makes equal groups of 8 pins on her bulletin board.

   How many groups of pins can Caitlyn make?

   a. Draw a model of 56 split into groups of 8.

   b. Write an equation you can use to solve the problem. _____

   c. Answer the question. _____

2. Caitlyn also has 24 postcards and a scrapbook with 4 pages. She puts the same number of postcards on each page.

   How many postcards are on each page?

   a. Draw a model of 24 split into 4 equal groups.

b. Write an equation you can use to solve the problem. _____

c. Answer the question. _____

Write a story problem to match the equation.

3. $30 \div 6 = ?$

_____

_____

Answer the questions.

4. A bookstore has 48 copies of a book. There are an equal number of copies of the book on each of 6 shelves.

How many copies of the book are on each shelf? _____

5. Rick has 63 baseball cards. He puts 9 baseball cards on each page of a book.

How many pages can Rick fill? _____

6. Darla has 45 nickels. She places the nickels in 5 equal groups.

How many nickels does Darla place in each group? _____

Practice Solving Real-World Division Problems

Follow the steps to answer the question.

1. Dean makes a quilt from 54 squares of fabric. The quilt has 9 rows of squares.

   How many squares are in each row of the quilt?

   a. Draw an array with 54 squares.
      Make 9 equal rows of squares.

   b. Write an equation you can use to solve the problem. _____

   c. Answer the question. _____

Write a story problem to match the equation.

2. $20 \div 4 = ?$

   _____

   _____

Follow the steps to answer the question.

3. A pet store has 21 fish. There are an equal number of fish in each of 3 fish tanks.

   How many fish are in each tank?

   a. Write a division equation you can use to solve the problem.

      Use a question mark for the unknown number. _____

   b. Write a related multiplication equation you can use

      to solve the problem. _____

   c. Answer the question. _____

Answer the questions.

4. Amelia buys 42 cucumber plants for her garden. She puts the same number of plants in each of 6 rows.

   How many plants does Amelia put in each row? _____

5. A party store has 64 balloons. The store makes bunches of 8 balloons.

   How many bunches does the store have? _____

6. A bakery makes 24 bagels. Four bagels are put into each bag.

   How many bags of bagels does the bakery make? _____

Practice Solving Two-Step Division Problems

Follow the instructions to answer the question.

1. Kevin splits 35 sunflowers equally among 5 vases. Then he puts 3 roses in each vase.

   How many flowers are in each vase?

   a. List steps you can take to solve this problem.

   _____

   _____

   b. Write an equation that represents the problem. Use a question mark for the unknown number.

   _____

   c. Answer the question in a complete sentence.

   _____

Write a story problem that matches the equation.

2. $32 \div 4 - 6 = ?$

   _____

   _____

Follow the instructions to answer the question.

3. Lila bakes 6 batches of corn muffins. Each batch makes 6 muffins. She puts the same number of corn muffins into 4 baskets.

    How many muffins are in each basket?

    a. List steps you can take to solve this problem.

    _____

    _____

    b. Write an equation that represents the problem. Use a question mark for the unknown number. _____

    c. Answer the question in a complete sentence.

    _____

Answer the questions.

4. Cameron has 85 balloons. Four balloons pop. He then splits the remaining balloons into 9 equal bunches.

    How many balloons are in each bunch? _____

5. Sophia works for 4 hours and earns $10 each hour. Sophia spends the money to buy 5 shirts. Each shirt is the same price.

    What is the price of each shirt? _____

Exploring Shapes and Shared Attributes (A)

Practice Describing Two-Dimensional Shapes

Follow the instructions to describe the features of the shape.

1.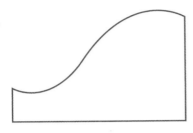

   a. Is this an open shape or a closed shape? Circle your answer.

   open shape   closed shape

   b. Fill in the blanks.

   This shape has _____ straight sides and _____ curved side.

   This shape has _____ vertices.

   This shape has _____ square corners.

2.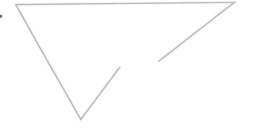

   a. Is this an open shape or a closed shape? Circle your answer.

   open shape   closed shape

   b. Fill in the blanks.

   This shape has _____ straight sides and _____ vertices.

   This shape has _____ square corners.

3.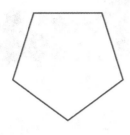

a. Is this an open shape or a closed shape? Circle your answer.

open shape   closed shape

b. Fill in the blanks.

This shape has _____ straight sides and _____ curved sides.

This shape has _____ vertices.

There are _____ square corners.

Describe the shapes.

4.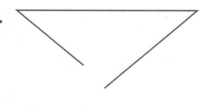

_____

_____

5.

_____

_____

6.

_____

_____

7.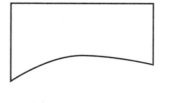

_____

_____

Practice Identifying a Shape with Given Features

Circle the shape that matches the description.

1. Which shape has 4 sides, 4 vertices, no right angles, and only 2 sides that are the same length?

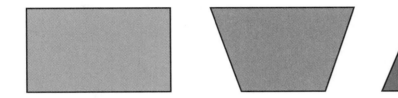

2. Which shape has 3 sides, 3 vertices, no sides that are the same length, and 1 square corner?

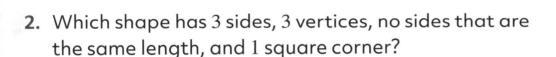

3. Which shape has 4 sides, 4 vertices, no sides that are the same length, and only 2 square corners?

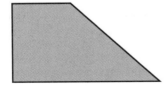

Draw a shape that fits the description.

4. An open shape with 3 straight sides, 2 vertices, and 1 square corner

5. A closed shape with 4 straight sides, 4 vertices, and only 2 square corners

6. A closed shape with 3 straight sides, 3 vertices, and no square corners

7. An open shape with 5 straight sides, 4 vertices, and no square corners

8. A closed shape with 4 straight sides, 4 vertices, 4 square corners, and opposite sides that are the same length

Exploring Shapes and Shared Attributes (C)

Practice Identifying Shared Features of Shapes

Fill in the blanks.

1. What features do these shapes have in common?

   a. Both shapes have _____ sides.

   b. Both shapes have _____ vertices.

   c. Both shapes have at least _____ sides that are the same length.

2. What features do these shapes have in common?

   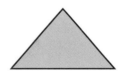

   a. Both shapes have _____ sides.

   b. Both shapes have _____ vertices.

   c. Both shapes have _____ sides that are the same length.

3. What features do these shapes have in common?

   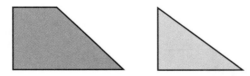

   a. Both shapes are _____ shapes.

   b. Both shapes have at least _____ square corner.

List the features that the group of shapes shares.

4.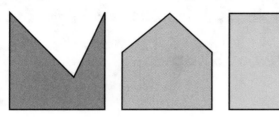

_____

_____

_____

5.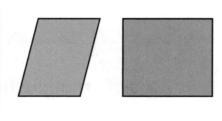

_____

_____

_____

6.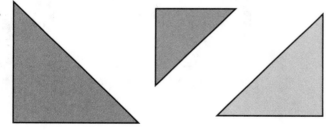

_____

_____

_____

7.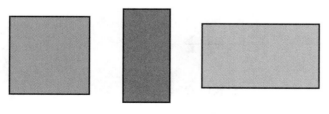

_____

_____

_____

Exploring Shapes and Shared Attributes (D)

Practice Classifying Shapes

Follow the instructions to sort the shapes.

1. This group of shapes can be sorted in different ways.

   a. Circle the shapes that have 3 sides.

   b. Shade in the shapes that have at least 1 square corner.

   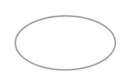

   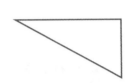

   c. Cross out the shapes that have 4 sides and 4 square corners.

2. This group of shapes can be sorted in different ways.

   a. Circle the shapes that have 6 sides.

   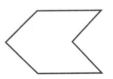

   b. Shade the shapes that have at least 1 square corner.

   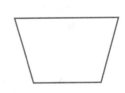

   c. Cross out the shapes that have *both* 6 sides and at least 1 square corner.

Fill in the blanks.

3. These shapes belong to the group

   of shapes with _____ sides and

   _____ square corners.

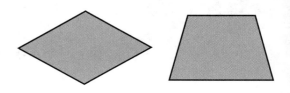

4. These shapes belong to the group
   of shapes with at least

   _____ square corner.

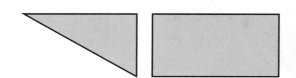

5. These shapes belong to the
   group of shapes with

   _____ sides.

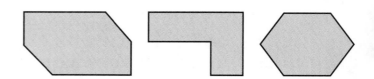

6. These shapes belong to the
   group of shapes with

   _____ sides and at least

   _____ square corner.

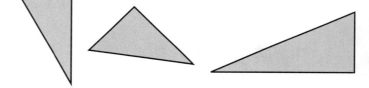

7. These shapes belong to the
   group of shapes with

   _____ sides and at least

   _____ square corner.

Practice Identifying Polygons

Answer the questions to decide whether the shape is a polygon.

1.

   a. Is this a closed shape? _____

   b. Does this shape have only straight sides? _____

   c. Does this shape have the same number of sides

   and vertices? _____

   d. Is this shape a polygon? Explain your answer.

   _____

2.

   a. Is this a closed shape? _____

   b. Does this shape have only straight sides? _____

   c. Does this shape have the same number of sides

   and vertices? _____

   d. Is this shape a polygon? Explain your answer.

   _____

3.

    a. Is this a closed shape? _____

    b. Does this shape have only straight sides? _____

    c. Does this shape have the same number of sides

    and vertices? _____

    d. Is this shape a polygon? Explain your answer.

    _____

Label the shape as a *polygon* or *not a polygon*. If it is not a polygon, explain why.

4.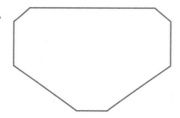

_____

5.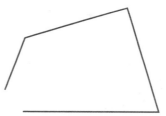

_____

6.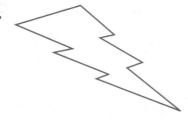

_____

7.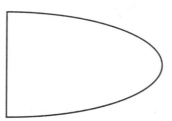

_____

Practice Classifying Polygons

Fill in the blanks.

1.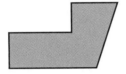

   a. This shape has _____ straight sides.

   b. This polygon is a _____.

2.

   a. This shape has _____ straight sides.

   b. This polygon is a _____.

3.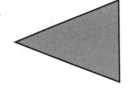

   a. This shape has _____ straight sides.

   b. This polygon is a _____.

4.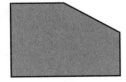

   a. This shape has _____ straight sides.

   b. This polygon is a _____.

5.

   a. This shape has _____ straight sides.

   b. This polygon is a _____.

Draw a shape that fits the description. Then name the shape.

6. A polygon with 6 sides and 6 vertices

_____

7. A polygon with 4 sides and 4 vertices

_____

8. A polygon with 3 sides and 3 vertices

_____

9. A polygon with 5 sides and 5 vertices

_____

Quadrilaterals (A)

Practice Identifying Types of Quadrilaterals

Fill in the blanks.

1. A rectangle is a quadrilateral with ___Side___ square corners.

2. A rhombus is a quadrilateral with ___angle___ sides that are the same length.

3. A square is a quadrilateral with ___Side___ square corners

   and ___angle___ sides that are the same length.

Fill in the blanks to answer the question.

4. What type of quadrilateral is this shape?

   a. This quadrilateral has ___Side___ square corners and ___angle___ sides that are all the same length.

   b. This quadrilateral is a ___parallelogram___.

5. What type of quadrilateral is this shape?

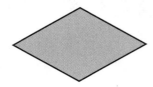

    a. This quadrilateral has ___Side___ square corners and ___angle___ sides that are the same length.

    b. This quadrilateral is a ___Trapozoid___ .

6. What type of quadrilateral is this shape?

    a. This quadrilateral has ___Side___ square corners and ___angle___ sets of sides that are the same length.

    b. This quadrilateral is a ___Parallelogram___ .

Name the quadrilateral.

7.

___Trapozoid___

8.

___parallelogram___

9.

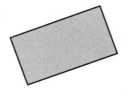

___Trapozoid___

10.

___parallelogram___

Practice Classifying Quadrilaterals

Follow the instructions to classify the quadrilateral.

1. **a.** Circle all the features of this shape.

   4 square corners   4 sides that are the same length

   b. Circle all the names that describe this shape.

   rectangle   rhombus   square

2. **a.** Circle all the features of this shape.

   4 square corners   4 sides that are the same length

   b. Circle all the names that describe this shape.

   rectangle   rhombus   square

3. **a.** Circle all the features of this shape.

   4 square corners   4 sides that are the same length

   b. Circle all the names that describe this shape.

   rectangle   rhombus   square

List all the names that describe the quadrilateral.

4.

_____

5.

_____

6.

_____

7.

_____

8.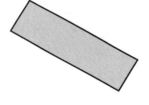

_____

9.

_____

10.

_____

11.

_____

Practice Describing and Drawing Quadrilaterals

Draw 2 sides to complete the quadrilateral.

1. A rectangle

2. A rhombus

Can you add sides to me to make a rhombus?

3. A square

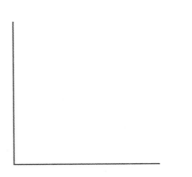

Draw a quadrilateral that fits the description.

4. A rectangle that is not a rhombus

5. A rhombus with 4 square corners

6. A rhombus with no square corners

7. A quadrilateral with 2 square corners and 2 sides that are the same length

8. A quadrilateral with 1 square corner and no sides that are the same length

9. A quadrilateral that is not a rectangle, rhombus, or square

Area Concepts (A)

Practice Understanding Area

Fill in the blanks.

1. Area is the amount of _____ on a flat surface.

2. Area is measured in _____ _____.

3. The area of a plane figure equals the number of unit squares that can cover the figure with no

   _____ or _____ .

Circle the answer.

4. Which figure shows the correct way to cover a rectangle with unit squares?

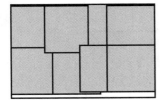 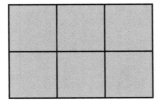 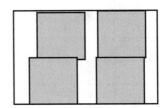

Find the area of the plane figure.

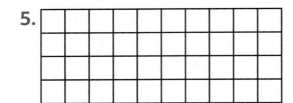 = 1 square unit

5.

Area = _____ square units

6.

Area = _____ square units

7.

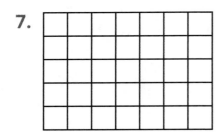

Area = _____ square units

8.

Area = _____ square units

9.

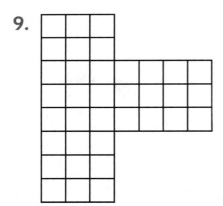

Area = _____ square units

10.

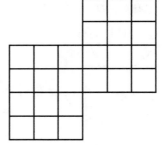

Area = _____ square units

Practice Understanding Area Units

Fill in the blanks.

1. Area is measured in _____ _____.

2. The area of a unit square with side lengths of 1 inch

   is _____ square inch.

3. The area of a unit square with side lengths of 1 yard

   is _____ square yard.

4. The area of a unit square with side lengths of 1 meter

   is _____ square meter.

> I wonder what the area of my book cover is.

5. The area of a unit square with side lengths of 1 unit

   is _____ square unit.

Find the perimeter and area of the figure.

6.

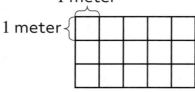

Perimeter = _____ meters

Area = _____ square meters

7.

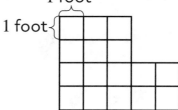

Perimeter = _____ feet

Area = _____ square feet

8.

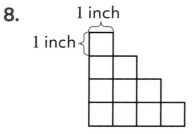

Perimeter = _____ inches

Area = _____ square inches

9.

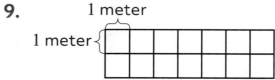

Perimeter = _____ meters

Area = _____ square meters

10.

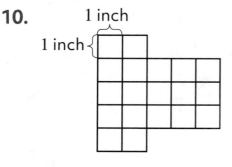

Perimeter = _____ inches

Area = _____ square inches

11.

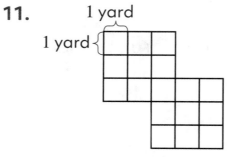

Perimeter = _____ yards

Area = _____ square yards

Measuring and Calculating Area (A)

Practice Finding Areas by Tiling

Follow the steps to answer the question.

1. What is the area of this rectangle?

   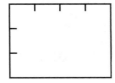

   a. Use a ruler to complete the lines inside the rectangle.

   b. Count the number of unit squares formed by the lines you completed.

   c. Fill in the blanks.

   This rectangle is covered by _____ unit squares, so the

   area of the rectangle is _____ square units.

2. What is the area of this rectangle?

   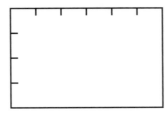

   a. Use a ruler to complete the lines inside the rectangle.

b. Count the number of unit squares formed by the lines you completed.

c. Fill in the blanks.

This rectangle is covered by _____ unit squares,

so the area of the rectangle is _____ square units.

Use a ruler to draw grid lines across the figure. Then find the area of the figure.

3.

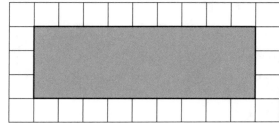

Area = _____ square units

4.

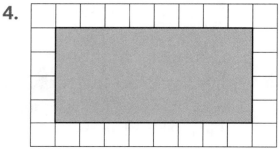

Area = _____ square units

5.

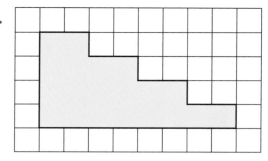

Area = _____ square units

6.

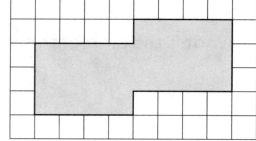

Area = _____ square units

Measuring and Calculating Area (B)

Practice Finding Areas with Units

Fill in the blanks.

1. This rectangle is covered with unit squares.

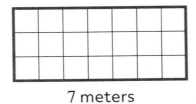

7 meters

a. The length of each unit square is ———— meter.

b. The area of each unit square is ———— square meter.

c. This rectangle is covered by ———— unit squares.

d. The area of the rectangle is ———— square meters.

Find the area of the figure. Include the correct unit in your answer.

2.

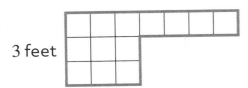

3 feet

————————————————

3.

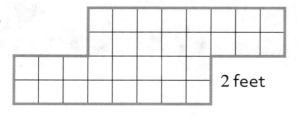

2 feet

_____

4.

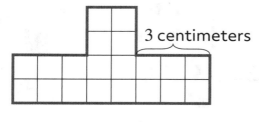

3 centimeters

_____

5.

3 inches

_____

6.

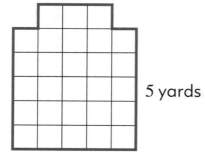

5 yards

_____

Area is the space inside a shape.

Measuring and Calculating Area (C)

Practice Multiplying to Find Area

Fill in the blanks.

1. The area of a rectangle is the product of the

   rectangle's _____ and its _____ .

2. The formula for area is $A =$ _____ × _____ .

Answer the question.

3. The post office sells a sheet of ten stamps. Each
   stamp has an area of 5 square centimeters.

   What is the area of the sheet of stamps?

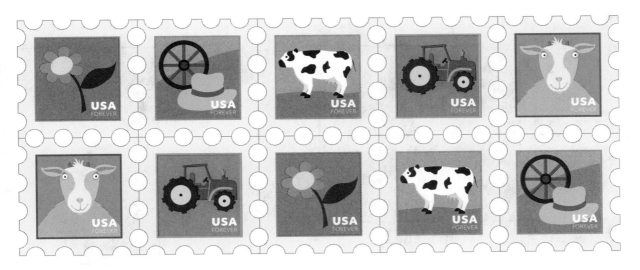

Find the area of the figure. Include the correct unit.

4.

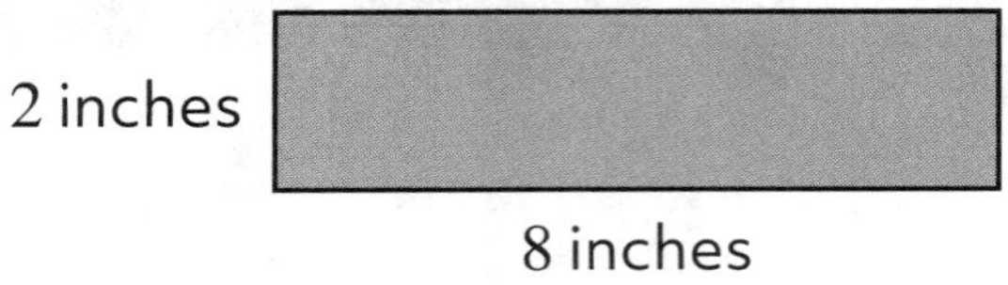

2 inches

8 inches

_____

5.

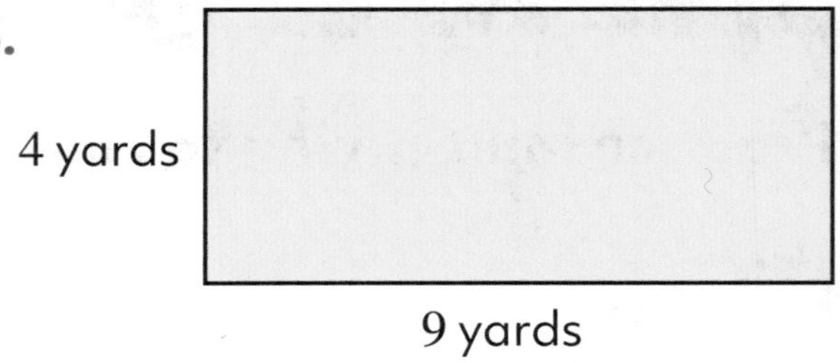

4 yards

9 yards

_____

6.

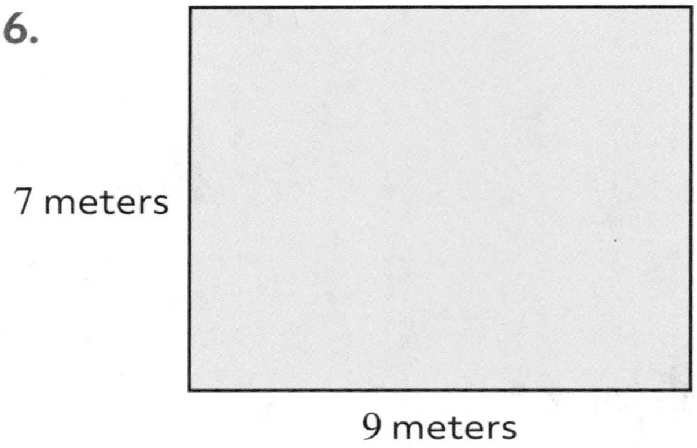

7 meters

9 meters

_____

7.

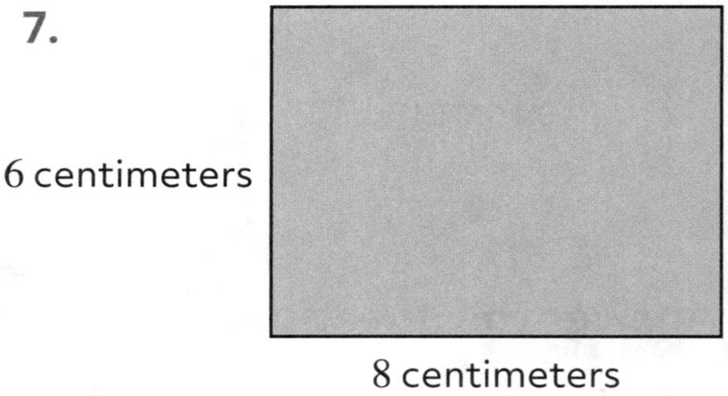

6 centimeters

8 centimeters

_____

8.

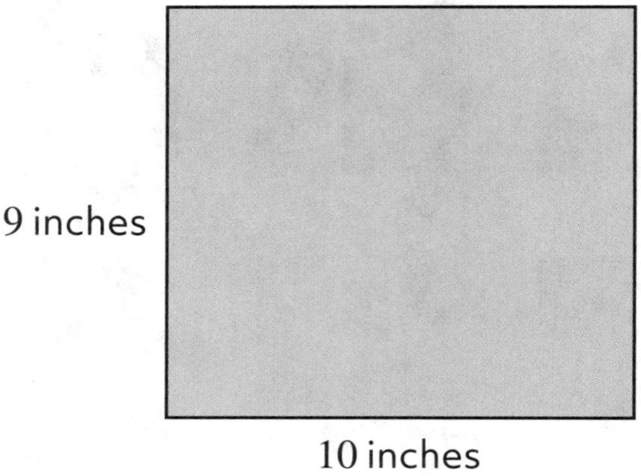

9 inches

10 inches

_____

9.

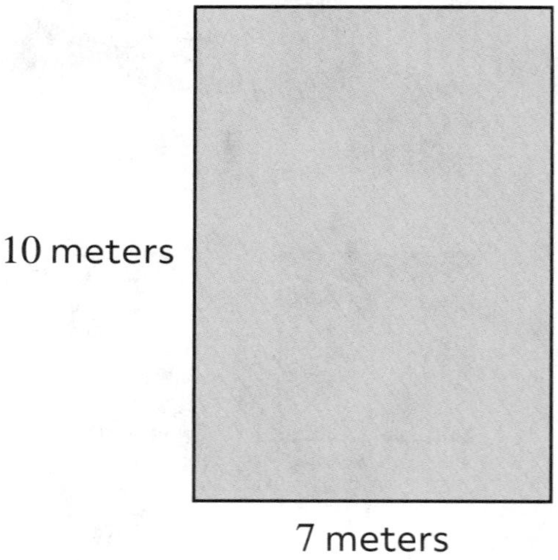

10 meters

7 meters

_____

Applying Formulas and Properties (A)

Practice Finding Areas of Different Shapes

Follow the steps to answer the question.

1. What is the area of this figure?

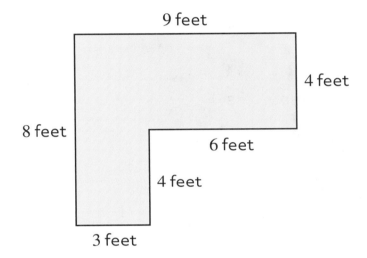

a. Draw a line on the shape to divide the rectangle into two smaller rectangles.

b. Find the area of each smaller rectangle. Show your work.

_____

_____

c. Add the areas of both smaller rectangles. Show your work.

_____

Find the area of the figure.

2.

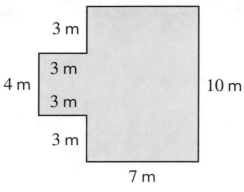

3 m
3 m
4 m
3 m
10 m
3 m
7 m

Note: *m* stands for "meters."

$A =$ _____ square meters

3.

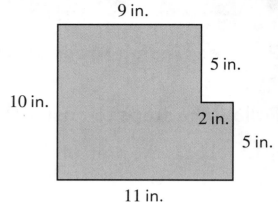

9 in.
5 in.
10 in.
2 in.
5 in.
11 in.

Note: *in.* stands for "inches."

$A =$ _____ square inches

4.

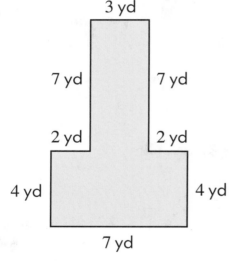

3 yd
7 yd   7 yd
2 yd   2 yd
4 yd   4 yd
7 yd

Note: *yd* stands for "yards."

$A =$ _____ square yards

5.

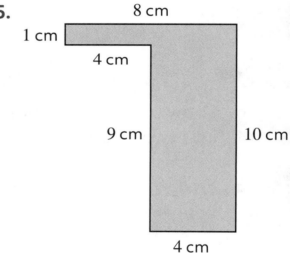

8 cm
1 cm
4 cm
9 cm   10 cm
4 cm

Note: *cm* stands for "centimeters."

$A =$ _____ square centimeters

Applying Formulas and Properties (B)

Practice Solving Area Problems Using Multiplication

Follow the steps to answer the question.

1. A poster is in the shape of a rectangle. The poster has a length of 7 feet and a width of 4 feet.

   What is the area of the poster?

   a. Draw a rectangle to represent the poster.

   b. Write a multiplication equation that you can use

      to solve the problem. _____

   c. Multiply to find the area of the poster. Include the

      correct unit in your answer. _____

2. A rectangular wall is 10 feet long and 9 feet tall.
   What is the area of the wall?

   a. Draw a rectangle to represent the wall.

b. Write a multiplication equation that you can use to solve the problem. _____

c. Multiply to find the area of the poster. Include the correct unit in your answer. _____

Answer the question. Include the correct unit in your answer.

3. Christian plants a garden in the shape of a rectangle. His garden is 9 meters long and 6 meters wide.

   What is the area of Christian's garden? _____

4. Lara tiles a floor in the shape of a rectangle. The floor is 7 yards long and 5 yards wide.

   What is the area of the floor? _____

5. A small notecard is 10 centimeters long and 8 centimeters wide.

   What is the area of the notecard? _____

6. An artist has a canvas. It is a rectangle that is 9 meters long and 5 meters wide.

   What is the area of the canvas? _____

Practice Solving Area Problems Using Division

Follow the steps to answer the question.

1. A picture is 10 inches long. It has an area of 80 square inches. How wide is the picture?

   a. Draw a rectangle to represent the picture.

   b. Write a division equation that you can use to solve the problem. _____

   c. Divide to find the width of the picture. Include the correct unit in your answer. _____

2. A desk in the shape of a rectangle is 2 feet wide. It has an area of 16 square feet.

   How long is the desk?

   a. Draw a rectangle to represent the desk.

b. Write a division equation that you can use to solve the problem. _____

c. Divide to find the length of the desk. Include the correct unit in your answer. _____

Answer the question. Include the correct unit in your answer.

3. A banner in the shape of a rectangle has an area of 81 square feet. The banner is 9 feet long.

   How wide is the banner? _____

4. A sidewalk has an area of 50 square meters. The sidewalk is 5 meters wide.

   How long is the sidewalk? _____

5. A window has 56 square feet of glass. The window is 8 feet long.

   How wide is the window? _____

6. A placemat in the shape of a rectangle has an area of 63 square inches. The placemat is 7 inches wide.

   How long is the placemat? _____

Practice Using Area to Model the Distributive Property

Complete the equation to represent the area of the rectangle.

1.

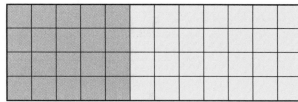

$$4 \times \boxed{} = \left(4 \times \boxed{}\right) + \left(4 \times \boxed{}\right)$$

2.

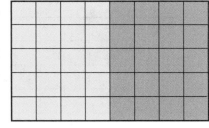

$$5 \times \boxed{} = \left(5 \times \boxed{}\right) + \left(5 \times \boxed{}\right)$$

3.

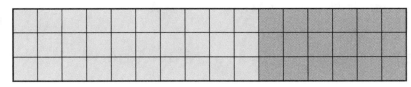

$$3 \times \boxed{} = \left(3 \times \boxed{}\right) + \left(3 \times \boxed{}\right)$$

Draw a line on the rectangle to model the equation.

4. $3 \times 9 = (3 \times 5) + (3 \times 4)$

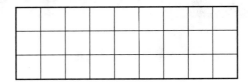

5. $4 \times 14 = (4 \times 10) + (4 \times 4)$

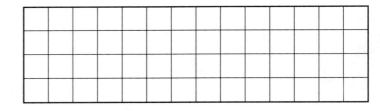

Follow the steps to answer the question.

6. What is the area of this rectangle?

a. Draw a line on the rectangle to divide the rectangle into two parts.

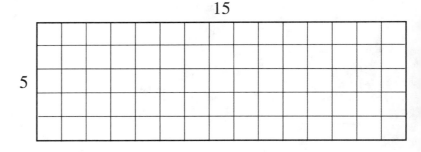

b. Fill in the boxes.

The equation $5 \times 15 = \left(5 \times \boxed{}\right) + \left(5 \times \boxed{}\right)$ represents the area of this rectangle.

The areas of the parts are $\boxed{}$ square units and $\boxed{}$ square units.

c. Answer the question in a complete sentence.

_____

Applying Formulas and Properties (E)

Practice Solving Problems with Perimeter and Area

Follow the instructions.

1. There are 3 different rectangles that have an area of 18 square units.

   a. Draw each rectangle on this grid.

   b. Complete the table for the 3 rectangles you drew in part **a**. Include the correct units.

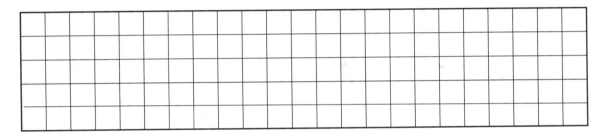

Length	Width	Perimeter	Area
			18 square units
			18 square units
			18 square units

   c. The area of these 3 rectangles is the same. Is the perimeter of each rectangle the same? Explain.

2. Some of these rectangles have the same perimeter.

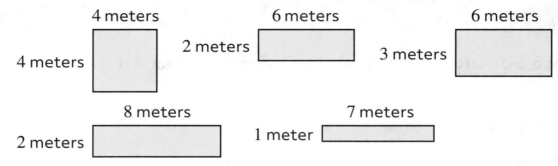

a. Circle the 3 rectangles that have a perimeter of 16 meters.

b. Complete the table for the 3 rectangles you circled in part **a**. Include the correct units for each measurement.

Length	Width	Perimeter	Area
		16 meters	
		16 meters	
		16 meters	

c. The perimeter of these 3 rectangles is the same. Is the area of each rectangle the same? Explain.

_____

Draw and label a rectangle that models the equation.

3. $3 \times 7 = 21$ **4.** $5 \times 2 = 10$

Unit Fractions (A)

Practice Working with Unit Fractions and Shapes

Fill in the blanks.

1. The denominator of a fraction is the number of _____ parts in the shape.

2. The numerator of a fraction is the number of _____ parts in the shape.

3. A fraction with 1 in the numerator is a _____ fraction.

Answer the question.

4. Does this rectangle correctly model $\frac{1}{3}$? Explain your answer.

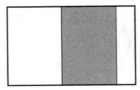

_____

_____

_____

Follow the steps to answer the question.

5. What are two ways to model $\frac{1}{2}$?

    a. Draw a line to split the square into 2 equal rectangles. Shade one part.

    b. Draw a line to split the square into 2 equal triangles. Shade one part.

Name the fraction of the shape that is shaded.

6.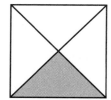

7.

8.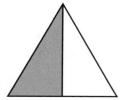

_____   _____   _____

Divide the shape into equal parts. Then shade the figure to model the unit fraction.

9. $\frac{1}{4}$

10. $\frac{1}{3}$

11. $\frac{1}{8}$

Unit Fractions (B)

Practice Working with Unit Fractions and Number Lines

Fill in the blanks to answer the question.

1. What are the steps for plotting a unit fraction on a number line?

   a. Divide the distance from 0 to 1 into equal parts. The

   _____ is the number of equal parts.

   b. Mark a point at the _____ tick mark after _____.

Answer the question.

2. Does the point on this number line correctly model $\frac{1}{4}$? Explain your answer.

_____

_____

Label the location of the point.

3.

4.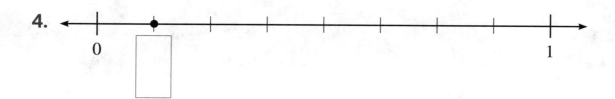

5.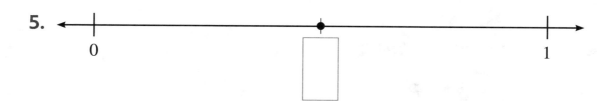

6.

Divide the distance from 0 to 1 into equal parts. Then plot the unit fraction.

7. $\frac{1}{2}$
    0   1

8. $\frac{1}{6}$
    0   1

9. $\frac{1}{3}$
    0   1

10. $\frac{1}{8}$
    0   1

11. $\frac{1}{4}$
    0   1

Practice Working with Unit Fractions and Sets

Fill in the blanks.

1. The denominator of a fraction is the _____ number of items in the set.

2. The numerator of a fraction is the number of _____ items in the set.

Answer the question.

3. Does this set correctly model $\frac{1}{3}$? Explain your answer.

_____

_____

Write the fraction that names the shaded part of the set.

4.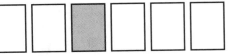

_____

5.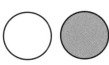

_____

6.  _____

7. _____

Shade items in the set to model the fraction.

8. $\frac{1}{4}$

9. $\frac{1}{2}$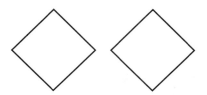

10. $\frac{1}{8}$

11. $\frac{1}{6}$

12. $\frac{1}{3}$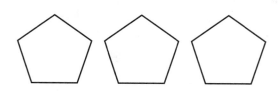

Non-Unit Fractions (A)

Practice Naming Fractions Modeled with Shapes

Fill in the blanks.

1. The denominator of a fraction is the number of _____ parts in the shape.

2. The numerator of a fraction is the number of _____ parts in the shape.

3. A fraction with a number other than 1 in the numerator is a _____ fraction.

Fill in the blanks to answer the question. Use words.

4. What fraction does this shape model?

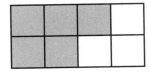

a. Each equal part of this rectangle represents one _____.

b. The model has _____ shaded parts.

c. This rectangle models the fraction _____.

Name the fraction of the shape that is shaded.

5.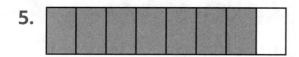

_____

6.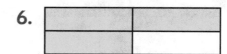

_____

7.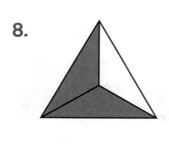

_____

8.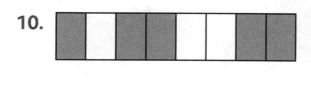

_____

9.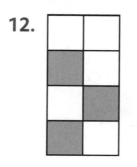

_____

10.

_____

11.

_____

12.

_____

Non-Unit Fractions (B)

Practice Representing Fractions with Shape Models

Fill in the blanks.

1. The denominator of a fraction is the number of _____ parts in the shape.

2. The numerator of a fraction is the number of _____ parts in the shape.

Follow the steps.

3. Model $\frac{2}{3}$ with this rectangle.

   a. The denominator is 3. Draw lines to make 3 equal parts in the rectangle.

   b. The numerator is 2. Shade any 2 equal parts.

Fractions can be fun!

4. Model $\frac{3}{4}$ with this rectangle.

   a. Fill in the blanks.

       The model must have _____ equal parts and _____ shaded parts.

   b. Draw lines to divide the rectangle into the correct number of equal parts.

   c. Shade the correct number of parts.

Shade the figure to model the fraction.

5. $\frac{4}{6}$

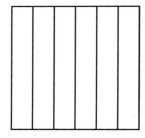

6. $\frac{5}{8}$

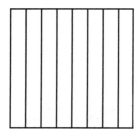

Divide the shape into equal parts. Then shade the figure to model the fraction.

7. $\frac{2}{4}$

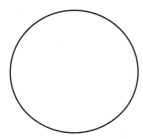

8. $\frac{2}{6}$

Practice Naming Fractions on a Number Line

Fill in the blank with a word.

1. The _____ of a fraction is the number of equal parts between 0 and 1 on a number line.

2. The _____ of a fraction is the number of hops starting from 0 on a number line.

3. What is the location of the point on this number line?

   a. The distance from 0 to 1 is divided into _____ .

   b. The point is _____ hops from 0.

   c. The location of this point is _____ .

Fill in the blank with a number.

4. What is the location of the point on this number line?

   a. The distance from 0 to 1 is divided into _____ equal parts.

b. The point is _____ hops from 0.

c. The location of this point is _____.

Label the location of the point.

5.

6.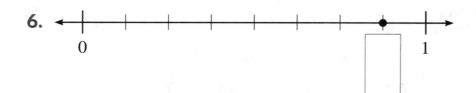

7.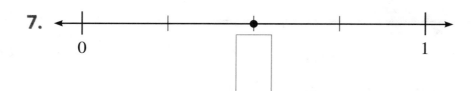

8.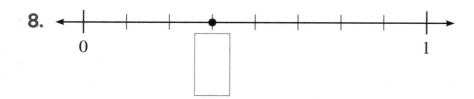

9.

10.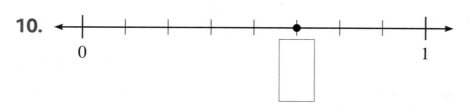

Practice Representing Fractions on a Number Line

Fill in the blanks to answer the question.

1. What are the steps for plotting a fraction on a number line?

    a. Divide the distance from 0 to 1 into equal parts. The

        _____ is the number of equal parts.

    b. Make hops starting at 0. Mark a point where the last hop

        lands. The _____ is the number of hops.

Follow the steps to plot the point.

2. Plot $\frac{3}{4}$ on this number line.

0   1

    a. Fill in the blanks.

        The distance from 0 to 1 must be divided into _____ equal

        parts. Make _____ hops starting from 0.

    b. Draw tick marks on the number line. Make the
        correct number of equal parts.

    c. Start at 0. Make the correct number of hops. Mark a point.

Divide the distance from 0 to 1 into equal parts. Then plot the fraction.

3. $\frac{4}{8}$

0   1

4. $\frac{3}{6}$

0   1

5. $\frac{6}{8}$

0   1

6. $\frac{2}{3}$

0   1

7. $\frac{5}{8}$

0   1

8. $\frac{2}{4}$

0   1

9. $\frac{7}{8}$

0   1

10. $\frac{4}{6}$

0   1

Reasoning with Fractions (A)

Practice Naming Fractions Modeled with Sets

Fill in the blanks.

1. The _____ of a fraction is the total number of items in the set.

2. The _____ of a fraction is the number of shaded items in the set.

**Fill in the blanks to answer the question.
Use numbers.**

3. What fraction does this set of apples model?

a. Each apple in this set represents _____.

b. The model has _____ shaded apples.

c. This set of apples models the fraction _____.

Fill in the blanks to answer the question. Use words.

4. What fraction does this set of circles model?

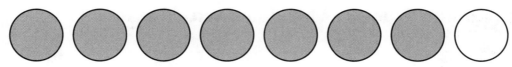

a. Each circle in this set represents one ___unshaded___.

b. The model has ___seven___ shaded circles.

c. This set of circles models the fraction ___8 / 7___.

Name the fraction of the set that is shaded.

5.

   ___8 / 3___

6.

   ___8 / 5___

7. ___6 / 5___

8. ___4 / 2___

9. ___6 / 3___

10.

    ___3 / 2___

Practice Representing Fractions with Sets

Follow the instructions.

1. Model $\frac{5}{6}$ with this set of triangles.

    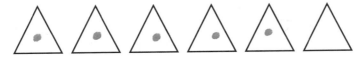

    a. Fill in the blanks.

    The model has __**6**__ triangles because the denominator is __**5**__.

    b. The numerator is 5. Shade any 5 triangles.

2. Model $\frac{2}{8}$ with a set of circles.

    a. Fill in the blanks.

    The model must have __**2**__ circles and __**8**__ of the circles are shaded.

    b. Draw the correct number of circles.

    c. Shade the correct number of circles.

Shade the figure to model the fraction.

3. $\dfrac{4}{6}$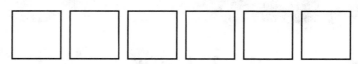

4. $\dfrac{2}{3}$

5. $\dfrac{5}{8}$

6. $\dfrac{3}{4}$

7. $\dfrac{2}{8}$

8. $\dfrac{2}{4}$

Draw and shade a set to model the fraction.

9. $\dfrac{3}{8}$

10. $\dfrac{3}{6}$

Reasoning with Fractions (C)

Practice Working with Fractions Modeled with Equal Groups

Fill in the blanks to answer the question.

1. What fraction does this set of circles model?

   a. The model has 12 circles split into _**12**_ equal groups.

   b. The model has _**8**_ groups that are shaded.

   c. This set of circles models the fraction _**12/8**_.

Name the fraction that is modeled.

2. _**3/8**_

3. _**12/6**_

Follow the instructions.

4. Model $\frac{1}{4}$ with this set of squares.

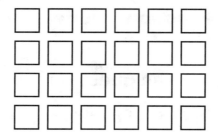

    a. The denominator is 4. Divide the set into 4 equal groups.

    b. The numerator is 1. Shade the squares in 1 of the equal groups.

Divide and shade the set to model the fraction.

5. $\frac{5}{6}$

6. $\frac{1}{3}$

7. $\frac{5}{8}$

8. $\frac{3}{4}$

Practice Identifying Equivalent Fractions

Fill in the blanks to answer the question.

1. Is $\frac{3}{4}$ equivalent to $\frac{6}{8}$? Explain your answer using the models.

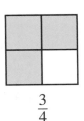

$\frac{3}{4}$

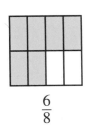

$\frac{6}{8}$

a. The squares are the _____ size.

b. The _____ amount of area is shaded in each model.

c. Equivalent fractions name the

_____ amount, so

$\frac{3}{4}$ is _____ to $\frac{6}{8}$.

Answer the question.

2. Is $\frac{1}{2}$ equivalent to $\frac{4}{8}$? Explain your answer using the models.

$\frac{1}{2}$

$\frac{4}{8}$

_____

_____

_____

_____

Decide whether the two fractions are equivalent. Write Yes or No on the line.

3.

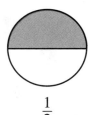 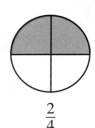

$\frac{1}{2}$ $\frac{2}{4}$

_____

4.

$\frac{4}{6}$ $\frac{1}{3}$

_____

5.

$\frac{2}{8}$ $\frac{2}{6}$

NO
_____

6.

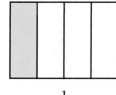 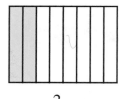

$\frac{1}{4}$ $\frac{2}{8}$

Yes
_____

Shade the shapes to model each fraction. Then decide whether the fractions are equivalent. Write Yes or No on the line.

7.

$\frac{1}{3}$ $\frac{3}{6}$

NO
_____

8.

 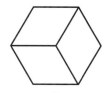

$\frac{4}{6}$ $\frac{2}{3}$

Yes
_____

Fraction Equivalence (B)

Practice Finding Equivalent Fractions

Follow the steps to answer the questions.

1. What number makes this equation true?

      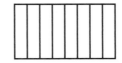

    $$\frac{3}{4} = \frac{\boxed{}}{8}$$

    a. Notice the amount of shaded area in the first model.
        Shade the same amount of area in the second model.

    b. Count the number of parts you shaded. Fill in the
        box to make the equation true.

    c. Explain how you know the fractions are equivalent.

    _____

    _____

2. What number makes this equation true?

    $$\frac{3}{6} = \frac{\boxed{}}{2}$$

    a. Fill in the blanks: _____ out of 6 apples is the same as

        _____ out of 2 groups of apples.

    b. Fill in the box to make the equation true.

Fill in the box to make the equation true. Shade the model to support your answer.

3. $\dfrac{4}{6} = \dfrac{\boxed{}}{3}$

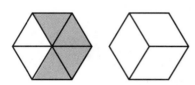

4. $\dfrac{1}{2} = \dfrac{\boxed{}}{6}$

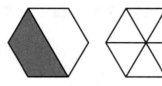

5. $\dfrac{2}{8} = \dfrac{\boxed{}}{4}$

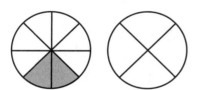

Fill in the box to make the equation true. Shade the fraction strips to support your answer.

6. $\dfrac{2}{3} = \dfrac{\boxed{}}{6}$

$\dfrac{1}{3}$	$\dfrac{1}{3}$	$\dfrac{1}{3}$

$\dfrac{1}{6}$	$\dfrac{1}{6}$	$\dfrac{1}{6}$	$\dfrac{1}{6}$	$\dfrac{1}{6}$	$\dfrac{1}{6}$

7. $\dfrac{4}{8} = \dfrac{\boxed{}}{4}$

$\dfrac{1}{4}$	$\dfrac{1}{4}$	$\dfrac{1}{4}$	$\dfrac{1}{4}$

$\dfrac{1}{8}$	$\dfrac{1}{8}$	$\dfrac{1}{8}$	$\dfrac{1}{8}$	$\dfrac{1}{8}$	$\dfrac{1}{8}$	$\dfrac{1}{8}$	$\dfrac{1}{8}$

Practice Using Number Lines to Identify Equivalent Fractions

Answer the questions.

1. Is $\frac{2}{3}$ equivalent to $\frac{4}{6}$? Explain your answer.

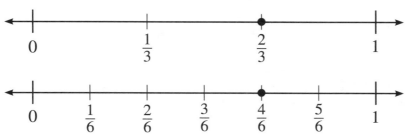

Yes They are the Same amount

2. Is $\frac{3}{6}$ equivalent to $\frac{3}{8}$? Explain your answer.

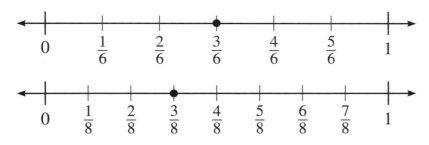

3. Jemma says $\frac{3}{4}$ and $\frac{5}{8}$ are equivalent fractions.

   Is Jemma correct? Explain your answer.

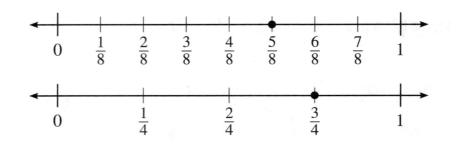

No _____

_____

Decide whether the pair of fractions is equivalent. Write Yes or No on the line.

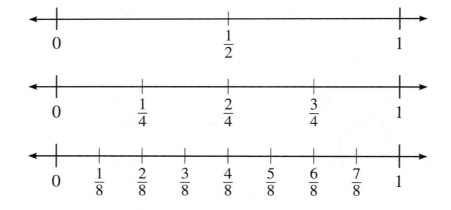

4. $\frac{1}{2}$ and $\frac{2}{4}$ __Yes__

5. $\frac{3}{4}$ and $\frac{4}{8}$ __No__

6. $\frac{1}{4}$ and $\frac{1}{8}$ __No__

7. $\frac{2}{4}$ and $\frac{4}{8}$ __Yes__

Fraction Equivalence (D)

Practice Using Number Lines to Find Equivalent Fractions

Follow the steps to answer the question.

1. What number makes this equation true?

$\frac{1}{3} = \frac{2}{6}$

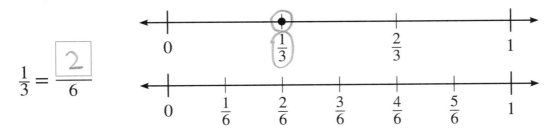

a. Notice where the point is on the first number line.

b. Plot a point on the second number line that is the same distance from 0.

c. Fill in the box to make the equation true.

d. Explain how you know your answer is correct.

They are same distance between 0 and 1

Write a number in the box to make the equation true.

2. $\frac{2}{4} = \frac{3}{6}$

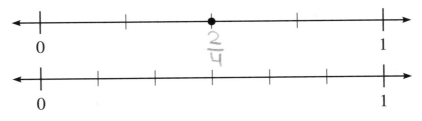

3. $\dfrac{4}{6} = \dfrac{\boxed{2}}{3}$

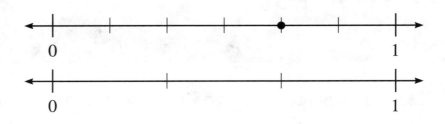

4. $\dfrac{1}{2} = \dfrac{\boxed{2}}{4}$

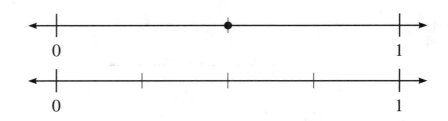

5. $\dfrac{6}{8} = \dfrac{\boxed{3}}{4}$

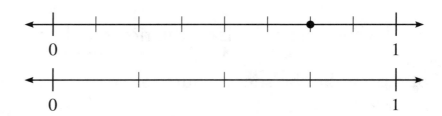

6. $\dfrac{3}{6} = \dfrac{\boxed{4}}{8}$

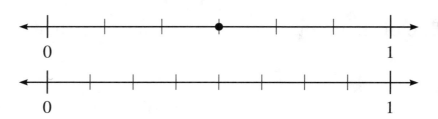

7. $\dfrac{1}{4} = \dfrac{\boxed{2}}{8}$

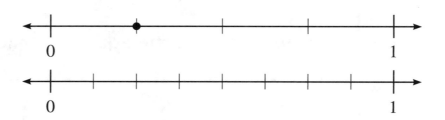

Practice Writing Whole and Mixed Numbers as Fractions

Fill in the blanks.

1. A _____ _____ has a numerator that is less than its denominator.

2. An _____ _____ has a numerator that is greater than or equal to its denominator.

3. An _____ _____ and a _____ _____ can both be used to describe an amount greater than 1.

4. A fraction with the same numerator and denominator always

   equals _____ .

Answer the question.

5. What is true about a fraction that is equal to 1 whole? Explain.

   _____

   _____

Fill in the box to make each equation true.

6. Each model shows a whole number.

a.  $0 = \dfrac{\boxed{}}{4}$

b. $\boxed{} = \dfrac{4}{4}$

c. $\boxed{} = \dfrac{8}{4}$

d. $3 = \dfrac{\boxed{}}{4}$

Name the shaded part of each model as an improper fraction and as a mixed number.

7.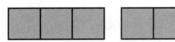

_____   _____

8.

_____   _____

9.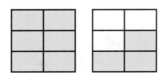

_____   _____

10.

_____   _____

Fractions and Whole Numbers (B)

Practice Plotting Whole and Mixed Numbers on Number Lines

Follow the instructions.

1. The point on this number line is located at the whole number 1.

   a. Fill in the blanks.

   Each whole on this number line is split into _____ equal parts.

   The point is located _____ hops after 0.

   The point on this number line is located at the fraction _____.

   b. Each whole number on this number line is also a fraction. Label each whole number on the number line with a correct fraction.

2. Label the location of each point on this number line as a mixed number.

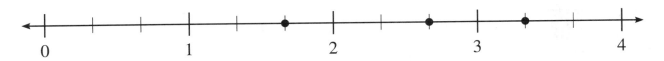

3. Label the location of each point on this number line as an improper fraction.

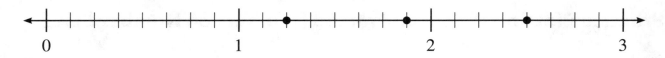

Plot and label each point on this number line.

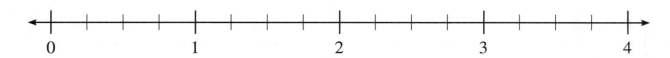

4. $\dfrac{7}{4}$ **5.** $2\dfrac{2}{4}$ **6.** $\dfrac{12}{4}$

Plot and label each point on this number line.

7. $\dfrac{9}{6}$ **8.** $\dfrac{0}{6}$ **9.** $3\dfrac{5}{6}$

Plot and label each point on this number line.

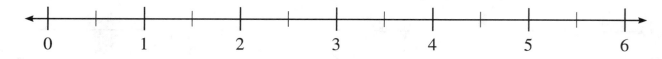

10. $3\dfrac{1}{2}$ **11.** $\dfrac{3}{2}$ **12.** $\dfrac{10}{2}$

Practice Comparing Fractions with the Same Denominator

Answer the question.

1. A fraction of each shape is shaded. Can these fractions be compared? Explain.

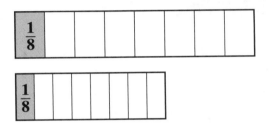

_____

_____

Follow the instructions to answer the question.

2. A fraction of each shape is shaded. How do these fractions compare?

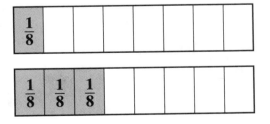

a. Fill in the blanks: The wholes are the same size and each whole

has _____ equal parts. Compare the _____ .

b. Fill in the boxes with <, >, or = to make the sentence true:

1 ☐ 3, so $\frac{1}{8}$ ☐ $\frac{3}{8}$.

Compare the fractions. Use <, >, or =.

3.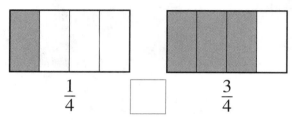

$\frac{1}{4}$ ☐ $\frac{3}{4}$

4.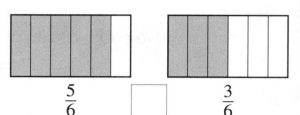

$\frac{5}{6}$ ☐ $\frac{3}{6}$

5.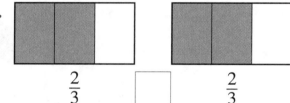

$\frac{2}{3}$ ☐ $\frac{2}{3}$

6. $\frac{7}{8}$ ☐ $\frac{5}{8}$

7. $\frac{1}{6}$ ☐ $\frac{2}{6}$

8. $\frac{1}{2}$ ☐ $\frac{1}{2}$

9. $\frac{3}{4}$ ☐ $\frac{2}{4}$

10. $\frac{4}{8}$ ☐ $\frac{3}{8}$

11. $\frac{1}{3}$ ☐ $\frac{2}{3}$

Compare Fractions (B)

Practice Comparing Fractions with the Same Numerator

Answer the questions.

1. A fraction of each shape is shaded. Can the fractions be compared? Explain.

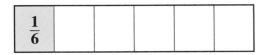

_____

_____

2. A fraction of each shape is shaded. Can the fractions be compared? Explain.

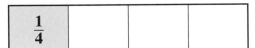

_____

_____

Compare the fractions. Use <, >, or =.

3.

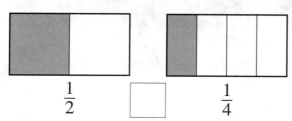

$\frac{1}{2}$ ☐ $\frac{1}{4}$

4.

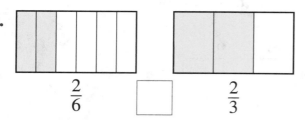

$\frac{2}{6}$ ☐ $\frac{2}{3}$

5.

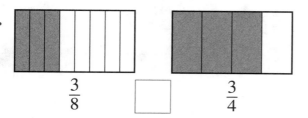

$\frac{3}{8}$ ☐ $\frac{3}{4}$

Fractions are fabulous!

6. $\frac{5}{6}$ ☐ $\frac{5}{8}$

7. $\frac{1}{4}$ ☐ $\frac{1}{4}$

8. $\frac{4}{6}$ ☐ $\frac{4}{4}$

9. $\frac{2}{6}$ ☐ $\frac{2}{4}$

10. $\frac{3}{4}$ ☐ $\frac{3}{8}$

11. $\frac{1}{4}$ ☐ $\frac{1}{3}$

Clock Time and Units of Time (A)

Practice Expressing Time

Fill in the blanks.

1. The longer hand of the clock tells the _____ .

2. The shorter hand of the clock tells the _____ .

Follow the instructions.

3. This clock shows a time.

   a. Fill in the blanks.

   The hour hand is between _____

   and _____ .

   The hour is _____ .

   Start at 12 and count the minutes by 5 and then by 1.

   The minutes are _____ .

   The time shown on the clock is

   _____ : _____ .

b. Write the time shown on the clock two different ways in words.

_____   _____

Write the time in numbers and in words.

4.

_____

_____

5.

_____

_____

6.

_____

_____

Draw the time on the clock.

7. 3:23

8. 12:28

9. five minutes to nine

Clock Time and Units of Time (B)

Practice A.M. and P.M. and Elapsed Time

Fill in the blanks.

1. Times between noon and midnight should be labeled _____.

2. Times between midnight and noon should be labeled _____.

3. _____ _____ is the amount of time that passes between two events.

Write the time that each activity happens. Include a.m. or p.m.

4. Jada wakes up in the morning at the time shown on the digital clock.

   _____

5. Eric eats dinner at the time shown on the analog clock. _____

6. Eloise has a snack at a quarter to 10 in the morning. _____

Follow the instructions.

7. Use the number line to find the elapsed time from 8:40 to 9:08.

_____ minutes

Find the elapsed time.

8.   Start   End

_____ minutes

9.   Start   End

_____ hours and

_____ minutes

10. Start: 2:17 p.m.
End: 5:48 p.m.

_____ hours and _____ minutes

11. Start: 2:00 p.m.
End: 8:00 p.m.

_____ hours

Clock Time and Units of Time (C)

Practice Solving Time Problems Using Addition

Follow the steps to answer the question.

1. A store clerk starts taking inventory at 9:05 a.m.
    It takes the clerk 27 minutes to finish.

    What time does the clerk finish taking inventory?

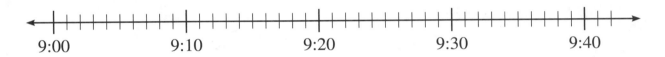

9:00   9:10   9:20   9:30   9:40

   a. Label the start time on the number line.

   b. Count on 27 minutes from the start time. Count by
       5, 10, and 1.

   c. Label the end time on the number line.

   d. Fill in the blank: The clerk finishes taking inventory at _____ a.m.

2. The store clerk starts stocking
    shelves at 9:45 a.m. It takes
    the clerk 50 minutes to finish.

    What time does the clerk
    finish stocking the shelves?

    a. Draw the start time.

Start   End

b. Count by 5 or 10 to find the end time.

c. Draw the end time.

3. The store clerk starts working at the cash register at 11:05 a.m. The clerk works at the cash register for 1 hour and 36 minutes.

What time does the clerk finish working at the cash register?

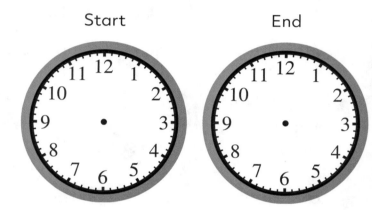

Start   End

a. Draw the start time.

b. Count by 5, 10, or 1 to find the end time.

c. Draw the end time.

Answer the question. Include a.m. or p.m.

4. Luis goes for a run. He starts at 3:25 p.m. and runs for 49 minutes.

What time does Luis finish his run? _____

5. A train leaves the station at 8:53 a.m. The train takes 1 hour and 38 minutes to travel to the next station.

What time does the train arrive at the next station? _____

Practice Solving Time Problems Using Subtraction

Follow the steps to answer the question.

1. Laurel walks for 45 minutes to her local library.
   She arrives at the library at 11:17 a.m.

   What time did Laurel start walking?

10:30   10:40   10:50   11:00   11:10   11:20

   a. Label the end time on the number line.

   b. Count back by 10s, 5s, or 1s to find the start time.

   c. Label the start time on the number line.

   d. Fill in the blank: Laurel started walking at _____ a.m.

2. Will and John play a board
   game. They stop playing at
   12:11 p.m. It took them
   1 hour and 7 minutes to
   finish the game.

   What time did they start
   playing the game?

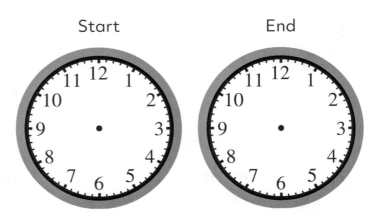

Start   End

   a. Draw the end time.

b. Count back by 5s, 10s, or 1s to find the start time.

c. Draw the start time.

Answer the questions. Include a.m. or p.m.

3. Matt's soccer game starts at 3:15 p.m. It will take him 1 hour and 27 minutes to get to the field and warm up.

   What time does Matt need to leave his house? _____

4. A business meeting ends at 10:38 a.m. The meeting lasted 1 hour and 12 minutes.

   What time did the meeting begin? _____

5. A pizza chef takes a pizza out of the oven at 6:03 p.m. The pizza cooked for 18 minutes.

   What time was the pizza put in the oven? _____

6. Maeve takes a train to visit her cousin. The train arrives at 5:26 p.m. The train trip was 3 hours and 42 minutes.

   What time did the train leave? _____

7. Mrs. Chen arrives at work at 8:31 a.m. It took her 48 minutes to drive to work.

   What time did Mrs. Chen leave her home? _____

Measuring Length (A)

Practice Measuring and Estimating Length

Fill in the blanks.

1. A _____ is a tool that can be used to measure length.

2. You can use a _____ to estimate length.

Answer the question.

3. What is a common benchmark for an inch? _____

Fill in the boxes to label each ruler mark.

4.

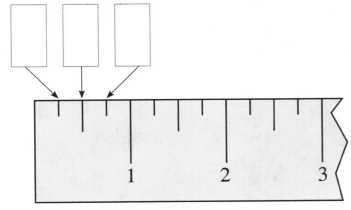

Use a benchmark to estimate the length of each object.

5.

about _____ inches

6.

about _____ inches

7.

about _____ inches

Use this ruler to measure the length of each object.

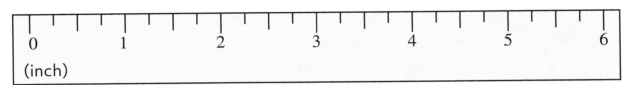

8.

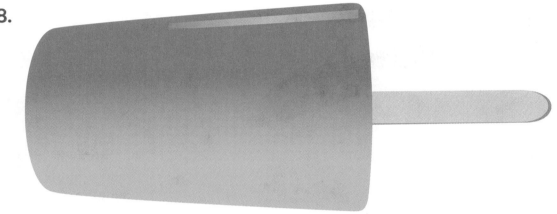

_____

9.

_____

10.

ERASER

_____

11.

_____

12.

_____

I use a ruler to measure length!

Practice Solving Length Word Problems with Multiplication

Follow the steps to answer the question.

1. Ava is playing with her toy train set. She makes a train using 7 train cars. Each train car is 4 inches long.

   How long is Ava's toy train?

   a. Let t be the length of the train.

      Write an equation to model the problem. _____

   b. Use your equation to find t.

      $t =$ _____

   c. Answer the question in a complete sentence.

      _____

2. Nico has a rope that is 53 feet long. He cuts three equal pieces from the rope. Each piece is 9 feet long.

   How much rope is left?

   a. Draw a diagram to model the rope.

b. Find the total amount of rope Nico cut off. Show your work.

_____

c. Find the amount of rope left. Show your work.

_____

d. Answer the question in a complete sentence.

_____

Answer the question.

3. A librarian lines up 9 books on a shelf. The spine of each book is 4 centimeters wide.

   What is the total width of the books? _____

4. Lin has 8 pieces of red string. Each piece of red string is 9 inches long. She also has 3 pieces of blue string. Each piece of blue string is 10 inches long.

   What is the total length of the string Lin has? _____

5. A carpenter has a piece of wood that is 72 inches long. The carpenter cuts 4 pieces that are each 8 inches long from the wood.

   How long is the piece of wood that is left over? _____

Practice Solving Length Word Problems with Division

Follow the steps to answer the question.

1. A store has a chain that is 63 inches long. The store separates the chain into 7 equal pieces.

   How long is each piece?

   a. Let p be the length of each piece of chain.

      Write a division equation to model the problem. _____

   b. Use your equation to find p.

      $p =$ _____

   c. Answer the question in a complete sentence.

      _____

2. Rey puts ribbon along 4 sides of a box that is shaped like a pentagon. Each side of the pentagon is the same length, and the perimeter of the pentagon is 20 feet.

   What is the total length of ribbon Rey uses?

   a. Draw a diagram to model the problem.

b. Find the length of each side of the pentagon.
Show your work.

_____

c. Find the amount of ribbon Rey uses. Show your work.

_____

d. Answer the question in a complete sentence.

_____

Answer the questions.

3. Mila runs a total of 54 miles. She runs the same distance each day for 9 days.

   How far does Mila run each day? _____

4. An electrician places wire around 3 sides of a square window. The perimeter of the window is 24 feet.

   How long is the wire the electrician uses? _____

5. Luis walks a nature trail 4 times. He walks a total distance of 28 miles.

   How long is the nature trail? _____

Liquid Volume (A)

Practice Measuring Liquid Volume

Answer the questions.

1. What is a common benchmark for 1 liter? _____

2. To the nearest liter, how much pudding is

   in this bowl? _____

4 Liters —
3 Liters —
2 Liters —
1 Liter —

3. To the nearest liter, how much water is

   in this pot? _____

— 5 Liters
— 4 Liters
— 3 Liters
— 2 Liters
— 1 Liter

Think about the liquid volume of the container.
Fill in the blank with *about*, *less than*, or *more than*.

4.

_____ 1 liter

5.

_____ 1 liter

6.

_____ 1 liter

Circle the answer.

7. Which item holds about 5 liters?

coffee mug

small
measuring cup

bucket

8. Which item holds about 50 liters?

car gas tank

watering can

drinking cup

9. About how much water is in this fish tank?

4 liters

40 liters

400 liters

10. About how much water is in this sink?

2 liters

20 liters

200 liters

Practice Adding and Subtracting with Liquid Volume

Follow the steps to answer the question.

1. Debra is making batches of fruit punch for a dance. She buys 18 liters of grape juice, 22 liters of cranberry juice, and 17 liters of apple juice.

    How many liters of juice does Debra buy in all?

    a. Use the information in the problem to fill in the parts and symbols in this chart.

Part	+ or −	Part	+ or −	Part	=	Whole
					=	

    b. Use your answer from part **a** to find the whole. Fill in the whole in the chart.

    c. Answer the question using a complete sentence.

2. A tank has 389 liters of water. Water is drained out of the tank to fill a pool that holds 226 liters of water.

    How much water is left in the tank?

a. Use the information in the problem to fill in the start, change, and symbol in this chart.

Start	+ or −	Change	=	Result
			=	

b. Use your answer from part **a** to find the result. Fill in the result in the chart.

c. Answer the question using a complete sentence.

Answer the question using a complete sentence. Show your work.

3. A doctor's office has two fish tanks. The larger tank holds 208 liters of water. The smaller tank holds 151 liters of water.

   How much more water does the larger tank hold than the smaller tank?

---

4. A bathtub has 129 liters of water in it. Then, 107 liters of water are added to the tub.

   How many liters of water are in the tub now?

Practice Multiplying and Dividing with Liquid Volume

Follow the steps to answer the question.

1. Jan buys a large bottle of cleaning solution. The bottle has 10 liters of cleaning solution. Jan splits the solution equally among 5 small bottles.

   How much cleaning solution is in each small bottle?

   a. Write an equation to solve the problem.

   _____

   b. Solve the problem. _____

   c. Answer the question using a complete sentence.

   _____

2. Julio makes 5 batches of soup. Each batch is 3 liters of soup.

   How much soup does Julio make in all?

   a. Write an equation to solve the problem.

   _____

   b. Solve the problem. _____

c. Answer the question using a complete sentence.

_____

Answer the question using a complete sentence.
Show your work.

3. Maria is having a party. She needs 3 liters of iced tea
   for each table of guests. There are 6 tables.

   How many liters of iced tea does Maria need in all?

_____

4. Marco has 24 liters of water. He pours the same
   amount of water into each of 8 bottles.

   How much water is in each bottle?

_____

5. Ann's aquarium holds 45 liters of water. She uses a
   5-liter container to fill the aquarium.

   How many times does Ann fill the container in order
   to fill her aquarium?

_____

_____

Practice Measuring Mass

Answer the questions.

1. What is a common benchmark for 1 gram?

   _____

2. What is a common benchmark for 1 kilogram?

   _____

3. What is the mass of this loaf of bread?

4. What is the mass of this watermelon?

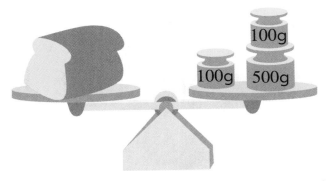

Note: *g* stands for "grams."

_____

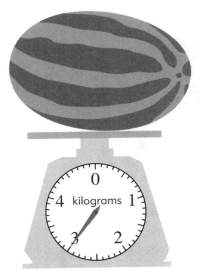

_____

Circle the answer.

5. Which measurement tool should be used to measure mass?

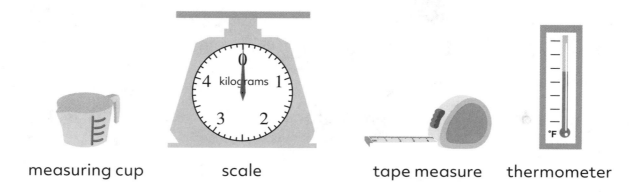

measuring cup   scale   tape measure   thermometer

6. Which object has a mass of about 5 grams?

   a car   a book   a nickel   a dog

7. Which set of objects has a mass of about 15 kilograms?

8. What is the approximate mass of a can of soup?

   35 grams   35 kilograms   350 grams   350 kilograms

Practice Adding and Subtracting with Mass

Follow the steps to answer the question.

1. Aisha and Alison each have a box. The mass of Aisha's box is 56 grams. The mass of Alison's box is 35 grams.

   How many more grams is Aisha's box than Alison's box?

   a. Describe a strategy you could use to solve the problem.

   _____

   b. Use your strategy to solve the problem. Show your work.

   _____

   c. Answer the question using a complete sentence.

   _____

2. Mariah has 429 grams of grapes. Jordan has 223 fewer grams of grapes.

   How many grams of grapes does Jordan have?

   a. Describe a strategy you could use to solve the problem.

   _____

b. Use your strategy to solve the problem. Show your work.

_____

_____

c. Answer the question using a complete sentence.

_____

Answer the question using a complete sentence. Show your work.

3. An aquarium has 289 grams of sand in it. Kim pours 240 more grams of sand into the aquarium.

   After Kim pours in all his sand, how much sand is in the aquarium?

   _____

   _____

4. A baker buys 23 kilograms of flour and 11 kilograms of sugar.

   a. How much flour and sugar does the baker buy in all?

   _____

   _____

   b. How much more flour than sugar does the baker buy?

   _____

Practice Multiplying and Dividing with Mass

Follow the steps to answer the question.

1. Damian makes a stack of 8 bricks. The mass of each brick is 5 kilograms.

   What is the mass of Damian's stack of bricks?

   a. Write an equation to solve the problem. _____

   b. Solve the problem. _____

   c. Answer the question using a complete sentence.

   _____

   _____

2. A garden store has 56 kilograms of potting soil. The store packages the soil in bags with a mass of 7 kilograms each.

   How many 7-kilogram bags of soil does the store have?

   a. Write an equation to solve the problem. _____

   b. Solve the problem. _____

   c. Answer the question using a complete sentence.

   _____

Answer the question using a complete sentence.
Show your work.

3. Otto buys a 36-kilogram package of horse pellets. He separates the pellets into 9-kilogram servings and pours each serving into its own plastic bin.

   How many plastic bins does Otto use?

   _____

   _____

4. A pencil has a mass of 7 grams.

   What is the total mass of 5 pencils?

   _____

   _____

5. A bakery has 6 bags of flour. Each bag has a mass of 10 kilograms.

   How many kilograms of flour does the bakery have in all?

   _____

   _____

6. Min has a stack of 7 graham crackers. The mass of each cracker is 6 grams.

   What is the total mass of Min's stack of graham crackers?

   _____

Picture and Bar Graphs (A)

Practice Working with Frequency Tables

Follow the steps to answer the question.

1. Raj counts the marbles in his collection. The tallies in this frequency table show his results.

   How many marbles of each color does Raj have?

   a. Count the tally marks in each row.

   b. Record the total for each row in the Frequency column.

Raj's Marble Collection		
Color	**Tally**	**Frequency**
green	卌 卌 IIII	
red	卌 I	
blue	卌 III	
yellow	卌 卌 I	
orange	卌 卌 卌	

Answer the questions.

2. Amy keeps track of the number of sit-ups she completes each day for four days. This frequency table shows her results.

   a. How many sit-ups does Amy complete on Friday and Saturday combined?

Amy's Sit-Ups	
Day	**Frequency**
Friday	15
Saturday	18
Sunday	21
Monday	24

b. This frequency table shows a pattern. How many more sit-ups does Amy complete from one day to the next? _____

c. The pattern continues for 3 more days. How many sit-ups does Amy complete on Tuesday, Wednesday, and Thursday?

_____   _____

_____

3. A group of people choose their favorite type of bagel. This frequency table shows the results.

Favorite Bagels	
Flavor	**Frequency**
plain	24
whole wheat	19
everything	16
cinnamon raisin	22

a. What is the most popular bagel flavor?

_____

b. What is the least popular bagel flavor? _____

c. How many people choose whole wheat or everything as their favorite bagel? _____

d. How many fewer people choose plain as their favorite bagel than whole wheat or everything combined? _____

TRY IT

Picture and Bar Graphs (B)

Practice Working with Scaled Picture Graphs

Use the scaled picture graph to answer the questions.

1. Anthony sells snacks to raise money. This scaled picture graph shows how many of each snack he sells.

Snack Sale	
Type of snack	**Amount**
cupcake	★ ★ ★ ½★
banana	★ ★ ★
doughnut	★ ½★
apple	★ ★ ★ ★ ½★

Key: Each ★ = 4 snacks

a. How many snacks is each half symbol? Explain.

____

b. How many pieces of fruit does Anthony sell?

Show your work. ______________________________

c. How many more pieces of fruit than cupcakes does

Anthony sell? Show your work. ______________________

2. A theater sells tickets to a play for one week. This scaled picture graph shows the ticket sales for the first 4 days.

Ticket Sales	
Day	Amount
day 1	■ ■ ■ ■ ■
day 2	■ ■ ■ ■
day 3	■ ■ ■
day 4	■ ■ ■

a. Each ticket sells for $8. How much money did the theater collect on day 3? Show your work.

_____

b. This picture graph shows a pattern.   Key: Each ■ = 5 tickets

How many fewer tickets are
sold from one day to the next? _____

c. The pattern continues for the rest of the week.

How many tickets are sold on day 5? _____

Complete the scaled picture graph.

3. Matt goes to pick berries. He picks 40 blueberries, 60 raspberries, 50 blackberries, and 25 strawberries.

Matt's Berries	
Type of berry	Amount
blueberry	
raspberry	
blackberry	
strawberry	

Key: Each ◯ = 10 berries

Practice Working with Scaled Bar Graphs

Use the scaled bar graph to answer the questions.

1. A bicycle store has a 5-day sale. This bar graph shows the number of bicycles sold on the first 4 days of the sale.

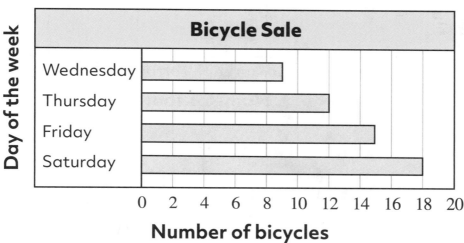

a. How many more bicycles are sold on Thursday than Wednesday? Show your work. $12 - 9 = 3$

b. How many fewer bicycles are sold on Friday than Saturday? Show your work. $18 - 15 = 3$

c. This graph shows a pattern. The pattern continues for the whole sale. How many bicycles should the store expect to sell on Sunday? Explain. 9, 12, 15, 18 it grows by 3. 21 on Sunday

2. A group of students are asked to name their favorite sport. This scaled bar graph shows the results.

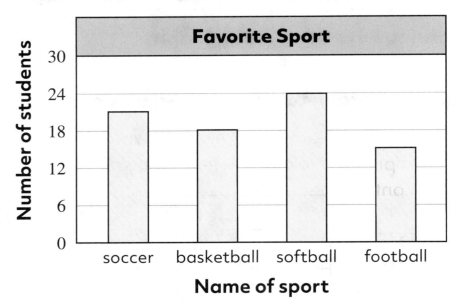

a. Which sport is named as favorite by the most students? Explain. _Softball 24 kids like it_

b. How many more students name softball than football? Show your work. _24−15=9_

c. How many fewer students name basketball than soccer? Show your work. _21−18=3_

d. How many fewer students name soccer than basketball and football combined? Show your work.

Picture and Bar Graphs (D)

Practice Drawing Scaled Bar Graphs

Follow the steps to complete the scaled bar graph.

1. Nellie, Kyobok, Marc, and Dale participate in a music contest. This picture graph shows the number of votes each contestant receives.

   a. Write the total number of votes each contestant receives on the picture graph.

Music Contest	
Contestant	**Votes received**
Nellie	✔✔✔✔✔ 50
Kyobok	✔✔✔✔✔✔ 60
Marc	✔✔✔ 30
Dale	✔✔✔✔✔✔✔✔✔ 90

   Key: Each ✔ = 10 votes

   b. Draw a bar for each contestant to complete this bar graph.

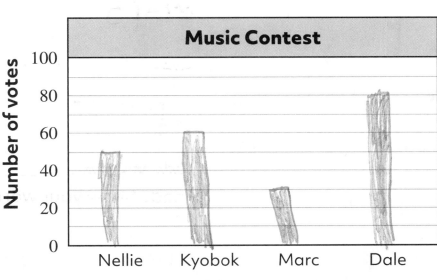

Complete the scaled bar graph.

2. This frequency table shows the number of pets sold at Pete's Pet Store in a month.

Pets Sold	
Type of pet	**Frequency**
bird	25
cat	15
fish	35
dog	10
hamster	30

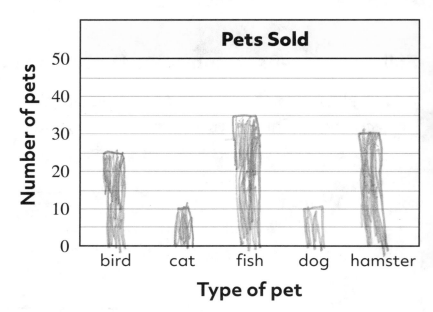

3. A petting zoo has 14 goats, 18 sheep, 8 llamas, 12 rabbits, and 6 pigs.

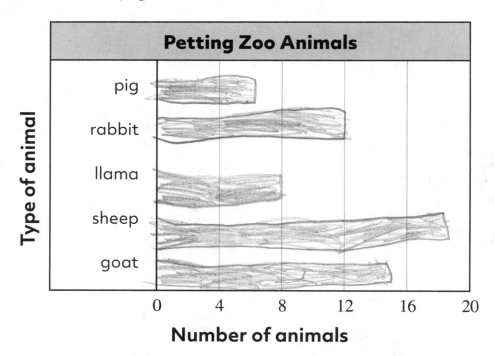

Line Plots (A)

Practice Interpreting Line Plots

Use the line plot to answer the questions.

1. Amelie's family goes fishing. This line plot shows the length of each fish they catch and release.

Fish Lengths

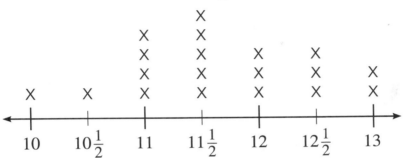

Length (inches)

a. What is the most common fish length? Explain.

   11 1/2

b. What is the maximum fish length? Explain.

   13 in.

c. What is the minimum fish length? Explain.

   10

d. How many fish did Amelie's family catch? _19 fish_

2. This line plot shows the distances people traveled to get to the library one morning.

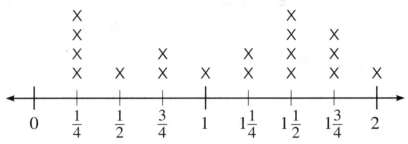

Distances to the Library

Length (miles)

a. What are the most common distances traveled to the library? _1, 1/2_ _____ _1/4_ _____

b. How many people traveled 1 mile to get to the library? _1 person_ _____

c. How many people traveled less than 1 mile to get to the library? _10 people_ _____

d. How many people traveled more than 1 mile to get to the library? _____

e. How many more people traveled more than 1 mile than less than 1 mile? _3 people_ _____

Line Plots (B)

Practice Drawing Line Plots Involving Whole Numbers

Follow the steps to create a line plot.

1. Astrid collects sticks in her yard after a storm. This frequency table shows the lengths of the sticks Astrid collects.

Stick Length	
Length (centimeters)	Frequency
28	1
29	0
30	5
31	3
32	5
33	2
34	2
35	1
36	1

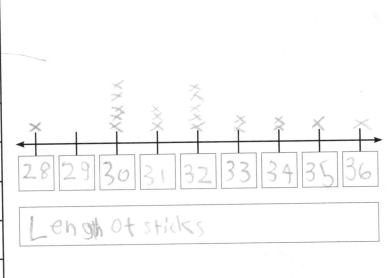

Length of sticks

a. Label the numbers below the number line. Use the numbers in the frequency table as a guide.

b. Label the number line. Fill in the box below the numbers you wrote in part **a**.

c. Choose a title for the line plot. Write it in the box above the line plot.

d. Make marks to represent the data in the frequency table. You can use a dot or an X for each mark.

Complete the frequency table. Then create a line plot.

2. Rami weighs each rock in his rock collection to the nearest gram. These are his measurements.

18 grams   15 grams   19 grams   19 grams   20 grams   17 grams

19 grams   19 grams   20 grams   18 grams   19 grams   16 grams

Rami's Rocks	
Mass (grams)	Frequency
15	l
16	l
17	l
18	2
19	5
20	2

Rami's Rocks

Mass (grams)

Practice Drawing Line Plots Involving Halves and Quarters

Follow the steps to create a line plot.

1. Jennifer measures the pencils in her pencil box to the nearest quarter inch. This frequency table shows her results.

Jennifer's Pencils	
Length (inches)	Frequency
$3\frac{1}{2}$	2
$3\frac{3}{4}$	3
4	2
$4\frac{1}{2}$	1

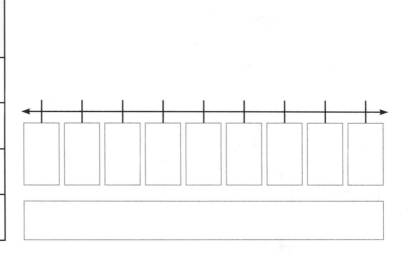

a. Label the numbers below the number line. Use the numbers in the frequency table as a guide.

b. Label the number line. Fill in the box below the numbers you wrote in part **a**.

c. Choose a title for the line plot. Write it in the box above the line plot.

d. Make marks to represent the data in the frequency table. You can use a dot or an X for each mark.

Complete the frequency table. Then create a line plot.

2. Amal records the amount of water she drinks, to the nearest quarter of a liter, for 12 days. These are her results.

$1\frac{1}{2}$ liters $1\frac{3}{4}$ liters $2\frac{3}{4}$ liters   2 liters $2\frac{1}{4}$ liters   2 liters

$2\frac{1}{2}$ liters $1\frac{1}{2}$ liters $2\frac{1}{4}$ liters   2 liters   2 liters $2\frac{1}{4}$ liters

Amal's Drinking Water	
Amount (liters)	Frequency
$1\frac{1}{2}$	
$1\frac{3}{4}$	
2	
$2\frac{1}{4}$	
$2\frac{1}{2}$	
$2\frac{3}{4}$	

Amal's Drinking Water

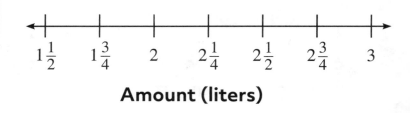

Amount (liters)

You can display data in many ways!

Glossary

a.m. – a label for times between midnight and noon; stands for *ante meridiem*

addend – one of the two or more numbers that are added to find a sum

algorithm – a step-by-step way to solve a problem

analog clock – a clock that displays the time with an hour and a minute hand

area – the amount of space on a flat surface, most often measured in square units

area model – a model for multiplication that shows the product of two factors as the total number of squares on a rectangular grid; one factor is the number of rows and the other factor is the number of columns

array – a set of rows with the same number of objects in each row

associative property – a rule that says no matter how you group three numbers to add them two at a time (or three numbers to multiply), the answer will not change

associative property of addition – a rule stating that grouping three addends in different ways does not change their sum

associative property of multiplication – rule that says no matter how you group factors to multiply, the product will not change

bar graph – a graph that uses bars to show how much of a given category is in the data

closed shape – a shape that starts and ends at the same point

commutative property – a rule that says no matter what order you use to add two numbers (or multiply two numbers), the answer will not change

commutative property of addition – a rule stating that changing the order of two addends does not change their sum

commutative property of multiplication – a rule that says no matter what order you use to multiply factors, the product will not change

compatible numbers – numbers that are easy to compute using mental math

data – numerical information that has been gathered

denominator – the number in a fraction that is below the fraction bar

difference – the answer to a subtraction problem

digital clock – a clock that uses numerals to display time, with hours and minutes separated by a colon

distributive property – a rule that says that multiplying a number by a sum gives the same answer as multiplying the number by each addend of the sum and then adding the products

dividend – the number to be divided; the dividend divided by the divisor equals the quotient

division – an operation to share equally or group an amount into equal parts

divisor – the number that divides the dividend; the dividend divided by the divisor equals the quotient

elapsed time – the amount of time between a beginning time and an ending time

equation – a number sentence; two expressions that are shown as equal to one another

equivalent fractions – fractions that name the same amount, such as $\frac{1}{2}$ and $\frac{3}{6}$

estimate (n.) – a very good guess or rough calculation of an answer when the exact answer is not necessary

estimate (v.) – to make a very good guess or rough calculation of an answer when the exact answer is not necessary

evaluate – to find the value of an expression

expanded form – a way to write a number that shows the place value of each of its digits; for example, $543 = 500 + 40 + 3$ or 5 hundreds + 4 tens + 3 ones

factor – one of two or more numbers that are multiplied

factor pairs – two numbers that multiply to give a particular product; factor pairs of 6 are 6×1 and 3×2

fraction – a number that represents a part of a whole or a part of a set

frequency table – a table that shows the number of times pieces of data occur

gram (g) – the basic metric unit of mass

half hour – a fraction of an hour, equal to 30 minutes

half inch – one-half of the distance between the zero mark and the one-inch mark on a ruler

hexagon – a 6-sided polygon

hour (h) – the unit for measuring time that equals 60 minutes

identity property of addition – a rule that says that the sum of a number and zero is always the original number

identity property of multiplication – a rule that says that the product of a number and one is always the original number

improper fraction – a fraction in which the numerator is larger than the denominator

inch (in.) – the basic English, or customary, unit for measuring length

inverse operations – opposite operations that undo each other; subtraction and addition are inverse operations; division and multiplication are inverse operations

kilogram (kg) – the metric unit for measuring mass that equals 1,000 grams

kilometer (km) – the metric unit for measuring distance that equals 1,000 meters

line plot – a number line that shows all the pieces of data with a mark or marks above each piece of data to show how many times that piece of data occurred

liquid volume – the amount of liquid a container will hold; the measure of liquid capacity

liter (L) – the basic metric unit for measuring capacity

mass – the amount of matter in an object

maximum – the greatest value for a data set

midnight – another name for 12:00 at night

minimum – the least value for a data set

minuend – a number from which another number is subtracted

minute – the amount of time it takes for the minute hand on an analog clock to move one tick mark

mixed number – a whole number and a proper fraction that show a single amount

multiple – the product of a given number and any whole number

multiplication fact family – a set of four related multiplication and division facts that use the same set of three numbers

multiply – to use the shortcut for adding the same number over and over a certain number of times

non-unit fraction – a fraction with a numerator that is any number except 1, such as $\frac{2}{3}$ or $\frac{5}{8}$

noon – another name for 12:00 during the day

numerator – the number in a fraction that is above the fraction bar

open shape – a shape that starts at one point and ends at a different point

p.m. – a label for times between noon and midnight; stands for *post meridiem*

pentagon – a 5-sided polygon

perimeter – the distance around the edge of a shape

picture graph – a graph that shows information using picture symbols

place value – the value of a digit depending on its position, or place, in a number

plane figure – a flat shape with only two dimensions: length and width

polygon – a closed shape that has three or more sides

product – the answer to a multiplication problem

proper fraction – a fraction in which the numerator is less than the denominator

quadrilateral – a polygon with four sides

quarter hour – a fraction of an hour, equal to 15 minutes

quarter inch – one-fourth of the distance between the zero mark and the one-inch mark on a ruler

quotient – the answer to a division problem; the dividend divided by the divisor equals the quotient

rectangle – a quadrilateral with four square corners and opposite sides that have equal length

rhombus – a quadrilateral in which all sides are the same length

round (v.) – to change a number to the nearest place value asked in a problem; for example, rounding 532 to the nearest ten would be 530

square – a quadrilateral that has four square corners and four sides that are the same length

square corner – a corner in a flat shape that is formed by two line segments and is the same shape as the corner of an index card

square unit – a unit used to measure area; equal to the area of a square that is one unit on each side

standard form – the usual way of writing a number using digits

subtrahend – a number that is subtracted from another number

sum – the answer to an addition problem

triangle – a polygon with three sides

unit fraction – a fraction with a numerator of 1, such as $\frac{1}{3}$ or $\frac{1}{7}$

unit square – a square that has a length of one unit on each side

vertex – the point where two sides of a shape meet; the plural of *vertex* is *vertices*

volume – the amount of space taken up by a three-dimensional object; measured in cubic units

zero property of multiplication – a rule that says that the product of a number and zero is always zero